Rita Mae Brown

Twayne's United States Authors Series

Frank Day, Editor

Clemson University

TUSAS 615

RITA MAE BROWN
Photograph by Mark Homan, courtesy of Bantam Books

Rita Mae Brown

Carol M. Ward

Clemson University

Twayne Publishers • New York
Maxwell Macmillan Canada • Toronto
Maxwell Macmillan International • New York   Oxford   Singapore   Sydney

Rita Mae Brown
Carol Ward

Twayne Publishers   Maxwell Macmillan Canada, Inc.
Macmillan Publishing Company   1200 Eglinton Avenue East
866 Third Avenue   Suite 200
New York, New York 10022   Don Mills, Ontario M3C 3N1

Library of Congress Cataloging-in-Publication Data

Ward, Carol Marie.
  Rita Mae Brown / Carol M. Ward.
      p.   cm.—(Twayne's United States authors series ; TUSAS 615)
  Includes bibliographical references and index.
  ISBN 0-8057-4000-7
  1. Brown, Rita Mae—Criticism and interpretation.   I. Title.
II. Series.
PS3552.R698Z93   1993
813'.54—dc20   92-26821
                                                    CIP

10 9 8 7 6 5 4 3 2 1

The paper used in this publication meets the minimum requirements
of American National Standard for Information Sciences—Permanence
of Paper for Printed Library Materials, ANSI Z39.48-1984. ⊚™

Printed in the United States of America.

Contents

Preface

The successful literary career of Southern author Rita Mae Brown illustrates popular culture's assimilation and absorption of the ideals espoused by the women's movement and the gay liberation movement of the seventies as well as the nation's continued fascination with the history and culture of the American South. Although her novels, essays, poetry, and screenplays are not necessarily the most polished in terms of their artistic style, her treatment of the themes of contemporary feminism, lesbianism, and Southern identity makes her an important and influential author of her times. Often using conventional literary forms and revealing her connection to the Mark Twain humorist tradition, Brown nonetheless forges her own unique style to deal with such controversial subjects. The memorable characters and communities that she creates and the organic fictional forms that she evolves reflect not only her liberal ideology but also her traditional Southern values. Through her fast-paced narratives and subversive humor she makes eccentricity palatable for a mass audience while retaining a strong cult following.

Most of Brown's philosophy about feminism, lesbianism, and history can be found in her early political essays; these pieces contain the ideas about individuals, society, and art that she develops and demonstrates in her subsequent fiction. For all of her talk about change and about the necessity of the unpredictable, Brown is amazingly consistent in her own view of the world from these youthful revolutionary essays to her increasingly mainstream novels. After a careful examination of these important but not easily accessible essays, I attempt to trace in this study how her philosophy is translated into fiction as well as to explore other biographical connections between Brown's life and her work. Her books are treated chronologically with the exception of *Bingo*, which although a later work is considered as a sequel to *Six of One*. Having drawn extensively on her writer's manual *Starting from Scratch* I have not included a separate analysis of this work. Because of the unavailability of her screenplays and some of their filmed versions, I was forced to omit consideration of this fascinating aspect of her career.

Although her books have achieved popular success and she herself is rather a celebrity, especially in the women's community, Brown has not received the scholarly attention that her books deserve. Book reviews, several critical articles, and some published interviews are the main sources of information outside of what she has written. I hope that this broad overview with its bibliography of available source materials will provide a starting point for further critical analyses of her life and work.

Acknowledgments

I would like to thank Margaret Duggan for suggesting this project to me, Frank Day for editing often messy copy and exhibiting great patience waiting for the final draft, John Padgett and Sharon Jones for research assistance, Elizabeth Lienert for indexing the manuscript, Peter Dakutis for reading my rough drafts and giving me his honest appraisals, and Silvia Morales for keeping up my enthusiasm. In addition, grateful acknowledgment is made to Rita Mae Brown, who read and commented on the manuscript.

Chronology

1944   Rita Mae Brown born November 28. Adopted in infancy by Ralph and Julia Brown in Hanover, Pennsylvania.

1955   Family moves to Fort Lauderdale, Florida.

1961   Ralph Brown dies 13 August.

1962   Brown graduates from Fort Lauderdale High School.

1964   Brown's scholarship to University of Florida is revoked for her involvement in civil rights movement and her open lesbianism. She hitchhikes to New York City.

1965   Receives A.A. degree from Broward Junior College.

1967   Forms Student Homophile League at Columbia and New York University.

1968   Receives B.A. degree in English and the classics from New York University. Earns certificate in cinematography from School of Visual Arts (Manhattan). Cofounder of theater group FREE (Feminist Repertory and Experiment Ensemble).

1969   Photography editor for Sterling Publishing Company. Delivers speech at First Congress to Unite Women. Joins Redstockings, a women's group.

1970   Co-authors "Woman Identified Woman" for Radicalesbians. Resigns from N.O.W. Stages demonstration with Lavender Menace at Second Congress to Unite Women.

1971   Organizing member of Furies Collective in Washington, D.C. Founding editor of *Quest*. Lecturer at Federal City College (D.C.). Research fellow at Institute for Policy Studies (D.C.) *Hrotsvitha: Six Medieval Latin Plays. The Hand That Cradles the Rock.* Begins friendship with Alexis Smith.

1972   Forced to leave Furies collective on 6 March.

1973   *Songs to a Handsome Woman. Rubyfruit Jungle.*

1974   Receives Massachusetts Council on Arts and Humanities Fiction grant and N.E.A. Creative Writing fellowship.

1975   Sagaris College opens.

1976 *A Plain Brown Rapper. In Her Day*. Receives Ph.D. in English and political science from Institute for Policy Studies.

1977 Teaches at the Women Writers Center in Cazenovia, N.Y. Bantam edition of *Rubyfruit Jungle*.

1978 *Six of One*. Moves to Charlottesville, Virginia.

1979 Meets Martina Navratilova.

1981 Navratilova ends relationship; Brown moves to Los Angeles temporarily to work as scriptwriter. Founder and president of American Artists, Inc. (Formerly Speakeasy, Inc.), a company that options novels for television and film.

1982 *Southern Discomfort. Slumber Party Massacre. I Love Liberty*. Returns to Charlottesville. Death of cat Baby Jesus.

1983 *Sudden Death*. Death of mother Julia Brown on 13 August.

1985 Death of former fiancé Jerry Pfeiffer. Narrates *Before Stonewall. The Long Hot Summer*.

1986 *My Two Loves. High Hearts*.

1988 *Starting from Scratch. Bingo*.

1990 *Wish You Were Here*.

1992 Relationship with Judy Nelson, Navratilova's ex-lover. *Rest in Pieces*.

Chapter One

Rita Mae Brown: The Woman and the Writer

The formative event of Rita Mae Brown's childhood was her adoption as an infant by Ralph and Julia Brown. Brown's natural mother deposited the infant at an orphanage shortly after her birth on 28 November 1944, because she "couldn't manage" and Julia, despite a bad case of pneumonia, sent her husband and sister to retrieve the three-month-old baby and bring her back to York, Pennsylvania.[1] Brown has never cared to locate her "illegitimate parents," even though her natural father, from the Venable family of Charlottesville, Virginia, lived in her hometown, and her mother, from the Young family, also lived in the area.[2] Brown must partly blame them for the struggles that she underwent as a child when other children taunted her, leading her into fistfights over her status as a "bastard" (Maupin, 50). The themes of adoption, of finding one's place in a community, of coming home are important components of Brown's fictions.

She considers the Browns her true family and credits them for their role in rearing her. Ralph's background as a Dunkard from the North and Julia's Southern heritage provided her with the best of both worlds: "it was wonderful drawing from both cultures."[3] From Ralph, whom she compares to actor Andy Griffith, she inherited her "agrarian mentality"; from Julia, Brown learned her "survival skills," such as "to watch what people do and not pay attention to what they say" (Fleischer, E2; Horn, C13). As a child she also shared her mother's Lutheran faith: "I'm drenched in the church. I'm drenched in Bach. All Lutherans are drenched in Bach," Brown now admits.[4] Brown has nothing but praise for the way these loving parents prepared her for life: "They loved me, too, but I was not the center of attention. They didn't try to be my best friend. They were my parents and to them that meant teaching me right from wrong, teaching me good work habits, and doing anything they could to get me the best public education available" (*Starting from Scratch*, 6).

Brown was a precocious student, learning to read at the age of three and frequenting the public library before she started elementary school. Even at that age she knew she wanted to be a writer and her desire was reinforced by her parents, their friends, and her kindergarten teacher. She was such a good student that, after scoring well on an IQ test in the third grade, Brown was transferred from a rural school to an upper-middle-class school filled with the children of doctors and lawyers: "I despised them. They were competitive, snotty backbiting toads. . . . My revenge against them was to get straight A's."[5] With this youthful knowledge of class and regional differences, at age eleven Brown migrated with her adopted family, which included four boys, to Fort Lauderdale, Florida.

High School and College Years

In Fort Lauderdale, Brown excelled academically and athletically. Although she made good grades at school, Brown tried not to let others know, so that she could maintain an active social life.[6] Part of her social activities revolved around sports, especially tennis, for which she won prizes as a member of the high-school tennis team. Then, as now, she sees sports as the "way I connect to people" (Ransom, 1). Around the age of fifteen, Brown lost her father. One of her fondest memories of him was his last birthday gift to her, a new typewriter he managed to buy despite the family's lack of money: "I still don't know what my father sacrificed to give me this wonderful typewriter" (*Starting from Scratch*, 9).

It was at this time also that her sexuality was beginning to emerge. Brown recalls how she would "truss my little titties up and try to look older" in order to attract the attention of the college boys on vacation. Ironically, Fort Lauderdale at this time was the site for the filming of the quintessential beach movie, *Where the Boys Are* (Maupin, 50). Admittedly "pansexual," Brown experimented sexually with both males and females. When she was sixteen, a friend's father discovered the love letters that Brown had written to his daughter and "threatened to shoot me on sight."[7] She lost many of her friends, lost her seat on the student council, and suffered the abuse of classmates and teachers when her lesbianism was made public.

Although she was accepted to several colleges, she selected the University of Florida because of the scholarship money it offered and the school's proximity to her family. Brown admits to having had many fights with her mother while she was at college but now attributes their difficulties to Julia's lingering grief over Ralph's death. Although Brown enjoyed college and her sorority, she found herself in trouble in 1964 when she became actively involved with the civil rights movement. When one of her Delta Delta Delta sorority officers criticized her for associating with "nigras" and asked her if she wanted to marry one, Brown rejoined, "I don't care if I fall in love with a black or a white or a man or a woman or an old or young person" (Jackovich, 81). When word of her controversial reply got to the dean of women, Brown was charged with being a lesbian and her scholarship was taken away from her. She was forced to undergo daily therapy with the campus psychiatrist and was placed under what amounted to "house arrest" in the dorm. Years after this incident, Brown still reacts with hostility and bitterness at this great injustice: "Those sons of bitches weren't going to say this was due to my civil rights involvement. Still make me mad? How could you tell? . . . Christ, I've never been in so much trouble in my life, plus getting beat up for it. The violence was easier to take than the hypocrisy" (*Starting from Scratch*, 11).

Without money she could not remain at the university, so she hitch-hiked to New York City in the summer of 1964. Her first address was an abandoned car she shared with a black gay man who was also exiled from the South and an orphan cat she named Baby Jesus. Brown then worked as a waitress for a while and finally earned a scholarship to New York University where she studied the classics and English. She received her bachelor of arts degree in 1968. Although she did appreciate the museums and the many free plays, Brown did not particularly like living in New York; as she wrote in an autobiographical essay, "Take a Lesbian to Lunch," "If you are young, female and poor, New York City is worse than Dante's Inferno. You are walking game for all manner of sick hunters. Looking back on those days, I'm not quite sure how I survived" (*Rapper*, 84–85). Interested in a possible filmmaking career, she continued her studies, receiving a certificate in cinematography at the School of Visual Arts in Manhattan. This experience later helped her to get a job as photography editor for Sterling Publishing Company.

Activist and Writer

During her years in New York City as a student and survivor, Brown became involved in gay and feminist issues, forming the Student Homophile League at New York University and Columbia University in 1967 and helping to open a women's center on the Lower East Side. An

early, active member of the National Organization for Women, Brown
was disappointed by N.O.W.'s class pretensions and its refusal to address
the issue of lesbians in the women's movement: "N.O.W. was, to make
a long story short, full of shit. A women's movement is for women. Its
actions and considerations should be for women not for what the white,
rich, male heterosexual media finds acceptable" (*Rapper*, 87). Outspoken
about her lesbianism, Brown managed to win enough respect from the
other women to become editor of the organization's newsletter and
administrative coordinator for the national office. Frustrated by her
position as token lesbian and critical of N.O.W.'s "sexist, racist and class
biased attitudes," Brown blasted the group's leadership in the January
1970 newsletter before she resigned to join a more radical feminist
group, the Redstockings (*Rapper*, 91). When they, too, had difficulty
accepting her lesbian feminism, she became involved with Gay Liberation, a radical homosexual organization of men and women. But Brown
became disillusioned with this group because of the lack of political
awareness of the lesbians and the different political agendas of the male
gays. After these experiences, Brown moved hesitantly in the direction of
radical lesbian separatism: "This is a call for a separatist movement of
Lesbians? Yes and No. No, (speaking for myself) because I do not want to
be separate from any women. Yes, because until heterosexual women
treat Lesbians as full human beings and fight the enormity of male
supremacy with us, I have no option but to be separate from them just as
they have no option but to be separate from men until men begin to
change their own sexism" (*Rapper*, 94–95).

Her evolving political philosophy led her to Washington, D.C., to
participate in a communal living experiment, the Furies Collective,
modeled on the Bolshevik cell. Brown was a lecturer at Federal City
College (1970–71), a research fellow at the Institute for Policy Studies
(1971–73), and wrote political essays for *Quest* and other feminist journals. For a number of reasons, which she details in her "Introduction" to
A Plain Brown Rapper, Brown was voted out of the collective on 6 March
1972. She learned a lot about herself and about feminist politics from her
experience. Along with Brown, other women in the collective contrib-
uted significantly to the feminist movement. Charlotte Bunch, a longtime fellow at the Institute for Policy Studies, currently holds the Laurie
New Jersey Chair in Women's Studies at Douglass College, Rutgers
University. Involved in the formation of *Quest*, she has edited and written
several books about various aspects of the women's movement, lesbian
feminism, and global feminism. Coletta Reid and Nancy Myron were

founding members of the feminist Diana Press (which would soon publish some of Brown's work). Ginny Berson and Jennifer Woodhul helped start Olivia Records, a successful distributor of women's music. Joan Biren began Moonforce Media, a feminist filmmaking and distribution company.

Brown began her writing career around this time, publishing not only many essays for feminist journals, but also a translation, *Hrotsvitha: Six Medieval Latin Plays*, and her poetry collection *The Hand that Cradles the Rock*. Both books were published by New York University Press in 1971. Her second volume of poetry, *Songs to a Handsome Woman* (1973), and her collected essays, *A Plain Brown Rapper* (1976), were published by Diana Press. With the encouragement of actress Alexis Smith (for whom her second volume of poetry was written) and with the purchase of an expensive Mont Blanc Diplomat fountain pen ("my magical pen"), Brown began writing her first work of fiction, a novel based on her youthful experiences. *Rubyfruit Jungle*, rejected by mainstream presses, was first published in 1973 by Daughters Press, a small, feminist publishing house, and later reprinted by Bantam Books in 1977 after Bantam purchased the rights for about a quarter of a million dollars, which they paid to Daughters, who gave Brown half of the money.[8] With Bantam's purchase of *Rubyfruit Jungle*, Brown was finally able to write full-time. She had previously supported herself with grant funds and by teaching writing at the Women Writers Center in Cazenovia, New York, and at Goddard College in Vermont. In 1973, she was involved with the planning of Sagaris, an independent feminist institute, and taught a session on leadership when the collective opened in the summer of 1975.[9]

Rubyfruit Jungle was followed by *In Her Day* (1976). Brown made the transition to mainstream press with the hardcover publication of *Six of One* (1978), published by Harper and Row, who has published several of her subsequent novels. In her interviews given during this period, Brown proclaimed loudly that she did not want to be considered a lesbian author: "Look, calling me a lesbian writer is like calling Baldwin a black writer. I say no; he is not: he is a great writer."[10] She did not want to be pigeonholed or stereotyped by the narrow category of gay writer: "My whole message is that we're *not* different. Sure, there are some things different about being gay or poor, or black or old, but they're not so monumental as to be impediments to human communication. Next time anybody calls me a lesbian writer I'm going to knock their teeth in. I'm a writer and I'm a woman and I'm from the South and I'm alive, and that is that" (Holt, 16). Because her books do speak to family and human issues with compassion and humor, they have found mainstream acceptance despite their many outrageous characters and controversial situations.

Return and Romance

In 1978 Brown made an important move to Charlottesville, Virginia, back to her roots in the South. She claims to have wanted to move to Virginia since she was five years old, her natural father's family having "a deep taproot in Charlottesville."[11] There, she shared a house with actress/writer Fanny Flagg (*Coming Attractions, Fried Green Tomatoes at the Whistle Stop Cafe*) before she met tennis champion Martina Navratilova. Brown talks about their relationship in several interviews; Navratilova writes about it in her 1985 autobiography. Looking at both sides of the story carefully, one is able to piece together what brought these two strong, intelligent women together and what caused them to separate so painfully after two years together. They met through a mutual friend in Richmond on 8 August 1979, but it was not until several months later that they renewed contact and began their relationship. Soon thereafter they bought a large home on the outskirts of Charlottesville.

Brown's first impression of Navratilova was a foreshadowing of what would later drive them apart; as she tells her friend Armistead Maupin in 1982, "She was a nice young girl in a limiting profession; where you can make a lot of money but know very little" (Maupin, 50). Since Brown had always been attracted to older, more sophisticated and mature women, Navratilova's youth and emotional inexperience were constant impediments in their relationship. As Brown's mother warned, "Honey, *have* a child, don't marry one" (Maupin, 50). Another issue was Martina's "limiting profession"; Navratilova felt that Brown had very little respect for the game of tennis as a career, seeing her own work as a writer to be very much more important than Navratilova's need to practice and compete. As Navratilova writes, "Rita Mae had a way of putting it [tennis] down, almost to the point where if I was working hard, I was doing something wrong."[12] Brown stimulated Navratilova's intellectual growth, one of the major reasons for Navratilova's attraction to her, but this encouragement to read books, visit museums, discuss politics, and collect books about architecture eventually seemed a subtle means of criticizing her sport and career.

After the Billie Jean King palimony scandal, more attention was focused on lesbianism in the sports world, causing fear among Navratilova and other players that sponsorship might be affected. Openly and publicly gay, Brown was less personally bothered than Navratilova when reporters began to pursue this topic. Brown was critical, however, of the hypocrisy implied in the search for lesbians when gay men were not being equally exposed and when there were more gay professionals than gay sports stars.[13] Navratilova, an immigrant, was particularly concerned about her citizenship status, which might be endangered, she felt, by scandal. Brown blames the breakup partly on Navratilova's new relationship with basketball star Nancy Lieberman, although Martina still insists that Lieberman was simply a coach helping her improve her tennis game and winning attitude. On the other hand, Navratilova sees the main problem as Brown's interference, however unintentional, with her tennis dreams. When they spent time together in Charlottesville, Brown insisted on privacy for her work, but according to Navratilova, Brown would make Martina feel guilty for practicing tennis and keeping in shape: "After a while, it got to the point where it was better if she stayed home instead of accompanying me on the tour. It was easier for me to go about my business, to play my matches, when I didn't have to worry about Rita Mae getting her peace and quiet" (Martina, 213). The stress on their relationship from the conflicting demands of their separate careers eventually affected Martina's game: "What was wrong was my attitude. I had lost the singleness of purpose I'd had when I was first coming up. I had become ambivalent about tennis, ambivalent about myself, ambivalent about my career" (*Martina*, 213). Blaming much of this ambivalence on Brown's influence, Navratilova turned to Lieberman, who promised to help her overcome this attitude and rededicate herself to winning. Brown, however, perceives another element of career conflict in their relationship; "when she left me, she said very simply, 'I'm tired of being your second banana'" (Maupin, 50). When at parties, Navratilova might start out being the center of attention, but people eventually gravitated to Brown because of her wit and social skills (poise that Brown claimed she had gained by virtue of her Southern upbringing) (Maupin, 50).

One point of contention between the lovers was the manner in which the breakup occurred in April 1981. Brown insists that she first heard about it after Navratilova gave a press conference in which her manager told the press that Martina was no longer under "the influence of this terrible older lesbian and she [the manager] was going to teach her [Martina] how to be straight."[14] Brown says that the reporters broke the news to her on her front lawn the next day. "I felt like I'd been blindsided and I guess I was really stupid" (Julian, 38). Not even her friends in

Charlottesville who knew the couple predicted this outcome. Navratilova
tells a different version. She reveals that Brown overheard her talking on the
telephone to Lieberman, and a violent physical, emotional fight erupted
when Navratilova expressed her determination to leave: "She was hurt,
anybody would be, and we got into one of the nastiest, most physical
arguments I ever hope to be in. We stormed around the house raging at each
other, from room to room, until I couldn't take it anymore" (*Martina*, 220).
She eventually gave cautious interviews about her relationship with Brown
and was upset when they were published against her wishes. The next
painful aspect of their breakup was the financial settlement and physical
separation. When Navratilova moved to Dallas to share an apartment with
Lieberman, Brown could not afford to stay in their mansion and moved to
Los Angeles for a while to work on scripts to support herself. After the
trauma of the divorce was complete, however, Brown and Navratilova were
able to become friends again; as Brown marvels, "That's what's so incredible
about our friendship. We've done the worst we can do to one another, and I
love her more now than I did then" (Julian, 38). Navratilova reminisces
fondly, "Even now I think about Rita Mae, and I know she was someone very
special. God, there are times when I'm talking about something, and I can't
quite get the facts right, and I think to myself, Rita Mae would have the
answer" (*Martina*, 220).

Brown as Scriptwriter

Brown was hired by Norman Lear to write part of his ABC special "I
Love Liberty," which aired on 22 March 1982. Working with other
writers on the script, Brown learned how to "scale down" her style to suit
television demands (*Starting from Scratch*, 17). The show won the Writers
Guild of America Award and earned an Emmy nomination for the
writers. Nineteen-eighty-two also saw publication of her fourth novel,
Southern Discomfort, and the release of a horror film based on a script she
had written several years earlier. Her script, entitled *Sleepless Nights*, was
intended to be a spoof of the horror genre, but the final product, called
Slumber Party Massacre, possessed more gore than wit. Although directed
by a woman, Amy Jones, the film was produced by Roger Corman,
notorious for his low-budget horror films. When criticized for her
participation in such a sexist genre, Brown defended her original script:
"It's a feminist film—in the end, the girls save themselves. There's no
deus ex machina."[15] For many years there had been talk of a film version
of *Rubyfruit Jungle*; several interviews indicate that Brown had adapted a
script from her novel with Arnie Reisman and that Joan Tewkesbury

(famous for her script for Robert Altman's classic film *Nashville*) was scheduled to direct (Horn, C13). The film was never made. Brown was disappointed that the rights to her work had been sold, leading her to attempt to raise the money to buy back her option so that she could pursue her own production (Julian, 36).

After her separation from Navratilova, Brown underwent further emotional stress with the death of her seventy-eight-year-old mother, her seventeen-year-old cat Baby Jesus, sportswriter Judy Lacy (for whom she wrote and published the tennis novel *Sudden Death*, 1983), and former fiancé Jerry Pfeiffer (of AIDS). Again, several film projects kept her busy during this difficult time and helped her clear away some debts while she was researching her Civil War novel, *High Hearts* (1986). In 1985 she narrated a landmark documentary, *Before Stonewall*, which charts the history of homosexual life in America. She wrote the script for part one and co-wrote part two with Dennis Turner for the television remake of the 1958 film *The Long Hot Summer*, which was originally based on William Faulkner's *The Hamlet*. With Reginald Rose she co-wrote *My Two Loves* for the ABC Monday Night Movie. This controversial project explored a recently widowed woman's (Mariette Hartley) discovery of her sexuality as she is torn between loyalty to her deceased husband's best friend (Barry Newman) and her newly discovered passion for her lesbian co-worker (Lynn Redgrave).

New Directions

Brown experimented with new forms in her work, including a writer's manual entitled *Starting from Scratch* (1988), a sequel to *Six of One*, entitled *Bingo* (1988), and a murder mystery called *Wish You Were Here* (1990). At the time of this writing, she completed the sequel to *Wish You Were Here*, entitled *Rest in Pieces*, and plans to continue her Kitty Crime Series; she was also conducting research for a historical novel on the life of Dolly and James Madison and completing a novel to be called *Venus Envy*. Continuing to write teleplays and film scripts, Brown was awarded a grant by the American Film Institute for a film project.

Brown plans to remain in Charlottesville. The lovely countryside, the intellectual life at the University of Virginia, and the Piedmont Women's Polo Club (of which she was president and founder) have kept her infatuated with the region as well as providing much needed diversion from her regular writing schedule. Rising before dawn, Brown feeds her animals then begins writing; after lunch she heads for the stables for her afternoon ride. Living on a farm keeps her in touch with her environment: "I'm much more tied to natural cycles and the weather defines what I can do and what I can't, when I can plant and when I can't. And when you get away from that, for me, it would be disconnecting" (Ball, 9). Although she tours with each new book, Brown's activism is restricted to donating to her causes—money for AIDS research ("We are all becoming widows now, whether we are gay or straight. We are losing our men"), for the Society for the Prevention of Cruelty to Animals ("I believe other women will fight for children and that leaves me free to fight for the animals"), and for arts organizations ("My first priority is the arts because it's everybody else's last priority") (Ransom, 3B).

After Navratilova's departure, Brown lived alone for a decade, preferring the solitude that she needs as a writer: "I'm not a person who is driven to be coupled. I'm a lone wolf. I get along fine with people but I don't want them around me all the time, and I'm pretty sure I don't want them under my roof."[16] Her dedication to her writing, however, was not the only stated impediment to romance: "What woman wants me? Think about it. The kind of woman that would interest me would never, ever be seen with me. . . . Someone who loves her career, is bright, self-sufficient, and on a similar economic level to mine. . . . Anybody like that isn't going to risk coming out. I don't think I'm going to meet that kind of person and I'm not interested in someone who's going to be dependent and just follow me around" (Julian, 82). After many years of solitude, in an unusual twist of fate, Brown became romantically involved with Judy Nelson, the ex-lover of Brown's ex-lover Navratilova. When Nelson sued Navratilova after a widely publicized break up, Brown served as a go-between in the out of court settlement.[17] As Brown had previously written in *Six of One*, "love is the wildcard of existence." Nelson and Brown share a love of horses, their continuing friendship with Navratilova, and a house in Charlottesville.

When asked about her future as a writer, Brown exuberantly lists the many projects she wishes to accomplish: "When I sit down at the typewriter, I'm in love with literature; I'm in love with the English language; I'm not thinking about belonging to anybody or any movement. I'm thinking about writing the best book I'm capable of writing at that moment" (Carr-Crane, 4).

Chapter Two

Essays and Poetry: "Fingerprints on the Shape of Things to Come"

Written from the fall of 1969 to the winter of 1975, during the formative years of the women's movement, Rita Mae Brown's collection of essays, entitled *A Plain Brown Rapper* (1976), evokes the tumultuous history and heady emotions of the era. Not only were women fighting to gain political and economic power, but they were also battling each other within various women's organizations over the definition and achievement of their goals, the political role of gays in the movement, and the needs of working-class women and women of color. This era coincided with increasing student activism, the so-called "sexual revolution," and the gay liberation movement. In these essays Brown attempts to define herself in light of the changing attitudes of the times, reflecting in her exuberant writing the general excitement of the period, her hope for change, and her disillusionment with certain movement priorities and divisive factions. Despite her many frustrations with aspects of these revolutionary movements, Brown embodies a firm commitment to principle and to the power of activism. Stylistically, her essays also employ the broad humor, the social satire, the maddening contradictions, and the overall optimism of much of her later fiction. In fact, the essays contain the kernels of most of the ideas that she will develop in her fiction and espouse throughout her career. Though often marred by youthful, hotheaded extremism and simplistic solutions to complex problems, they provide a fascinating background for and introduction to her work. The pieces reveal that even in her early works Brown was indeed putting her "fingerprints on the shape of things to come."[1]

A Plain Brown Rapper: The Personal Is Political

Believing, as did many feminists, that the personal is political, Brown reveals elements of her physical and spiritual biography as she examines her life in the context of the important sociopolitical upheavals of her day. As she notes in her introduction, these "essays are as much a chronicle of the decade as of my own development" (*Rapper*, 22). The volume's title emphasizes her alliance with the working class ("plain") as well as her belief in consciousness-raising strategies and the discovery of women's political voice through association with black radical elements ("rapper"). Her introduction for the volume details her involvement with various political groups during the turmoil of the sixties. Noticing parallels to Sappho's revolutionary commitment in ancient Greece, Brown sees herself in the tradition of women committed to change for all women: "We are all daughters of those distant mothers" (*Rapper*, 9). Like Alice Walker and other contemporary feminist authors, Brown believes in the importance of continuity over the generations, especially the unwritten history of women. Her study of the classics confirmed her belief in the irrepressibility of the human spirit: "Every day I hit on some fantastic idea full 2000 years old and I recall even now the marvel I experienced at the continuity of human life" (*Rapper*, 12).

Brown attributes her first revolutionary rage to witnessing Candice Bergen during a film shoot in New York City. She noticed the discrepancies between Bergen, an artist raised in wealth and secure in a movie-making career, and herself, a destitute working-class woman, about the same age, making it on her own, filled with confidence and potential but without the means to easy success. As a result, Brown felt an extreme sense of injustice, not only for herself but for others who would not be able to achieve their dreams because of accidents of birth, race, or class. These democratic leanings soon blossomed into full-fledged political action. Brown disliked the student anti-war protesters and the self-righteous whites in the civil rights movement. She preferred to work on the grass roots level for feminist causes—establishing day care centers, schools, health care, and other services for women in the community. This preference for local action eventually led her and her characters back to the South, to their roots, to lead productive lives as models for the future.

Her second politicizing experience was her experiment with communal living with the Furies Collective in Washington, D.C. This arrangement was disappointing for several reasons. Brown tried to live what she preached but encountered conflicts with the middle-class women who were less open in their communication, especially of their emotions, and who felt threatened by Brown's competency and brash manner. She finally realized that "style is as important as content, politically and individually" (*Rapper*, 15). After her disillusionment with the Furies, it was hard for Brown to perceive their successes, though in time she learned to see the good in their attempts: "We are the bridge generation between the desert and the promised land. If we don't build it no one gets there . . ." (*Rapper*, 19). Despite her personal frustration with this communal arrangement, Brown felt compelled to dedicate the volume of essays to these women. These two turning points are emblematic for Brown and her generation—anger from perceived injustice is followed by commitment/activism that often leads to disappointment. In retrospect, Brown realizes: "Change, it becomes apparent, is not a convulsion of history but the slow, steady push of people over decades" (*Rapper*, 13). She exhibits a still strong belief in principle after her temporary setbacks, compromises, and failures. Brown attributes her strength to being not alone; she is encompassed by a "circle of flesh" of other women to whom she feels bound; the volume is implicitly dedicated to all women (as she dedicates her first book of poetry "to women everywhere").[2]

Brown, feminism, and the women's movement. The collection serves as a chronicle of the evolution of her activism. Beginning her first piece, a speech entitled "Violence" (Fall 1969), by questioning whether violence or passive resistance is more effective as a method of political change, Brown establishes a rhetorical pattern that she uses in other essays of asking questions, saying that she has no answers, then making a bold statement that one assumes is indeed her opinion of or "answer" to the question posed. In "Violence" she refers to her speech as "one horizontal question mark," but she ends with an italicized bold statement: "*No power group ever performs any action—no matter how beneficial to the people—unless it is in their self interest to do so*" (*Rapper*, 26). This same rhetorical strategy is followed in the two closing essays (which were apparently written for the collection, since credit for their prior publication is not given). "This Lady's Not for Burning" uses double entendre in the title to express not only the fear of feminists becoming witch hunters when they insist that everyone think and speak alike but also the proviso that this author no longer advocates violent solutions to problems. The essay asks how society can be changed but admits there are "no easy answers, no magic solution" (*Rapper*, 215); in the next chapter "Conclusion," however, she outlines very specific programs to feminize the patriarchal system.

As her involvement with the movement increased, Brown concentrated on writing about particular meetings, events, and issues instead of the generalized harangue, like "Coitus Interruptus," characteristic of the early pieces. The specific activist experiences that inspired the essays "Yale Break," "Something About 'Walk a Mile in My shoes,'" "Say It Isn't So," and "August 26, 1970, N.Y.C." helped Brown to formulate her views on feminist education, the nature of leadership, and the significance of political history. "Yale Break" describes the Women's Liberation Conference held 27 February to 1 March 1970 on the Yale University campus. A bastion of rich white male privilege, Yale provided a unique symbolic atmosphere for the conference of feminists. Brown contrasts the two featured speakers, Kate Millet and Naomi Weisstein, in terms of their presentation style. Brown appreciates Millet's ground-breaking efforts in such works as *Sexual Politics*, but her academic style of conveying her ideas is criticized. As Brown will later explore in her writings about education, the academic lecture approach is part of the partriarchal system that women should try to change. On the other hand, Naomi Weisstein's "personalized and intimate" talk brought the women to their feet in applause: "When she finished she was no longer a star but a flesh and blood woman and we knew we could touch her."[3] This humanized sharing would be a much better model for future education that the pontifical dispensing of knowledge associated with male aca-demia, what Brown terms "dessicated intellectual trips" (*Rapper*, 39). Calling for a learning collective, "a real, living place where we can come together and learn from each other," Brown recalls a workshop experi-ence where women suspended "the typical male forms of judgement and disapproval" in order to communicate truly in a playful but warm way with each other (*Rapper*, 38–39). Brown had learned the lesson of humor from her past as a lesbian; she knew people were more likely to accept controversial ideas if she were funny, not morbid, about her lifestyle. Humor is used to humanize the situation, to diffuse differences of opinion, and allow for more open communication: "We got away from the heavy, heavy political raps where words replace fists and sentence structure masquerades as reality. We spoke from inside and we laughed from inside also" (*Rapper*, 40). This emphasis on humor as a means of revolution is crucial in understanding Brown's later fictional works. Brown's interest in the development of a learning collective would lead to her involvement with Sagaris, a feminist model university.

   Brown not only shows that honest communication is important to the movement, but she also shows a commitment to action. "Operation Hassle," conducted during the conference, is described in "Something About 'Walk a Mile in My Shoes.'" The women learn from their playful assaults of males on campus that "no male in America wants to be in the position of a woman (dehumanized sex object) for even two minutes" (*Rapper*, 43). Subjecting men to the kind of sexist ogling and crude remarks that women face every day walking down a city street, the women experience the power of group action while putting men in their place. The whole episode sounds very much like one of Brown's later fictional anecdotes where roles are reversed and conventions are defied.

Complaints about male academic traditions and concern for activism recur in Brown's analysis of a feminist meeting in Boston in "Say It Isn't So." Marlene Dixon and Roxanne Dunbar are criticized for their imitation of the "let-me-tell-you-something approach" that "reeks of male identification" in "our academic whorehouses" (*Rapper*, 47). At this meeting, Brown belligerently challenges these two speakers during the discussion session after the lectures by comparing male oppression to the women's movement's own inability to accept lesbianism. Brown argues that women should not be inhibited by male strictures against homosexuality: "To love without role, without power plays, is revolution" (*Rapper*, 49). Dunbar responds by evading the issues: "Women can love each other but they don't have to sleep together" (*Rapper*, 50). She sees homosexuality as a "chosen oppression" that should remain hidden, while Brown wants to liberate women by bringing all oppressions into the open (*Rapper*, 50). Brown later criticizes Dunbar for her opinions of the relationship of the working class to the women's movement in "Roxanne Dunbar" (January 1972). Although in this essay Brown is careful to state that hers is "a political criticism, not a personal attack," Brown does claim that Dunbar's heterosexuality prevents her from seeing the political points being made by lesbians (*Rapper*, 119). Brown challenges her to "break through the brainwash of male supremacist ideology in her own head or she and other women like her will find themselves deeply betrayed by their own analysis" (*Rapper*, 128).

The importance of women's history to Brown is also revealed in the dramatic details of "Say It Isn't So." While Dixon lectures on women's history, Brown senses the connection between the current discussion and the gilt-framed pictures of the founding fathers surrounding lecture hall. The women at the meeting are being treated like the women in a portrait of the orator Daniel Webster, sitting speechless and powerless in the gallery. She ends the essay with another historical example in order to relate current activism to the past abolitionist movement, also led by women. When angry men attacked the hall where the abolitionists were meeting, the white women saved the blacks who were attending by taking their hands and individually leading them through the mob. This tactic is later used by the women's movement to display the solidarity of heterosexual and homosexual elements, but at this Boston meeting, the Dixon/Dunbar liberationists discreetly abandon the hall to the lesbian contingent in order to avoid the lesbian issue.

Brown, feminism, and class struggle. In "August 26, 1970, N.Y.C.," another historical example is used to establish the connection of the current movement to past struggles, this time to the movement for women's suffrage in the early twentieth century. The seventies' struggle for equal rights is plagued by the same mistakes that the suffragists encountered. Class, instead of lesbianism, is the divisive issue in the battle for equal rights. The suffragists, as well as the supporters of the Equal Rights Amendment (E.R.A.), were trying to gain privileges for the white middle-class women within the male establishment rather than fighting to end male oppression over all women. E.R.A., like the right to vote, is reformist rather than revolutionary. The day that provides the title for the essay was emblematic of the class problems facing the women's movement. The N.O.W. supporters of E.R.A. had organized a picket of the Stock Exchange, a lunch at a posh male-populated restaurant, and speeches in Battery Park for a visible media event of protest. On the same day, however, a group of waitresses went on strike for better working conditions without the publicity or support of N.O.W. At the N.O.W. rally there were "no cheers for the Wall Street workers, no cheers for the Black sisters thrown into jails, no cheers for the lesbians beaten senseless on the streets. The cheers were all for a future of projected goodies and for that old Equal Rights Amendment, the bandaid to heal the gaping, festering wound of rich, white, American male politics" (*Rapper*, 60). Despite her criticism of N.O.W. and the disappointment that women have not learned from the history of their struggles, Brown still ends her essay with the hope that truly oppressed women "will bypass rhetoric and make a revolution" (*Rapper*, 60). In her descriptions of these events, Brown shows her usual keen eye for contrasting details and social satire.

The movement's misperceptions about the needs of the working-class women enrage Brown in "The Last Straw" (Winter 1972). For her, the working class is much more than the foundation for Marx's theories of production. Identifying herself closely with the working class, Brown knows that class attitudes infect every aspect of a person's thought and behavior, often without that person's being aware of their influence. They certainly color Brown's personal and fictional perceptions of life. Middle-class women typically ignore the effect of class consciousness when they oversimplify the significance of a college education. According to Brown, just because a working-class woman goes to college, middle-class feminists often mistakenly believe that one has overcome one's background and is now just as privileged as the middle/upper class. Conversely, influenced by the New Left's glorification of the simple life, many middle-class feminists see downward mobility as a means of removing class differences. Brown is furious about this affront: "I don't want to live with mattresses on the floor, ragged clothes, dirt and spaghetti for supper every night. How anyone can imitate poverty and give it the flavor of 'inness' is so alien to me that it is disgusting. . . . Downward mobility is the greatest insult yet devised by middle-class people against the working class" (*Rapper*, 103). Neither attitude about education or downward mobility really solves the problems created by differences in class. Women must try to alter their behavior to eliminate ideas of privilege given to them through the rich, white, male, heterosexual elite: "Our collective responsibility as lesbians is to annihilate, smash, destroy male supremacy and build a New World. . . . If you are serious you will begin by changing yourself" (*Rapper*, 106).

Brown will continue to align herself with working-class values in her fiction, targeting the rich for her most scathing satire. Believing strongly that hard work will bring results, she refuses to apologize for wanting expensive material possessions when her writing career takes off. She is put in the strange position of justifying her possession of a Rolls Royce (she owned a 1964 Rolls Royce Silver Cloud in 1981), her country club membership, her fox hunting, and other seemingly elitist pursuits; as one of her critics writes, "Brown is not, of course, the first working-class revolutionary to find her intellectual commitment to socialism in conflict with her need to protect herself by acquiring material possessions."[4] In reponse ot her critics, Brown will essentially repeat the arguments of "The Last Straw." She will criticize the irresponsible wealthy while condoning her own hard earned privilege. Because of her roots in poverty, she is reluctant to see herself as privileged even after her writing career becomes financially successful. These contradictory views are translated into her novels as a certain ambivalence about wealth. Brown, however, is not concerned that she might contradict herself, for as she repeatedly comments, contradictions make life interesting.

Her working-class bias and her belief in grass-roots activism appear also in "Hanoi to Hoboken: a round trip ticket" (March 1971), in which Brown criticizes feminist activists who expend their energy working in Vietnam when they are needed much closer to home to work on America's own problems. She considers a visit to Hanoi to be a more "glamorous" or fashionable or exotic gesture than organizing workers to end discrimination in Hoboken, New Jersey: "By flying to Hanoi, you win attention of the male left. By working in Hoboken you attract no attention at all and by working with Lesbians you are quickly dismissed as irrelevant and sick" (*Rapper*, 64). Instead of fighting imperialism there, women need to work on the root cause of that imperialism—sexism. As Brown's activism and essays become more focused, she begins to explore possible actions to improve the condition of women in America. In order for women to achieve political power, women of privilege must rescue women without privilege with health care centers, day care, food, shelters, and other programs for survival. Next, re-education must be accomplished through consciousness-raising and feminist media. Feminists must then face the crucial issue of lesbianism before they also consider the explosive issues of race and class. Recognizing the enormity of the work projects she has outlined, Brown is realistic enough to comprehend that there are no easy solutions. Even so, women must begin the difficult work of changing the social conditions of all women: "Let's begin the slow and tedious labor here in our own backyard that will eventually change the world" (*Rapper*, 71).

Brown, feminism, and the media.   In a number of the essays in *A Plain Brown Rapper*, Brown advocates the beginning of social change through the formation of feminist media that will counteract the repressive male-dominated images that surround us all. In "The Last Picture Show," "A Manifesto for the Feminist Artist," and "I Am a Woman," Brown looks more specifically at the problem of sexist art and possible solutions to this social manipulation. Brown castigates Peter Bogdanovich's 1971 hit movie *The Last Picture Show* for its dishonesty in style and characterization and its absurd propagandistic version of life. Brown, like many lesbians and feminists, feels disinherited by media which ignore the problems of race, class, and sex in all of their "art rot, this media sabotage of our lives" (*Rapper*, 159). Not only do the filmmakers force their "white, middle-class, heterosexual male version of life" onto the public, but they have created degrading versions of women, blacks, and homosexuals that distort truth and fulfill the fantasies of those who control the images (*Rapper*, 154). In the case of *The Last Picture Show*, this coming-of-age movie is treated as serious art, with its dishonest and insulting black and white cinematography: "The shabby technical work is collaborated with the shabby storyline which is the archetypal relationship: two male friends. This time it's Sonny and Duane. Let's follow Sonny and Duane in their adventures. So we do. They get drunk. They hurt a deaf-dumb friend. They screw girls. They fight each other. From these activities Sonny's 'manhood' emerges, and understanding of life" (*Rapper*, 154). The film ignores racial issues and presents women as vacuous sex objects for the boys. There is no attempt to explain why all the characters are so shallow and so unhappy in their existence. As angry as Brown is about the portrait of women in the film, she is even more puzzled about why men glorify and rhapsodize over such insincere, adolescent portraits of themselves: "The men in this movie are not sensitive to anything except what is connected to their concept of self. They have zero ability to empathize with a woman's life and only the tiniest ability to empathize with each other. . . . The only time in the movie when a male character is not centered on himself, when he is drawn into another human life, is at death. . . . Is death what it takes to get men to realize they love somebody?" (*Rapper*, 156–57).

The only solution Brown sees to this problem of media propaganda is "to make our own films. We have to convey the truth of our own life experiences to the mass public" (*Rapper*, 159). Having gone to film school herself (she details her struggles in *Rubyfruit Jungle*, written at the same time as this essay), Brown knows how difficult it is to break into the sexist film industry, yet she has faith that feminist art can prevail: "Get yourself together and help build our own media. Write, paint, dance, speak, sing, act—it doesn't matter what you do as long as you do something" (*Rapper*, 160). If enough individual artists are creating, an impact will be felt in society. In the introduction to her novels, Brown often encourages her readers to write their own stories. She does not see the artist as an elitist separate from the rest of the world but as an ordinary person who has taken the time to dedicate herself to the hard, lonely task of writing.

Brown continues her analysis of the role of art in society in "A Manifesto for the Feminist Artist" (June/July 1972). She criticizes the white, male, heterosexual media which offer only nostalgia and porno-violence as legitimate art. These two dominant themes originate in "emptiness, starvation of creativity and hope, and incredible self-indulgence" (*Rapper*, 163). In contrast to an art that systematically rapes individuals and entire sexes / races, the feminist artist must provide "a vision for the future where no group rapes another, where force is not the heart of politics and egotism not the mind of art" (*Rapper*, 164). Despite her hope for the future of feminist media, Brown cannot blindly accept any art created by a woman as being automatically worthy of respect and emulation: "We do each other a disservice as artists if we pretend it's all quite marvelous and we weaken the intellectual growth of the entire Women's Movement which has too long fed itself the nectar of easy applause" (*Rapper*, 175). Though she finds it difficult to criticize a fellow woman artist, she does offer a critique of Viveca Lindfors's one-woman show *I Am a Woman* (in her October 1972 article by the same name) for its fairly exclusive focus on women's relationships to men only, its weak use of props, Lindfors's poor performance (in contrast to Colleen Dewhurst's powerful acting), and the one-woman format (which has been usurped by television). Brown is encouraged by this artistic failure, however, as she rallies women artists to create a feminist media: "Make your decision now to work with women, build, create our new art. Don't wait for an establishment actress to legitimize you. Many of you are as good if not better than Viveca Linfors [sic]. Develop your talent. Be energized by your strength. Support your sisters. Organize a media network" (*Rapper*, 179).

Another way in which the establishment media have manipulated the women's movement is through their creation of stars, as Brown details in her February 1972 essay "Leadership vs. Stardom." Brown defines the "star" as a very visible token symbol selected by the male media to represent what all women are thinking, but the star (such as Betty Friedan, Gloria Steinem, Germaine Greer, and other television talk show guests) has no political following and is no real threat to the power structure. On the other hand, "a leader, for us, is a woman who comes from the ranks of the movement. She works hard, has probably been responsible for political analysis and/or program. . . . is intensely concerned with helping other women become leaders" (*Rapper*, 142). Since the concept of leadership brings up images of aggressive, egotistical male models, many serious women fear becoming leaders themselves or attack the true leaders among them: the true woman leader "is much easier to attack than the oppressor so she provides some relief from the frustrations that accompany oppression" (*Rapper*, 144). Brown knows, however, that women must overcome the personal/psychological level to enter the political realm and thereby foster meaningful change. She advocates the formation of a political party, one that will differ from the male-structured politics but will nonetheless allow many women leaders, in many different areas, to emerge.

Brown, lesbianism, and sexuality. Most of the essays reveal Brown's attempts to explain the political significance of lesbianism, its place in the women's movement, and the nature of lesbian identity. For Brown, as for many radical feminists, lesbianism is the logical end of women's liberation. Many of the more moderate feminists, especially the heterosexual constituency, feared the recognition of the lesbian element in the movement because this sexual behavior would give reason to the white male patriarchy to dismiss the claims of the movement for equal pay and equal rights. Of course, one of the first responses the opposition uses to discredit the ideas and demands of any feminist is to call her a "dyke." In sexist male eyes, women want rights because they are too ugly to get a man to take care of them. Despite the initial controversy, many feminists, straight and gay, defended the right of lesbians to participate in the women's movement.

For the radical feminists, lesbianism redefines sexuality, challenges the system of sexism, and undermines the power of the patriarchy. Those are the real reasons that men are so threatened by women loving other women. Brown participated in the collective writing of what became the separatist manifesto of the times, "Woman Identified Woman," which, though not included in *A Plain Brown Rapper*, nevertheless reveals much about Brown's political stance in 1971. "Lesbian" is defined by the writers from the New York Radicalesbian group as "the rage of all women condensed to the point of explosion. She is the woman who, often beginning at an extremely early age, acts in accordance with her inner compulsions to be a more complete and freer human being than her society—perhaps then, but certainly later—cares to allow her."[5] Because the lesbian refuses to be socialized to the traditional female role, she comes into "painful contact" with the realities of a sexist society, which leads her into awareness of the "essential aloneness of life" and dispels "the reality of illusions" ("Woman Identified Woman," 87). This "tortuous journey" into self-discovery can teach the lesbian that "the liberation of self, the inner peace, the real love of self and of all women, is something to be shared with all women—because we are all women" ("Woman Identified Woman," 87).

Since a sexist society is responsible for the artificial and "inauthentic" categories of heterosexuality and homosexuality, the label of "lesbian" will be used to try to keep women within the bounds of traditional sex roles as long as men retain power in society. Until the common definition of "woman" includes the characteristics of strength, independence, and active definition of self, "lesbian is the label invented by the Man to throw at any woman who dares to be his equal, who dares to challenge his prerogatives (including that of all women as part of the exchange medium among men), who dares to assert the primacy of her own needs" ("Woman Identified Woman," 87). Thus, lesbianism is seen as an expression of rebellion against the status quo, of the assertion of the freedom of the individual in an essentially oppressive society.

The essay also grapples with the problem of women being defined only by their sexuality. Homosexual and heterosexual women are both defined by men in relation to their sexuality, how women respond to men, not by how they define themselves as human beings. Even some feminists perceived lesbianism as an alternative to sex with men, thus still defining female sexuality as a response to men. Since at this time the women's movement was trying to deny the importance of lesbianism as a feminist concern, the essay insists that "until women see in each other the possibility of a primal commitment which includes sexual love, they will be denying themselves the love and value they readily accord to men, thus affirming their second-class status" ("Woman Identified Woman," 88). The writers call for the creation of a new sense of cultural and individual identity for all women. In their second-class status in an oppressive male-dominated society, women are afraid to identify with other women: "For to confront another woman is finally to confront one's self—the self we have gone to such lengths to avoid. And in that mirror we know we cannot really respect and love that which we have been made to be" ("Woman Identified Woman," 88).

Just as lesbians are forging their new identities through sisterhood with other women, so should all women turn toward other women to discover their true selves, freed of definitions created by the male superstructure. Only when women discover their individual identities will society at large be able to change: "It is the primacy of women relating to women, of women creating a new consciousness of and with each other which is at the heart of women's liberation, and the basis for the cultural revolution" ("Woman Identified Woman," 89). If women in the movement spend all of their energies trying to be recognized as equals to men, when men refuse to allow that equality, women will lose the opportunity to create new patterns of behavior and thought that will truly liberate them.

"Woman Identified Woman" not only defended the place of the lesbian in the women's movement but also laid the foundation for the separatist philosophies to follow. The influence of these ideas about lesbian identity and politics is evident in Brown's essays in *A Plain Brown Rapper*, although she eventually decides against separatism as a permanent answer to sexism. "Coitus Interruptus" (February 1970) describes the basic sexual incompatibility of men and women. Brown seems influenced by "The Myth of the Vaginal Orgasm" by Anne Koedt, a significant essay based on Masters and Johnson's sexual research, as well as feminist revisions of Freudian theories of penis envy.[6] Men and women want different things from a relationship: "The male seeks to conquer through sex while the female seeks to communicate. Put the two together and you breed hate" (*Rapper*, 29). A sexist society is detrimental to both men and women for it denies them full expression of their complex humanity outside of stereotypical roles. A sexist society demonstrates America's underlying hatred of sexual activity in general and its hatred of women in particular. Men refuse to see that sexism is political because they benefit from the system and because men are not defined by their sexual function alone as women are. The issue of female identity is crucial to Brown's thesis; women who accept a definition based on sex alone "accept spiritual lobotomy" (*Rapper*, 30). Critical of feminists who fear being defined as lesbians (because of what men might think), Brown tries to counter the male definition of lesbians as women who cannot attract men or who have been hurt by men. Males cannot accept the lack of conquest in female relationships: "To sleep with another woman is to confront the beauty and power of your own body as well as hers. You confront the experience of your sexual self knowledge. You also confront another human being without the protective device of role" (*Rapper*, 32). Though Brown is aware of the divisive aspect of male/female roles, how the roles prevent people from seeing life in human terms, she refuses to play the role of educator/nurturer for men. Too much woman energy has already been spent trying to teach men to become better human beings: "Men must educate themselves" (*Rapper*, 34).

Despite a degree of sensitivity to the harm that sexism causes all human beings, Brown displays in her sarcastic style a hostility toward men, both gay and straight. Straight men, whether conservative corporate businessmen or enlightened liberals, possess egos which "can swell up like a bloated tick, gorged on his various conquests" (*Rapper*, 29). The parasitic nature of man's existence implied in this grotesque image is developed later in Brown's poetry describing the decay associated with male civilization. Man can proudly display himself as a sexual being, using the "prick as proof of his manhood, the locus of this identity as a male" (*Rapper*, 30). The bitterness that she feels toward men who try to discredit women as lesbians is clear: "When you think about it, what is so terrible about two women loving each other? To the insecure male, this is the supreme offense, the most outrageous blasphemy committed against the sacred scrotum" (*Rapper*, 31). She later refers to male sexuality as "cock privilege" (*Rapper*, 31). Gay men are also criticized for their misunderstanding of lesbians: "The more [lesbians] look like traditional

female sex objects, the more accepted they are" by the male gay community (*Rapper*, 33). Part of her hostility can be explained by the personal
anecdote that closes the essay. After receiving a threatening phone call
from a man who charged her with being a lesbian, Brown wishes that she
were not hurt by such vengeful violent gestures, but in a sexist society it
seems that personal identity as a lesbian still makes one vulnerable to the
group in power.[7]

While many of her fellow feminists used the woes of sexual repression
to call for a lesbian nation, Brown refused to support permanent separatism as a solution to sexism: "Separation is what the ruling rich, white
male wants: female vs. male; black vs. white; gay vs. straight; poor vs.
rich. I don't want to be separate from anyone—that just keeps the Big
Man on top of all of us" (*Rapper*, 95). Using this appropriately sexual
image, Brown interprets separatism as a capitulation to patriarchy.
Groups need to unite in common cause to defeat the forces of sexism,
instead of rejecting the politics of lesbian feminism: "The last thing that
I want is separatism. . . . Together we can change the entire society
and make a better life for ourselves individually and collectively" (*Rapper*, 95). In her essay, "The Shape of Things to Come" (January 1972),
Brown targets heterosexual women for holding on to their male-
sanctioned privileges and preventing unity by wasting their energy on
men: "Heterosexuality keeps women separated from each other. Heterosexuality ties each woman to a man. Heterosexuality exhausts women
because they struggle with their man—to get him to stop oppressing
them—leaving them little energy for anything else" (*Rapper*, 111).
Against this anti-heterosexual litany, Brown posits the virtues of lesbianism, including freedom, equality, self-discovery, true intimacy: "Lesbianism also offers you the freedom to be yourself. It offers you potential
equal relationships with your sisters. It offers escape from the silly,
stupid, harmful games that men and women play, having the nerve to
call them 'relationships.' It offers change" (*Rapper*, 112).

Although this statement about the possibility for change sounds
unrealistic and naive, Brown is astute enough to realize that change will
not be easy. "The Good Fairy," published in the summer of 1974, refers
to the legendary creature that can instantly transform someone into a
princess or a toad without the slow painful process of change. Since there
is no way to perform this instantaneous transformation in real life, the
women's movement has to face some tough truths about the nature of
personal and political change. Americans in general fear change and
differences as threats to the status quo, so feminists must make women

aware of how influenced they are by the assumptions of their culture. Whereas feminists often gather around issues that create changes in material status, lesbian-feminists support changes on the emotional/ spiritual level that encourage woman identification. The personal changes that Brown delineates in the essay are ones that also express a fundamental change in attitude that can eventually further political goals. Brown is especially interested in non-verbal communication, how women use space, eye contact, voice, and posture as a reflection of their values and internalized self-esteem. Women must first reclaim their bodies, their sexuality, outside the prescribed roles, then political changes can follow: "The external reflects the internal. As the feminist demands more physical space and reclaims her strength, so too, she seeks increased political space. She is no longer willing to be defined by men, sexually or politically" (*Rapper*, 189–90). An avid tennis player and horseback riding enthusiast, Brown celebrates the body and its significance to women's acquisition of political power. Life is a process of continual change, of becoming: "I wouldn't want it any other way, would you?" Brown concludes with enthusiasm (*Rapper*, 191).

Throughout these essays, Brown describes a lesbian identity that is aligned with the positive traits of freedom and self-knowledge. Despite her belief in the need for an individual's internal change, in "It's All Dixie Cups to Me" (Winter 1975), Brown warns against the dangers of pop psychology's disposable identity, the false illusion that we can build an identity: "The need for conscious identity is a manufactured item. The fact that so many people are dismantling and refurbishing themselves turns this phenomena [sic] into a bizarre assembly line" (*Rapper*, 194). Though she advocates continual change as the natural process for the growth of the individual, too much self-analysis can alienate one from experience or make a person too self-absorbed ("narcissistic paralysis") (*Rapper*, 194). For the feminist, the self must include a "conception of the past and a possibility of the future," a reconciliation with the history of women under matriarchy and partriarchy (*Rapper*, 196–97). Brown defines her own sources of "root self" as emotion (love and fear) and work. Both of these areas allow her to forget her "social self" (built on comparison and awareness of difference) and to become unselfconscious, at one with her fundamental being. Similarly, woman identification helps women to achieve personal and political freedom, when they see how their individual selves are united to other selves in common goals: "Slowly, heightened self-consciousness fades as we connect, understand, love and breathe the lives of our sisters. . . . Within the goal of women's freedom we find our more personal goals" (*Rapper*, 200). In her novels, Brown focuses more on the expression of the individual lesbian female identity than on the larger political identity. In particular, as we shall see, the characters must shed their false notions, their socially defined roles, in order to discover their true "root selves."

From non-fiction to fiction. Throughout these essays, Brown displays a righteous rage against all forms of injustice, based on an understanding of her personal experience and of social/economic history. She is idealistic yet practical in her approach to the problems that face women. Believing in the validity of individual effort, Brown transforms the basic American/Protestant work ethic into dynamic social action. She espouses hard work as the solution to almost every problem she describes. Her politics reveal a grass-roots orientation; if the individual can improve herself, she can improve her small community, and she can make progress toward the improvement of society at large. Not only is change necessary, but it is the natural, fundamental condition of life. More importantly, change is possible. Though the pervasive sexism she describes seems overwhelming, Brown has faith that change can happen. In these essays, Brown embraces the challenge of life and displays her essential optimism about the human condition. Her faith in the future is rooted, in these essays as in her fiction, in her understanding of history, that we are influenced by what we have been.

In the essays, Brown is able to express much of her anger so that her novels are relatively free of the polemics that one finds here. Her early activism is channeled into her prose fiction as she follows the philosophy developed in these writings. She will use her fiction to create new communities where differences are tolerated and people learn to solve their problems individually and collectively. Her characters must rid themselves of false social identities and face life honestly. Individual change must occur before wider social change can take place. Thus, her withdrawal into her artistic career is not a betrayal of her principles of activism, but the first step that every concerned person must take. Often reprinted by small feminist presses in essay collections, Brown's pieces were important also for expressing a new, non-academic way of writing about politics. Since traditional academia was a target of feminists for its male intellectual bias, this new personalized form of essay based on interpretation of individual experience encouraged other women to share their own ideas as well. The small feminist presses provided an outlet for this important writing. Though Brown has sought a mainstream audience for her novels, so that she can influence more people with her subversive humor, she has always supported the specialized feminist press as an outlet for her political articles and poems. Whereas some feminists ardently believe that women should publish only in women's presses, Brown sees the value of reaching a wider audience with her work as a logical extension of the political philosophy expressed in these articles.

The Hand That Cradles the Rock: Poetry as Protest

"Dedicated to women everywhere," *The Hand That Cradles the Rock* conveys in its very title the issues of radical feminism and woman's social role in contemporary society that Brown will explore in her later fiction.[8] Instead of the traditional female role as mother, ruling the world through procreation, modern woman must gain political power through activism or even through violence, if necessary. Brown's poetry, like that of many feminist poets of the early seventies, expresses her radical social views. She criticizes the patriarchal system of institutionalized sexism for its oppression of the human spirit. Only after the destruction of that civilization can a new world be born, one that is modeled on the female principle. In this first volume of poetry, women are identified with nature, while men are defined by images of death, decay, and destruction. Brown seems to be searching for the common bonds between herself as a woman and the female of all species in her quest to reclaim women's history. As she writes in her introduction to the reprint edition of her two poetry volumes, "we must struggle for justice for ourselves and for others. Poetry is part of that struggle."[9] Part of this revolutionary function entails evolving a new language to express the love that dares not speak its name, the love between women.

Apocalyptic vision.   In the poem that opens the volume, "On the Rooftop Where All the Pigeons Go to Die: A Litany for the Male Culture," Brown establishes the imagery of death that will dominate her poems about society's male institutions.[10] Particularly at fault are universities and governments ("warmakers" in her vocabulary). In this apocalyptic vision the institutions of knowledge and leadership have degenerated into "incestuous crabs" that feed off the dead. The natural world has been sullied ("dirtied seagulls") or destroyed ("ghosts of pigeons," "senseless slaughter of insects") by contact with man's machines and wars. The tulips are no longer "fat and fine"; the tortoises no longer "phosphorescent" in the moonlight. Though men have advanced in abstract knowledge ("triplets of nucleotides dance in their head"), they have yet to understand the ecology of the planet and to accept their responsibility for nature: "they dig subways to ignore the pigeon dead." William Butler Yeats's rough beast slouching toward Bethlehem in "Second Coming" is transformed into "some lost dinosaur," who searches for her progeny through time. This female dinosaur "crawling out of a blistering egg" suggests a primal female force that will continue to survive in this new millennium, characterized by "great hulks of decomposed intelligence" on "wastelands of the sea." Knowledge and science have failed: "Men fall into doubt/Clutching it in lieu of the truth," the poem concludes.

A similar vision of the failure of male-defined culture is presented in "Necropolis." In a scathing diatribe against "stillborn, celibate intellects," Brown dismisses the significance of the monkish scholars who have been responsible for transmitting the accumulated wisdom of the ages ("translating ignorance into Latin and Greek") when they know nothing of love, life, or nature ("endlessly dissecting the cadaver of a nun"). She ironically challenges these "secure hypocrites" to "Lead on!" for it is "easy to be king/When all your subjects are dead." Her triple battle cry of "Lead on!" is transformed linguistically into a chant of "Drone, drone/Drone your dreary dithyrambs." In the closing line Brown calls down the "curse of the makers" on these foolish intellectuals.

Yet another apocalyptic vision is presented in her triptych "The New Lost Feminist"; this poem abandons the imagery of the ancient world for a prophetic look at the American landscape. The Center Panel in her portrait of the revolutions of the sixties and seventies takes place during the "twilight of the Supreme Court" when America's "rotting rib cage frames the gallows/Of her putrid goals." Government has failed to live up to its ideals of justice for all because Machiavellian tactics of expediency have permitted the means to "devour" the ends. The groups that have suffered the most from the staggering Goliath of government—blacks, women, and youth—must flee the "bloated corpse" of a dying civilization.

The far panels of this triptych vision of the end of our era describe the problems that feminists face in their attempts to restructure or transform society. The Right Panel describes the "leprous shadow" of a beast that causes women to fight among themselves. As in her political essays, Brown laments the divisive nature of feminist debates. Instead of perceiving the similarities that women share as an oppressed group, the women in the movement are divided by factors of class, race, sexuality, and philosophy and are thus prevented from discovering their true political identities. The second stanza questions the nature of that female identity. Since women have always been "limping on the edges of the History of Man," they have been denied access to their "forgotten and unknown selves." Though matriarchies have existed in the past, institutionalized sexism has wiped out individual and collective memory of woman's contributions to history. Brown's simple assertion "It's time to break and run" becomes a rallying call to action for the "new lost feminists" trying to find their way in the wilderness.

The Left Panel likewise deals with the discovery of woman's voice. Not only were feminists discovering the inherent sexism built into language, but they were also struggling to express themselves honestly and openly, to break the passive silence that deters women from participating in male-dominated arenas. As writer Judith McDaniel noted in 1977, "Language for me is action. To speak words that have been unspoken, to imagine that which is unimaginable, is to create the place in which change (action) occurs. . . . If feminism is the final cause— and I believe it is—then language is the first necessity."[11] The importance of the discovery of a new language is, in part, responsible for the proliferation of poetry in the early stages of the women's movement.[12] The "single, precious word" that Brown struggles to express is "Freedom." The images of violence and blood suggest not only the difficulty of trying to speak a new language ("Incoherent in the midst of men/I bleed at the mouth") but also the hostility which a woman will suffer for demanding her freedom. As long as freedom is "unrealized," women will bleed and die despite a "network of swollen blue veins/Large with my life force."

To celebrate the new epoch of the women's movement, Brown composed a poem entitled "Bullseye," which calls women to action. Images of time dominate as she describes how men throughout history have controlled human perceptions of time. Men attempt to harness nature by dividing what is eternal and fluid into rigid artificial demarcations. Woman, whom Brown associates with primal natural forces, must stop the old ways and begin a new era, measuring time by her heartbeats. In "For Men Only" Brown describes a similar view of time: Man is portrayed as a "creature of time," doomed to die, while woman is connected with the tide. The "I" in the poem is Brown speaking as an individual woman but also as a timeless elemental female force. In "Bullseye," time will become a vital living force not a prisoner of "dead men" who "climb pyramids to read the sky" or Indians who "calculate upon great golden calendars/Trapping time between betrayed stars." The woman to begin this new era is personified as a female centaur, who will use her bow and arrow to end the millennium. A mythological creature with the upper body of a man and the lower body of a horse, the centaur, with the exception of wise and gentle Chiron who was a tutor to many of the Greek heroes, was characterized by violence and aggression. In creating a female centaur, Brown makes a monster from a monster in order to break out of the boundaries of traditional female roles.[13] Women must tap into that primitive source of strength, to listen to their own heartbeats. This beating becomes a call to action at the end of the poem: "Woman, put your ear to your breast. / Hoofbeats."

Brown's wrath is not limited to the intellectual elite but also finds a target in the leftist liberal ranks. In "Radical Man" she condemns the male student liberals, as she had in her political essays, for their egocentricity. Brown saw firsthand the hypocrisy of many college radicals who espoused the principles of individual freedom (especially sexual) but wanted to treat women as sex objects.[14] Brown foresaw the connection between the student radicals and the "Me Generation" as she satirizes the male's "Eternal I, / A marvelous me of malevolence." Not only are men characterized by this enormous ego, but the whole era is infected by such selfishness.

Sisterhood is powerful.   In contrast to these poems that criticize the failures of male civilization, Brown incorporates in the volume a number of poems that extol the virtues of the female principle. The poems that deal more exclusively with women tend to be less strident in their tone, less complex in their structure, and more natural in their imagery than those poems that deliver political diatribes. Their simplicity is disarming yet deceptive. Though the tone is relaxed in these celebrations of women, the content is revolutionary in portraying lesbian / feminist issues. Some of the portraits of women can be perceived as references to sisterhood while most can also be interpreted as having a sexual subtext, thus revealing the contemporaneous debates within the women's movement. "The Disconnection" first seems a poem of sisterhood instead of one about sexuality, but it can easily work on both levels. The woman at first feels free to reach out to her sister (or lover) as "Strings and threads lay all about / And none of them connected / Or touched her outstretched hand." She seems temporarily to escape the bonds of the past or the social constraints of her rearing to connect with another woman. Soon, however, she discovers "strings and threads tie up her brain" and she retreats back into self-concern and self-absorption: "She sits and cradles her head / Afraid that it will roll away, / Too tired to cut it off." One's stability and sanity are threatened by the psychological constructs of one's social conditioning. Woman loses a chance for personal connection in a romantic relationship as well as political union with her sister in the women's movement.

The possibility of madness is very real for women trying to break out of years of submission and male control; freedom is frightening and dangerous. The suggestion of insanity is pursued in "For Sweet Ellen," a short poem whose alternate title explains its subject: "For a Brilliant Young Woman Who Lost Her Mind."[15] Brown appropriately uses the sea as symbolic of the female consciousness. Ellen was pulled under by the water into insanity, while Brown portrays herself as an amphibious creature, existing between the water and the shore. Brown's love of the sea as female symbol recurs often in her poetry, reflecting her background as a youth in Fort Lauderdale.

The individual relationship again becomes the collective experience in "The Invisible Sovereign." Brown sits on the trash heap of civilization like the princess on the glass hill waiting to be rescued by her lover or like "Man on the Dump" in Wallace Stevens's poem about the artist sitting on the trash heap of discarded images attempting to create fresh vision through his art. The "pile of broken bottles" is emblematic of the "smashed world" that "this decomposed glass city" portrays. In her poem "New York City" Brown likewise identifies images of glass with the hard, cold, brittle quality of city life. There she describes skyscrapers as "Great glass altars" and the city as a "flawed diamond / Aflame with imperfection." Through this nightmare world she follows the voice of a woman, who could be either a personal lover or, what is more likely here, a force of collective woman energy, "calling up the awesome world" that she has within herself. Blinded in this "forest of frightening familiars," Brown seems perched between two worlds, at the end of one life waiting to be reborn into the next.

The collective woman appears also in "Aristophanes' Symposium," existing as an eternal force searching through history for connection with "the one I knew / In thick clouds of prehistory," the primeval female. "Divided by some awful hand," the poem's persona longs for the day of union, when "I will know you as you know me / And one day you will call me, 'Woman.'" This sense of power that comes from a universal female life force is reflected in "Female of the Species." Brown compares herself to a wounded lioness, drawing upon all of her strength to continue the hunt though she knows she must "die on the run."

Most of the love poems in the collection, however, are personal and private, predicting the very personal tone of *Songs to a Handsome Woman*. She celebrates the physical love between women, the attempts to create a new language of love, and the romantic pangs of separation. "Canto Cantare Cantavi Cantatum" conjugates the poet's song to her lover. Awakening her passions, the woman charges the world with heat and light. But since she loves another, the fire that is burning in Brown is confined to a "lonely taper/In blackest night." In "The Midnight Caesura" Brown is confused by her lover's actions; "she kindly disengaged me/Or was I abandoned?" The difference of perspective as these lovers try to discover a common language ultimately does not matter to Brown; her main concern is having to go to bed alone, left to dream of her lover. Though physical connection is important to Brown, mental communion is equally valued. In "A Song for Winds and My Vassar Women," Brown celebrates the "beauty in the place/Lips touch" as all of nature begins to assume the form of woman's lovely body. But "minds miss the vital connection/And hearts wander" when total communication is not achieved.

The importance of communication is reiterated in "The New Litany," in which the "mute, prosaic Sappho" begs for the power of poetry, to "be blessed with song/To fling at the metaphors of darkness," "To bring the dawn and rein Time's ravenous mouth,/To spend the sacraments on sheets/Redeemed in a kiss." She must break out of her confused silence to be able to express the holiness that she wants from her love. When her lover does not hear her song, whether out of feigned deafness or simple rejection, the would-be lover poet is "left to pray/As Venus in her ascendency/Draws triangulations on reality." Love becomes a religion that redefines one's perceptions of reality. In this case, the mention of the triangle, used in the women's art of this period as symbol of the female genitals, suggests that this is not just abstract devotion, but a desire for sexual union with woman. The physical is deified when love becomes a religion for the lover.

Perhaps the most beautiful of Brown's poems to female love is "Song of My Wealth," which relies heavily on sea imagery for setting a symbolism. Her lover's ear becomes a nautilus shell as the poet transcends language to whisper "songs of dolphins dying in Floridean seas." These dying dolphins are transformed into jewelry to be displayed in Tiffany's aquarium-like window. Since the poet cannot afford such gifts for her lover, she offers a natural paradise of "cool sands," "tiny birds with invisible knees," and "night fish [that] flash fire under the moon." The moonlight shines on the naked lovers as they lie on the beach "Amid stars and starfish and shooting stars within us." The only jewel the poet can give is her soul, a pearl, "a piece of suffering enameled to joy." This lyric is paired, as are many of the other love poems, with a companion poem on the opposite page in the volume, "Song of a Poor Young Woman." The wealth that this "poor woman" possesses is also a connection with the natural world. Her body parts become birds, sea creatures, and rare gems. Because of her integration with the natural world, the woman gains strength to "burn for centuries unborn" with passion.

These poems are paired through their use of natural imagery and redefinitions of wealth in the context of lesbian relationships; "To My Wife" and "Dancing the Shout to the True Gospel" are companion pieces in their political statements about lesbian love. "To My Wife" extols a marital relationship that defies traditional heterosexual definitions of husband and wife since the lovers are two women. Again, language is inadequate to encompass this homosexual love; "wife" is a "paltry proper noun" that does not convey the depth of their bond. The sea provides a more appropriate description of their love: "Silently we are cementing our lives / As a coral reef is built / Blossoming into iridescence." The image of the reef reveals not only the slow process of establishing a lasting relationship, but also shows the foundation that couples create for other "sea orphans / Swimming in waters of absurdity." The political connection of the companion poem is shown in the subtitle: "The Song My Movement Sisters Won't Let Me Sing," that is, a sexual love poem to a beautiful woman. The poet's love causes her to tear through the darkness into the light that Brown associates with knowledge and passion. Her lover's breathing on her neck is "a luxury diminishing death."

Likewise, "St. Zita's Home for Friendless Women" and "Sappho's Reply" are paired to convey a political message. In the first, unwed mothers are victims of male sexual abuse and abandonment. Rather than turn to each other for support and reject men for their sexist behavior, the women "ignore each other / And steam to watery graves." Sappho's response to this situation is for women to unite to help each other: "an army of lovers shall not fail."

Songs to A Handsome Woman: "Kisses and Revolution"

After this diverse volume of political diatribes, feminist anger, and Latin satirical influence (Brown was studying Latin and acknowledges the strong influence of Horace on her work during this period), Brown's second volume of poetry explores the dimensions of romantic love. Because it was inspired by Brown's relationship with a specific woman, the actress Alexis Smith, *Songs to a Handsome Woman*[16] is more personal and intimate than *The Hand that Cradles the Rock*, which was dedicated to all women. But Brown refuses to separate the personal and the political. In her opening note to the reader, she knows that she cannot explain love although she is "fool enough to be open about [her] feelings" (*Songs*). The only certainty that she can express about love is that "it deepens experience, making all life exquisite and valuable" (*Songs*). When one individual loves another, then racism, classism, sexism are "doubly repulsive" (*Songs*). Love humanizes and calls one to action against the forces that would deny love and life. Written when she was also working on *Rubyfruit Jungle*, these love poems celebrate romantic love, a type of youthful adoration that Brown admits no longer interests her: "My typical preoccupation with romantic love has given way to a focusing on the love that lasts, or marathon love" ("Another Time," *Poems*).

Though the "handsome woman" is not identified in the poems, the references to the age difference, to her stage and movie roles, and specifically to "Follies," indicate Alexis Smith as the inspiration for these love poems. Born in 1921 in British Columbia, Smith specialized in playing "charming, resourceful, often cool and calculating leading ladies with aloof magnetism" in films of the forties and fifties.[17] She made her comeback in the early seventies on Broadway in Stephen Sondheim's musical *Follies*. Her avowed preference for experienced, aloof older women explains one reason for Brown's attraction to this beautiful and talented woman.[18] In "Follies" Brown praises Smith's accomplishments as she watches her performance on stage; the poem is a tribute to the artist who has "crossed the line between craft and creation." In "The Midnight Follies or Mary's Ass," Brown puns on the "ageless epiphany" of love that caused her "to follow a movie star" like the Wise Men followed the star to Bethlehem. The age difference is implied in "Travelogue" as Brown examines the lines in her lover's face as "the roadmap of her self." In both "Midnight Follies" and "Travelogue" the poet sees her relationship as a journey, one that leads to self-knowledge beyond the power of reason or logic.

The story of their relationship is most clearly established in "December 17, 1971 to December 17, 1972: A Narrative, of Sorts." Brown writes of meeting her, later having dinner with her and making a pass at her, and continuing to feel her presence when they were apart. Brown's political feminism seems to have been a stumbling block in their relationship. While Brown believes in activism and sees sexism as the underlying cause of all forms of oppression, her lover is politically incorrect because her consciousness has not been raised; she does not like to join organizations and thinks in terms of individual people instead of political movements. Language fails Brown as she tries to explain her lover's philosophy and as she tries to arouse her social consciousness: "This is no longer a poem/This is an effort/To find a form for the unspeakable." This conflict of the personal and the political will form the basis of the relationship depicted in *In Her Day*, in which an older closeted lesbian art professor has a troubled relationship with a fiery young feminist activist.

The age issue recurs in several poems as Brown explores the implications of age and experience in human relationships. In "Deja Vu: Watching Old Movies on the Late Night Show," Brown meditates upon seeing her lover in an early film when Smith was 27, the same age as Brown is at the time of writing the poem. Just as her lover is 51 and 27 simultaneously through the magic of the movies ("film makes time and history optional"), so Brown feels both 51 and 27 through her experience of empathy in love. She wants her lover to share her secret, forgotten dreams with her so that she "might grow rather than age." In "Broadway Delicatessan Lyrics for My Musical Lady to Sing in Her Shower," Brown depicts them as "identical strangers," who have both been at some time too young and inexperienced as well as both now being "old enough/To be caught between bed and bedlam." Not only can they share a common experience of time, but they can learn from each other. The younger Brown is "an apprentice to the future," while the older Smith can "find some remnant of [her] forgotten self" in the relationship. The teacher-pupil and mother-daughter stereotypes of lesbian relationships are implied but not exploited.

A number of the poems reveal sadness at feelings of rejection. When her lover refuses to speak to her, Brown has to control her youthful passion and learn to wait patiently, for "No woman born can be so cruel" ("The Ides of Age"). Though disappointed by one woman, Brown still has faith in the inherent goodness of women. When she is most dejected, she has "no gods to call on/Save a woman's heart" as she pleads for emotional comfort in the arms of her lover ("On Being an Orphan at Age 27"). When her lover is gone, the depressed poet asks for her lover to show mercy by returning to share her "flesh dreams" ("Mercy, Fairest Daughter of Thought and Experience").

As she indicates in her introduction to the reprint edition, Brown was attracted to Smith as a fellow artist: "I was drawn to a fine artist and nurtured my own art from her brilliance" ("Another Time," *Poems*). In "Beyond Vocabulary," Brown admires the actress's strong, fine hands that can communicate meaning, bypassing the need for words. She too wants to transcend language in her art as the poet expresses in "On Stage She Makes Thought Visible." Brown is somewhat ambivalent, however, about her lover's effect on her poetry. On the one hand, her love turns her into an ordinary woman as she loses her poetic voice in her awe of her lover's beauty ("True Confessions"). On the other hand, the lover functions as her Shakespearean "Dark Lady," inspiring her lyrical outpouring even as she feels rejected by love ("A Poet's Gift"). Feeling a kinship with Shakespeare's obsession, Brown continues to write because she knows that poetry will last and "These words carry what we were / And make us new." In "The Autograph of a Thought," however, the poet fears that her verse will become a "volume of forgotten love." Because her lover is silent toward her, Brown has "built empires with words / And cities of sounds." Having praised the actress in her first poem (entitled "Follies") for being able to cross "the line between craft and creation," Brown comes full circle in her final love poem as she recognizes that as an artist she too must take risks in order to succeed.

Though the volume is clearly dedicated to one woman, many of the poems still have relevance to other women in love. The passion, the fears, the pleasures of a romantic union are emotions with which other lovers can identify. Since there is a degree of role playing in all relationships, even the references to the actress / artist connect to a wider audience. Several poems also address issues of lesbian lovers in general. Attempting to explain her feelings to a woman who has not had a lesbian relationship, Brown poses a series of questions in "Dedicated to All Women Who Haven't Loved a Woman" that, in effect, show that sex with a woman is not that different from sex with a man. Though the woman's answer may differ from Brown's fervent lesbianism, she demands that the woman not avoid the question but seriously consider the issue. In another poem of the seduction of a heterosexual woman, "To My Dream Butch Straight Lady Who Bolts Her Doors but Leaves Her Windows Unlatched," Brown refuses to be quiet about her love: "It's not my fault we're both women / Why hold it against me?" The title implies that many straight women are tempted by the idea of a homosexual relationship and are at least partly open to experimentation.

Brown as Feminist Poet: "The Athenians Wrote Poetry, the Spartans Did Not"

Brown admits as she looks back on these early poems from the perspective of age and literary experience that she sees the volumes as the record of a brash young person, a recapturing of the spirit and events of those years in her life. Though some of the poems call to mind Wallace Stevens in the use of Floridean imagery or Stephen Crane in the use of the brief epigraph, or even William Butler Yeats in the use of apocalyptic landscape, the main merits of these poems are not literary. The significance of these works lies in their non-apologetic political stance and their unabashed celebration of women. Because of Brown's open politics, expressed vividly in her essays, and her vibrant lesbian sexuality, readers do not have to read between the lines to see what impact Brown's lifestyle had upon her artistic creations. The connections are clear, her sincerity unquestioned. The works were important, not only for their contribution to the feminist literary movement with its new emphasis on honesty, but also for their impact on Brown's perception of herself as a writer. Her first literary loves were poetry and theater. But Brown did not feel she could make a living at either of them ("Another Time," *Poems*). Despite her success as a novelist, she continues to write poetry as a mode of personal expression but does not consider it polished enough to publish. Like Anne Bradstreet, Brown sees these poems as unkempt children not ready to face the world.

The published poems assume a certain significance when seen in light of lesbian literature. As a vocal and well-known lesbian in the feminist movement, Brown was a visible role model for other poets and writers who wished to follow literary pursuits. Published both by an academic press (*The Hand That Cradles the Rock*) and by a feminist press (*Songs to a Handsome Woman*), Brown showed others the possibilities for publication. The early seventies saw the proliferation of poetry by women as the women's movement created a ready market for feminist writings. Brown was both a cause and a product of that era. But as Brown's colleague Charlotte Bunch notes in her essay "Reading and Writing for a Feminist Future," literature was essential to the evolution and spread of feminist ideology and was in fact a form of activism. Since the male hierarchy controls the mainstream presses, feminist publishing was the only alternative for most women writers, a way to distribute ideas in an inexpensive but creative way: "This creative rather than passive aspect of the written word is important for encouraging people to rebel and make change in society."[19] The activist component of women's literature at this time valued content over style, as women were struggling to find new ways of expressing themselves with newfound freedom.

Brown is not unaware of her own shortcomings as a poet. After starting out to write "a perfect poem," she eventually settled for writing good ones, "a few poems of which I was not ashamed" ("Another Time," *Poems*). She credits her classical training, her studies of Latin and Greek, and especially her admiration of Horace, for any qualities that her verse possesses. She criticizes her love poetry for being too emotional and uncontrolled: "occasionally the technique could carry the emotion, but usually the emotion spills all over the page" ("Another Time," *Poems*). This emphasis on content over literary style and merit is particularly evident in the poetry of the feminist movement. Jan Clausen has claimed that "poets *are* the movement," but she laments the uncritical approach that many readers and scholars take toward women's writing (Clausen, 5). Though poetry is like consciousness raising in that it breaks down the barrier between the personal and the political, helping women to discover their own voices, as the tradition of women's poetry evolves, more attention must be paid to the theory of feminist poetry.

The categories of poetic practice that Clausen outlines in her essay about the relationship of poetry to the feminist movement are relevant to an appreciation of Brown's verse. Brown's work was groundbreaking in its early emphasis on the theme of lesbianism, a topic that did not become prominent until the mid-seventies. Most of the early feminist poets proclaimed "I am a woman," while the next group of feminist writers proposed "I am a lesbian" as their central preoccupation in poetry (Clausen, 19). Like other writers of the times, Brown assumed that "feminist poetry is useful" (Clausen, 21). Brown recognized clearly the political implication of her anti-war and pro-woman poetry: "There's no such thing as an easy life and we must each struggle for justice for ourselves and for others. Poetry is part of that struggle. The arts alert us first to where the injustices hide and, of course, they hide in each of us" ("Another Time," *Poems*). She is critical of America because she hopes for change and she believes in the power of the arts to contribute to that change. With her usual emphasis on the continuity of history, Brown compares the modern women's movement to classical Greek civilization: "We have the ability to be the Athens of modern times as opposed to the militaristic Sparta. I remind you that the Athenians wrote poetry.

The Spartans did not" ("Another Time," *Poems*). The intellectual, cultural might of poetry is superior to the mere physical strength of the military.

   This desire for a "useful" poetry is implicated in the feminist quest for "the transformation of language as a key to the transformation of reality itself" (Clausen, 23). Adrienne Rich's dream of a common language is one shared by many feminist writers. Since poetry is such a language-intensive medium, it is only fitting that feminist poets concentrate on the power of language to express the self and to alter conventional ways of thinking. In "Poems Are Not Luxuries" Audre Lord writes, "I speak here of poetry as the revelation or distillation of experience, not the sterile word play that, too often, the white fathers distorted the word poetry to mean—in order to cover their desperate wish for imagination without insight" (in Clausen, 26–27). This discovery of the individual poetic voice and reclamation of poetic expression from male dominated practitioners have been both a blessing and a curse. As Rita Mae Brown discovers in her poetry, women must assert their identity through language, to break out of the traditional silences to which the sexist society has relegated them. But as Clausen realizes, expectations of feminist poetry can also inhibit the poet's creative freedom to deal with subjects outside the domain of feminist ideology. Writers are forced to be speakers for the movement in a collective voice as well as speakers for the personal individual conscience. Brown's volumes reflect this dichotomy. *The Hand That Cradles the Rock* presents the social view associated with the collective "we" experience of women, while *Songs to a Handsome Woman* responds directly and intimately to experience.

   The anti-critical response to feminist poetry, including Brown's, is a reaction against the traditional standards set by male critics and the male literary establishment. Two reviews of Brown's poetry reveal the typical bias against feminist work. One review mistakenly identified Brown as black, combining that stereotype with lesbian and feminist as a way to dismiss the work with no consideration of the content of *The Hand That Cradles the Rock*.[20] A reviewer of *Songs to a Handsome Woman* was sorely disappointed that the poems were not as sexually explicit as he was led to believe; therefore, he dismissed the works as "Victorian" and Brown as the "daughter of Matthew Arnold and Elizabeth Barrett Browning."[21] The "usual deafening silence" that greeted the publication of Brown's volumes is indicative of the feminist writer's quest for an audience ("Another Time," *Poems*). Should she expect only a feminist audience ("the world of feminist literature is sufficient unto itself; the feminist poet need look no further for inspiration, audience, or support"), or are women writers ultimately searching for mainstream acceptance (Clausen, 35)? As we shall see, Brown faces this feminist issue in her career as a novelist as she goes from cult phenomenon to mainstream best seller.

Chapter Three

Rubyfruit Jungle and *In Her Day*: "The Grand Canyon Between First Person Narrative and Third Person Narrative"

Although her political and poetical writings had made her well known in the feminist and lesbian communities, Rita Mae Brown first achieved national recognition with the publication of *Rubyfruit Jungle* (1973) by Daughters Press, a small feminist press that had just been founded in Vermont. The novel garnered such a cult following of enthusiastic readers (selling over 70,000 copies) that Bantam purchased the rights and brought out a paperback edition in 1977, subsequently reprinting the book a number of times. After having offered the manuscript to every major hardcover press in New York and having it rejected, Brown could finally claim a moral victory based on her book's financial success: "Eat your heart out. You all had your chance," she gloated over the publishing establishment (*Starting from Scratch*, 13). The experience of *Village Voice* critic Terry Curtis Fox explains the book's tremendous popularity despite the lack of publicity and its handling by a new feminist press: "After hearing about *Rubyfruit* at a conference on Women and the Law, it took Susan five bookshops to find a copy. When she finished it, I picked it off the coffee table, read the first chapter, and couldn't stop. That's how cults are made—by special interest word-of-mouth (in this case, feminist and gay) perseverance, and a talent which shows on page one and doesn't let up."[1] Despite the novel's overtly gay and feminist polemics, mainstream success was made possible by the book's humor, its daring heroine, and its reliance on traditional popular culture narrative formulae.

Rubyfruit Jungle: Overview of Critical Issues

Most contemporaneous reviewers noted the parallels between *Ruby-fruit Jungle* and the works of Mark Twain, Brown's avowed favorite author, focusing particularly on the humor and Southern background; they saw Molly Bolt as a feminist version of Huck Finn or Tom Sawyer. The use of the picaresque tradition also unites these authors as their protagonists journey through America on their way to adulthood, providing ample opportunities for their authors to criticize contemporary society along the way. Depending on one's perspective and critical biases, this entertaining story can be read as a lesbian coming-of-age novel,[2] a mother / daughter novel,[3] "the perfect document of the ME generation,"[4] feminine picaresque,[5] and as feminist social criticism (Chew, 195–213). These are all very valid ways of looking at this semi-autobiographical first novel, each providing special insight into the themes and artistry of the work.

An interpretation of the book as a picaresque novel, a *bildungsroman*, apprentice novel, *kunstlerroman*, or Horatio Alger fable depends on a particular understanding of the trajectory of the book's events and the narrator's development as a character. One of the consistent criticisms of *Rubyfruit* claims there is a lack of development in the character of Molly Bolt. Though in many ways she is a modern Huck Finn, according to some critics, she fails to grow or change in the course of her adventures: "she never learns anything new about the world; she is always uninhibited personally and sexually. She develops no new insights as a result of her experiences, whereas Huck comes to understand that his comrade Jim is a human being and is willing to risk his own soul to free Jim from slavery" (Fishbein, 156). True, Molly as narrator often speaks with the authority of someone who has survived the challenges of trying to succeed in a world that wants to deny her access to the full freedom of individuality and incorporates that knowledge into her account of her experiences in a hostile world, but there are subtle changes, real and implied, beneath the surface of the narrative. One of the problems of trying to deal with the novel as a coming-of-age narrative is that novels of female development generally differ from those that feature male protagonists. Whereas the male *bildungsroman* works toward the integration of the hero into society, feminist critics propose that the novel of female development necessarily is "essentially a novel of selfhood rather than of social conformity."[6] Because of rigid social definitions of female behavior, women do not mature in the same way that men do: "the orderly succession of stages characterizing the male *bildungsroman* is disrupted since the role requirements for women are antithetical to maturation" (Pratt, 34).

Symbolic Landscapes. The novel is divided into four sections characterized by changes in time, location, and sexual partners, that reveal some of the transformations in identity undergone by Molly. Part one focuses on her childhood in Pennsylvania, on the border between North and South, and her emerging sexuality as she experiments sexually with Broccoli Detwiler and Leota Bisland. Part two follows Molly and her family to Florida; we read of her high-school years, her associations with Leroy and with her cheerleader lover Carolyn, and her college romance with Faye. Part Three chronicles Molly's introduction to New York City through her friendships with Calvin and Holly. Part Four continues in New York City but explores her adventures in publishing and film school and her triangular affairs with Polina, Paul, and Alice before her reconciliation with her mother in Florida and her return to New York that ends the book.

The importance of place to Southern authors is by now a critical commonplace, and Brown clearly draws on this literary heritage to structure her character's journey and evolution. Brown begins *Rubyfruit Jungle* outside her hometown of York, Pennsylvania, close to the border between Maryland and Pennsylvania—a symbolic landscape for Brown, who frequently contrasts Southern and Northern locales. She is often critical of such artificial boundaries that separate people when they should be united in their common humanity. Coffee Hollow in *Rubyfruit* is a parodic version of Eden, where Molly undergoes her first fall from innocence. In an already begrimed world of "tarpaper houses filled with smear-faced children," an inverted paradise, Molly learns of her own status as a bastard.[7] With a truly American entrepreneurial spirit, young Molly decides that she can make money from her friend's uncircumcised penis by charging other children to see it, thus in an innocent manner revealing that successful capitalism/materialism involves sexual exploitation: "It is the phallus, that which is possessed by the male, that generates the income on which women are dependent" (Mandrell, 155). After learning that sex sells, Molly also learns another lesson of capitalism, that "money was power" (*Rubyfruit*, 5); if one had enough money, one could be free, not having to worry what other people think. It is this venture into capitalism, into a male-dominated world of power and success that so enrages Molly's adoptive mother, Carrie, that she tells Molly of her illegitimacy. Politically disinherited by not being a male in a patriarchal society, legally disinherited by not having a legitimate father, spiritually cursed by not being born in wedlock, and emotionally rejected by the only mother she has known, Molly is immediately cast as an outsider who must struggle to gain access to power and re-entry into the family that she has lost through the accident of her birth.

Her true fall from innocence is her knowledge that she has done nothing wrong to deserve the status of outsider to which society would relegate her. In order to deal with this primal rejection and cosmic injustice, Molly redefines her status; instead of being inherently evil (as in Carrie's Calvinistic view of fallen human nature), Molly knows that she is innocent: "When I was a little baby how could I have done anything wrong?" (*Rubyfruit*, 9–10). The past is not important even though "mothers and aunts tell us about infancy and early childhood, hoping we won't forget the past when they had total control over our lives and secretly praying that because of it, we'll include them in our future" (*Rubyfruit*, 3). Molly comes to believe totally in the present and its transformation into the future. Molly's refrain in the first chapter is "I'm here": "I can't see why it's such a big deal. Who cares how you get here? I don't care. I really don't care. I got myself born, that's what counts. I'm here," she exclaims in response to Carrie's rejection (*Rubyfruit*, 9).

Through this experience of being classified as a "bastard," Molly learns the social power of language to define one with labels and is later able to defend herself from the label of "lesbian." Instead of being exiled from home by her wicked stepmother, Molly leaves of her own free will. She runs away from home temporarily until a spider web frightens her, establishing a pattern of exile/return that will structure the other sections of the novel; one cannot escape the past and one's connection to family. The rural setting is intensified in chapter one by the contrast between shacks (where people live in society) and the woods (where she conducts her sex shows and escapes from family pressures). As in most American literature, there is a glorification of nature, a sense of freedom and escape, of spiritual healing, associated with the forest; yet there is an ambivalence, a feeling that the wilderness might also be evil through its loneliness, darkness, and ability to induce fear.

The contrast of natural versus man-made environments is developed in the remaining sections of the novel, particularly in Brown's choice of the Florida and New York City settings. Brown's personal love of the Florida beaches in her Fort Lauderdale childhood/adolescent home appears not only in her poetry but also in her biographical comments. She claims that she will one day return to write about that landscape, "but until that time I can only say how much I loved it. The subtropics, really, are my natural habitat" (*Starting from Scratch*, 9). Just as she confesses her love for the tropical Floridean environment, Brown is equally passionate in her reaction, albeit negative, to New York City: "After the lavish colors and smells of the subtropics, the city was cold, gray, and over-whelmingly ugly. No wonder Yankees are so mean" (*Starting from Scratch*, 12). Though she appreciates the cultural advantages of the city and knows that she has to experience it in order to succeed as a writer, Brown also realizes that the Southern landscape is more conducive to her creativity and her personality.

This love of the South and criticism of New York is apparent in *Rubyfruit Jungle* in the later sections. In section two, when Molly first moves to Fort Lauderdale, she is rather general about the environment, indicating only that she likes her new home. But later, after having lived in New York City, she is much more specific in her descriptions and feelings about her childhood home when she returns there to visit Carrie. As Brown describes New York City as "hell," so Molly as narrator conveys the coldness and impersonality of the city upon her arrival: "Faces were coming at me in all directions and I didn't know one of them. People were pushing and hurrying and no one smiled, not even a little grin. This wasn't a city, it was some branch of hell, the Hanging Gardens of Neon burning into my skull. Hell or not, there was no place for me to go so this would be my place" (*Rubyfruit*, 139). In typical Horatio Alger fashion, the small-town country bumpkin arrives in the big city unpre-pared (she is wearing her lightweight Southern clothes and has little money left) but has no other choice but survival. Survive she does, but in defiance of the city and the people that it has corrupted. After her dreadful experience with Polina and Paul, who represent the intellectual and spiritual dessication of the modern city, Molly dreams "of sewer lagoons underneath the skyscrapers where I could navigate a Con Edison raft to take me out of this crazy city with its crazy people" (*Rubyfruit*, 211–12). Her stream of consciousness questions where she belongs as she follows the imaginary sewer drainpipe to Miami Beach. In the depths of her depression, memories of her old Pennsylvania home rouse her from her stupor and force her to return there for the strength to survive: "Maybe the smell of the clover will get me through one more winter in this branch of hell. Maybe I can keep myself together with a day in the country. There's still no price on the sun" (*Rubyfruit*, 212–13).[8]

In the longest sustained natural descriptions in the novel, Molly

returns to the lost Eden of her childhood from Section One, creating an
idyllic setting of butterflies, fresh air, and rustic cabins. But the pond
that she visits is no perfect Walden Pond. Rimmed with green slime, it
is the home of pesky insects and belligerent frogs. Molly's contemplation
of her froggy companion leads to an understanding of her own human
nature: "Amphibians must think that we're inferior creatures since we
can't go in and out of the water the way they can. Besides being
biologically superior, that ole frog is more together than I am. That frog
doesn't want to make movies. That frog hasn't even seen movies and
furthermore that frog doesn't give a big damn. It just swims, eats, makes
love, and sings as it pleases. Whoever heard of a neurotic frog? Where do
humans get off thinking they're the pinnacle of evolution?" (*Rubyfruit*,
215). After her experiences with Polina, Paul, and Alice, Molly is in need
of reassurance about the basics of human existence. Like the frog, she
wants to live harmoniously, at peace with herself and the world, able to
do whatever she wants without artificial obstacles and social strictures.

Women's fictions persistently present this green world as a source of
spiritual strength for the female protagonist "in a quest for her lost
selfhood" (Pratt, 17). Because she has no real place in the mainstream of
society (as a woman she is denied full entry in the privileges and power of
society), woman "find(s) solace, companionship, and independence in
nature" (Pratt, 21). Since coming of age for a woman usually implies
submission to the demands of patriarchy instead of fulfillment of self, the
young heroine longs for natural union with the cosmos, a return to "a
state of innocence that becomes most poignant as one is initiated into
experience" (Pratt, 22). Molly's retreat into the natural world in search of
her lost innocence comes appropriately as she is on the verge of completing her degree requirements for film school and provides her with
enough rejuvenation and sustenance to encourage her next pilgrimage,
this time back to Fort Lauderdale to visit Carrie and resolve their
differences. Nature has marked the six years of her absence by phenom-
enal growth of the palms and the shrubs around her mother's house.
Carrie too has changed by forgetting the bitterness that had driven Molly
from their home, so she and Molly are able to come to terms with each
other in a loving if somewhat uneasy alliance, probably the only type of
bond possible between two such strong-willed and independent women.
Proving that one can go home again, Molly completes the cycle by
returning to New York City to begin her career, even though the sexism
of the film industry hinders her immediate success. When she thinks
about the injustice that she must suffer to achieve her goals, she remem-

bers the frog at the pond and longs for his wholeness and peace: "I wished I could get up in the morning and look at the day the way I use to when I was a child. I wished I could walk down the streets and not hear those constant, abrasive sounds from the mouths of the opposite sex. Damn, I wished the world would let me by myself" (*Rubyfruit*, 246). The lost Eden cannot be recaptured. Though the prodigal daughter might return, though she might be innocent of the crimes with which she is charged by social prejudices, she can only continue to assert her hard-fought identity, create art out of her experience, and express her open sexuality: "Watch out world because I'm going to be the hottest fifty-year-old this side of the Mississippi" (*Rubyfruit*, 246). In this concluding sentence Brown reminds us of the importance of the Southern setting in Molly's journey, one that began as a search for her beginnings, but continues as a quest into her future, reconciling past and present.[9]

Molly's sexual odyssey. In this overview of the significant locales of the novel, as Molly tries to find her place in the world, literally and figuratively, we can detect Molly's evolution on several different but clearly related levels—as a woman in a male-dominated society who must struggle for equality, as a sexually active gay who must assert her sexuality, as a daughter who must come to terms with her family, as a student who must complete her education, as an artist who must develop her talent, and as an individual who must preserve her individuality. None of these battles to establish her sense of self will be easy. Though Molly's strong sexual identity as a lesbian is central to her characterization, to the novel's interpretation, and to Brown's artistic intention, Brown interweaves Molly's sexual adventures in each section and location with both male and female partners.[10] In fact, Brown has been criticized for being too sympathetic to the male characters, for "Molly's closest relationships are with men rather than women" (Fishbein, 157). Her affection for Leroy, her friendship with the gay Calvin, her strong bonds to her father Carl are all portrayed in more sympathetic terms than Molly's affairs with most of the women in the novel. Those female relationships are sexually interesting but do not seem to evoke powerful emotional responses from Molly: "The book is no feminist tract because there is no genuine affection for women; Molly never truly loves the women with whom she sleeps. Women make good lovers, but they are not portrayed as friends" (Fishbein, 157). Brown's attempt to break taboos, to speak openly of "the love that dares not to speak its name," ironically creates the charge of being unemotional. The sexual liaisons, like those of many picaresque heroes, are meant as part of Molly's education of the world of both men and women. Brown concerns herself mainly with the physical nature of these relationships but will turn to the emotional aspects more in later works. Although at several points in the novel Molly proudly proclaims her affinity for women, her gay identity is not as easily defined as she would first have us believe. Examining in detail the sexual relationships developed in the novel, looking not only at the dialogue and action, but also considering the significant parallelism between her lovers, male and female, we will explore how Molly's sexual identity is formulated and expressed.

Section one contrasts Molly's introduction to sex in her childhood reactions to Broccoli Detwiler and to Leota Bisland. As we have seen, young Molly senses that the uncircumcised Broccoli is different and that the difference can be exploited for her profit. Her reaction to his "thing" might be seen as a comic inversion of the popularized Freudian notion of penis envy; as she honestly tells the boy, "All you got is a wad of pink wrinkles hangin' around it. It's ugly" (*Rubyfruit*, 4). This aversion to the boy's unusual penis is hardly meant to "explain" Molly's later lesbianism. Yet the section clearly parallels the encounters with Broccoli and Leota. The one situation leads Molly from the paradise of childhood innocence into an awareness of difference; the other normal childhood sexual experimentation with Leota arouses tantalizing physical sensations and begins to define Molly's preference for women. Both are punished with injustice and separation. For her behavior with Broccoli, Molly is rejected by her mother and classified as a bastard; after she experiences sexual union with Leota, Molly must move with her family to Florida (later her mother's discovery of Molly's lesbianism leads to the same sort of hysterical rejection occasioned by her discovery of Molly's sexual game with Broccoli). Though Broccoli casts her out of paradise, in a sense, Leota unwittingly sends Molly on a quest for fulfillment that eventually leads back to her in section four, near the end of the novel. Molly's seduction by Leota and their subsequent painful parting by chance circumstances establish the pattern of most of Molly's future relationships.

Section two continues Molly's sexual education, focusing on her cousin Leroy (not related by blood but, more importantly, by friendship), her high-school friends Connie and Carolyn, and her college roommate Faye. Uncertain about his own sexuality (as a child he loved theatrical makeup and later confesses to sexual encounters with an older local boy), Leroy blames his confusion on Molly: "How do I know how to act if you act the same way?" (*Rubyfruit*, 63). Leroy and Molly agree to have sex with each other, mainly as a way to help Leroy decide about his sexual preferences, but Molly also gets a chance to compare her sexual responses. Initially she prefers the physical intensity of her response to Leota, but like her picaro predecessors, she leaves the matter open for discussion: "I'm not gonna base my judgment on one little fuck with ole Leroy. We got to do it a lot more and maybe I'll do around twenty or thirty men and twenty or thirty women and then I'll decide" (*Rubyfruit*, 70). Leroy proves too bound by external social conventions to trust his instincts. He dislikes Molly's sexual aggressiveness, and he fears what his friends will do to him if they discover that he might be "queer." Though Molly counsels him to follow his feelings, wherever they might lead him, Leroy eventually becomes "like any other redneck. . . . very righteous in his heterosexuality" (*Rubyfruit*, 72). This same criticism will later be hurled at Leota when Molly returns to visit her. Bound by their common past, their friendship, their mutual interests (in motorcycles!), their ability to communicate with each other, Leroy and Molly are not suitable mates because Leroy has none of Molly's courage and ambition, nor does he share her intellect. Her logical arguments baffle and defeat him and her unconventional behavior disturbs his sense of normality.[11]

Molly's experimentation with Leroy is contrasted to her developing friendship with Carolyn and Connie. In her attempts to gain social success in high school, Molly uses her athleticism and humor to gain entrance into an elite group of cheerleader / football star friends. She is attracted to Carolyn because of her beauty and to Connie because of her irreverence toward authority. Connie shares her low opinion of sexual intercourse with men, her love of movies, and her dislike of social hypocrisy. The teenagers date the football guys because it is expected of them, but the trio of friends owe more allegiance to each other than to the boys: "in truth, none of the three of us gave a damn about any of them. They were a convenience, something you had to wear when you went to school functions, like a bra. . . . All this overt heterosexuality amused me. If they only knew. Our boyfriends thought they were God's gift because we were sleeping with them but they were so tragically trans-parent that we forgave them their arrogance" (*Rubyfruit*, 99).

When Carolyn sacrifices her virginity to her football stud after the team wins the big game, she seeks out Molly for advice and commisera-tion. In a fit of drunken playfulness, Carolyn gives Molly "kissing lessons" in a grounded blue jet in a park for children. No fear of flying here. As with her seduction by Leota, Molly seems an innocent victim of a girl more than willing to experiment at her expense. Using the liquor and the kindergarten atmosphere to absolve her of any real responsibility for her actions (in the style of Florence King's stereotypical Southern belle, a "self-rejuvenating virgin"), Carolyn refuses to believe that she could be a lesbian.[12] Like Leroy, she is so afraid of social pressures and so blinded by the stereotype of the lesbian as ugly and man-like that she cannot accept the sexual feelings that she has for Molly and for the camp counselor who had seduced her prior to this episode.

Molly's reaction to the affair is quite different. Her attraction to Carolyn, as to Leota, is purely physical. Admitting that she has more in common with Connie, Molly begins to feel "that warning signal in [her] stomach" when she notices Carolyn's similarity in appearance to the actress in a Paul Newman movie the friends had seen together (*Rubyfruit*, 77). In the blue jet, Molly thinks like a stereotypical male football player who is finally making it with the head cheerleader and soon-to-be prom queen. Her emotions are stimulated not only by Carolyn's physical beauty but also by her social status; Molly carefully notes the Villager blouse that Carolyn had stripped off from herself. Molly's teenaged sexual adventures with Carolyn (and later with Faye) seem to have as much to do with her social climbing as with her sexual self-definition.

As with Leota, Molly's sexual involvement leads eventually to separation, this time with more emotional trauma as the three friends part company over the affair. Connie becomes suspicious and then jealous of the emotional shift in the friendship as Carolyn is more overt in her attentions to Molly. Again, social strictures prevent Connie from being able to accept the new knowledge of Molly as a lesbian; she fears that Molly will try to rape her. Discussing the situation, significantly in the cockpit of the blue jet, Molly rejects Connie's attempt to label her simply as a "queer": "Why does everyone have to put you in a box and nail the lid on it? I don't know what I am—polymorphous and perverse. Shit. I don't even know if I'm white. I'm me. That's all I am and all I want to be. Do I have to be something?" (*Rubyfruit*, 107). As she is losing her closest friend, Molly reacts with an emotional tirade similar to her earlier response to Carrie's rejection of her. "I'm here" echoes in her "I'm me" claim. She does not want to be defined by any label or primary stereotype, neither "bastard" nor "lesbian." As in her political essays, Brown detests the artificial roles that separate people from each other.

Even though Molly knows that "college was going to be like high school, only worse" (*Rubyfruit*, 109), she is not totally prepared for how much worse it turns out to be emotionally for her. Her involvement with her wild college roommate Faye Raider begins very much like her relationship with Carolyn in that they are friends before they become lovers. But instead of exhibiting Carolyn's concern for propriety and social status and how things will be judged by others, Faye is spontaneous, reckless, and rebellious. Like Carolyn, Faye has the wealth, freedom, and status that Molly envies and aspires to achieve, but Molly seems less concerned about Faye's physical attributes. Whereas Carolyn and Leota are introduced with physical details, Brown does not mention Faye's "Southern belle gone co-ed" beauty until Faye takes Molly to a gay bar, as if Molly just realized that "Faye was worth cruising" (*Rubyfruit*, 118). After the friends pretend to be a couple to ward off curious gay women at the bar, Faye seduces a reluctant Molly in her childhood bedroom (*"Seventeen* gone raunchy") (*Rubyfruit*, 121). Molly hesitates to become involved after her tragic "experiences with non-lesbians who want to sleep with me" (*Rubyfruit*, 122), but soon succumbs to Faye's seriousness and her "logic": "So maybe part of it is curiosity but another part of it is that I have more fun with you than anyone else in the whole fucking world. I probably love you more than anybody. This is the way it should be, you know, a lover who is a friend and not that moonie crap" (*Rubyfruit*, 123). Although romance begins in a childhood setting (as had the relationships with Leota and Carolyn), Faye is the closest that Molly comes to a satisfying love relationship with a kindred spirit in *Rubyfruit Jungle*.

The differences between the two women become painfully apparent, however, after their relationship is discovered by their sorority sisters. Faye is mischievous enough to tell the secret of their love as well as to admit to others that she is a lesbian (unlike Carolyn), but she ultimately bends to the social pressures of the university and of her parents, who threaten to institutionalize her. Though she reluctantly parts from Molly, she feels that Molly will have a chance to succeed in the big city and sends her away with her blessing. Molly's reaction to this separation reveals the depth of her passion and resolve: "I left my books in my room except for my English book, left my term papers and football programs and my last scrap of innocence. I closed the door forever on idealism and the essential goodness of human nature . . ." (*Rubyfruit*, 131). That she could be so unfairly separated from her lover, not by the accidental circumstances (Leota) or the shallowness of a lover (Carolyn), but by the institutionalized prejudice of the entire social system is the last insult for Molly. Like Huck Finn, who declares, "All right, then, I'll *go* to hell," Molly finally confirms her sexual identity as a lesbian and marks the transition to her own version of hell, New York City; she deliberately chooses Washington Square as her purgatory because she had read in dime novels that outcast homosexuals gathered there.[13]

Section four continues Molly's sexual education by contrasting her relationships with significant men and women, both straight and gay. The Big City offers her the opportunity to become involved in the gay community as a means to establish firmly her woman-identification. This orientation to the gay subculture is accomplished by Calvin and by Holly, the male and female characters who are paralleled in this section. Both are black and openly gay, and both barter their sexuality for survival. They befriend the outsider Molly as she is initiated into the ways of the city. Calvin, who generously shares his space in an abandoned car in Washington Square, seems to equate homosexuality with personal freedom, in his case, freedom from a boring job, an unwanted wife and family, and from the general rat race of social conformity. To survive, Calvin has to hustle and encourages a skeptical and reluctant Molly to do the same. Sex and capitalism are again intimately related. He introduces her to the lesbian butch-femme bars, where the role playing of the gay women insults Molly's notions of what lesbian relationships should be: "What's the point of being a lesbian if a woman is going to look and act like an imitation man? Hell, if I want a man, I'll get the real thing not one of these chippies. I mean, Calvin, the whole point of being gay is because you love women" (*Rubyfruit*, 147–48). Because she wants to define her own unique identity, not mimic one based on stereotypical sex roles, Molly is offended by the "diesel dyke" that tries to make a move on her in the bar (*Rubyfruit*, 146). Instead of going home with one of the women, Molly shares emotional intimacy with Calvin as they tell each other their life stories. This sharing soon leads to their separation as Calvin determines to leave for San Francisco to seek his fortune; increasingly aware of the temporariness of human friendship, Molly reluctantly bids him farewell: "It was a very formal handshake, almost like a ritual" (*Rubyfruit*, 152).

After Calvin's departure, Molly is befriended by Holly, a beautiful lesbian who makes a pass at her at work. Emphasizing Holly's appearance in her descriptions, Molly interestingly does not mention that Holly is black until later in their friendship when they make love. Here as elsewhere Brown wants to challenge the reader's biases and preconceived notions. Molly's appreciation of Holly is not, however, limited to her statuesque beauty; they enjoy each other's company at work and after hours at the theater. Holly introduces Molly to the élite lesbian culture. Frustrated by the role playing at the secretary / truck driver bars, Molly is intrigued by this look at the wealthy gays. After being "spared the red velvet womb" of the bar that she has been frequenting, Molly is impressed by the huge, elegant, but friendly surroundings at the Penthouse, so much so that she grudgingly admits that New York can actually be beautiful, sometimes (*Rubyfruit*, 156). But her fierce independence and pride prevent her from succumbing to a famous archaeologist, Chryssa Hart, who wishes to help Molly with her education costs, "if only" (*Rubyfruit*, 167). Molly recognizes the sexist nature of Chyrssa's offer to buy Molly "the way she goes and buys a winter coat or a Gucci handbag. I'm a piece of meat. . . . She's no different from a construction worker, she's just got class and bread, that's all" (*Rubyfruit*, 168). Though Molly is clearly attracted to women of higher social status, she wishes to maintain her independence and perhaps deny to herself these betrayals of her honest working-class background.

Holly, who is satisfied with her relationship with an older actress, refuses to understand Molly's determination not to be a "kept woman." Despite their passionate orgasmic lovemaking, described in fairly detailed passages to emphasize Molly's loss of a sense of self in pure physical pleasure, Molly realizes their incompatibility in other ways. She confesses that she does not love Holly because Holly is a social climber who does not understand Molly's ambitions. Molly's strong principles upset Holly because they make her feel guilt about her own lack of ambition and her ethical shortcomings. Their relationship crumbles over this difference in values: Holly detests Molly's "wearing [her] poverty like a badge of purity," and Molly disapproves of Holly's "ritzy copout" of running away from her problems in order to "get [her] head together" (*Rubyfruit*, 176). Holly's irresponsible actions not only upset Molly's emotional balance but they cause her to lose her job as well. Getting involved with someone, even someone openly gay, is not a solution to Molly's situation.

As their rhyming names suggest, Holly and Molly are perhaps more related to each other than is at first apparent. Molly's holier-than-thou tone may reflect her own fears that she too might be the same social climber that she criticizes Holly for being, or Brown's criticism of Holly's affair with the older actress might comment on her own relationship at this time with the actress Alexis Smith, to whom the book is dedicated. Though she criticizes Holly's ritual of escaping her problems, Molly herself will later have to leave the city to get her own head together. Both Calvin and Holly connect homosexuality and racism to the patriarchal social system. As black gays in a white heterosexual society, they are doubly discriminated against, as Brown was well aware in her political essays of this period in her career. Through their contrasting lessons to her, Molly learns of the potential of her homosexuality to free her from conformity, but she also learns that it can make her economically or physically dependent on her sexuality.

The end of section three finds Molly once again watching a lover slip away from her as Holly confesses her love and takes a cab out of Molly's life. After the sexual ecstasy with Holly, in section four Molly seeks intellectual companionship, turning this time to Polina Bellatoni, an older college professor and author of *The Creative Spirit of the Middle Ages*. But this middle-aged woman proves to be even more creative than Molly could have imagined. A specialist in the study of Babylonian underpants, Polina achieves sexual satisfaction through fantasies of being a man in the john. Her sexual partner and counterpart, a professor who studies Yeats's use of the semicolon, Paul Digita has the inverse fantasy of desiring to be a woman in the ladies' room. Paul and Polina, as their similar names suggest, are variations of the same modern syndrome, the desiccation of the intellectual imagination that Brown in her political essays and poetry connects to the corruption of the city and the crumbling of the patriarchy. Molly's pursuit of Polina recapitulates some of her previous experiences with heterosexual women. Like Connie, Polina is embarrassed to find herself so prejudiced against lesbians and afraid of Molly's physical attack even though they had been comfortable as friends. Like Carolyn, Polina uses the wine as an excuse to experiment with Molly, whose boldness and gay perspective on life fascinate her. In her arguments with Polina, Molly reveals a stronger political lesbian identity than before. For the first time, Molly makes love in her own bedroom, taking the initiative in her physical seduction of Polina. Unfortunately, her affair is less than satisfying. After falling in love at first sight with Polina, Molly is disillusioned by her narrow-mindedness: "I liked Polina, maybe I even loved her a little, but this was hard to take. I didn't expect such an intelligent woman to be so classic a heterosexual bigot. I felt like a bug under a magnifying glass. Oh well, maybe the only beauty left in cities is in the oil slicks on the road and maybe there isn't any beauty left in the people who live in these places" (*Rubyfruit*, 200). In this passage Polina is clearly a symptom of the corruption of modern society, as represented by New York City in the novel.

Needing at this point in her education and initiation to look into the heart of this darkness, Molly continues with this bizarre affair even after she discovers Polina's disgusting fantasies. To her, being a lesbian is no more than the degrading cross-gender fantasy that she has been sharing with Paul. When Molly confesses that her only sexual fantasy involves her poetic perception of female genitals as a rubyfruit jungle, "thick and rich and full of hidden treasures," Polina concludes that Molly is a lesbian because of her "extremely immature sex life" (*Rubyfruit*, 203). Molly's morbid curiosity sends her to Paul, who is depicted as a "living study in human debris" and as an "ugly blob of protoplasm" (*Rubyfruit*, 196–97). When this "original human slug" fantasizes that he is a woman, Molly is so appalled that she must reject him as a medium through which to approach Polina (*Rubyfruit*, 209). Instead, she turns to Polina's daughter Alice for physical satisfaction in the face of Polina's weird sexual fantasies, but Molly quickly becomes a sexual go-between for mother and daughter. This incestuous liaison tortures Molly: "I was a kind of telestar for them to bounce messages off to each other. There were times when I felt lonelier with them than without them" (*Rubyfruit*, 211). She is relieved when Alice reveals their affair and Polina sends Molly out of their lives, back into her roach-infested apartment.

The perversity of this Polina-Paul-Alice triangle reflects not only the corruption of modern society but the hypocrisy of the heterosexual majority. Molly had been introduced to the bizarre nature of the so-called "normal" people when Calvin had secured her a one-night stand with Ronnie Rappaport, a wealthy businessman who got his thrills by having different people pelt him with grapefruits. With this episode, as with Molly's disillusioning relationship with Polina, Brown questions how the heterosexual majority can label lesbians as sick, disgusting, or immoral. Because she detests role playing and sexual stereotyping, Molly defends her love of women as a perfectly healthy impulse: "Women kissing women is beautiful. And women making love together is dynamite" (*Rubyfruit*, 201). From her sexual experimentation she learns the intensity of an emotional and physical relationship with a woman: "Men bore me. If one of them behaves like an adult it's cause for celebration, and even when they do act human, they still aren't as good in bed as women. . . . it's the difference between a pair of roller skates and a Ferrari—ah, there aren't words" (*Rubyfruit*, 198–99). Though Polina accuses Molly of being uncertain of her sexual identity, Molly is the most certain that she has been. But in order to test the validity of her decision, she must encounter the ghosts of the past: Leota and Leroy. These two former lovers had feelings and thoughts similar to hers at one time; using them as a measure Molly can mark the distance of her journey.

After her encounter with the frog back on the old homestead in

Pennsylvania, Molly visits the now-married Leota. Molly immediately notices the physical changes between the two women: "Same cat eyes, same languid body, but oh god, she looked forty-five years old and she had two brats hanging on her like possums. I looked twenty-four. She saw herself in my reflection . . ." (*Rubyfruit*, 216). Perhaps Molly too can see her own reflection in Leota, an unpleasant vision of what she might have become if she had opted for the traditional female career of marriage and family. Seeing marriage as a way to escape her family as a teen, Leota defines a good husband as one who "works hard, loves the kids. I couldn't ask for more" (*Rubyfruit*, 217). This vision of Leota's compromised horizons, coupled with Leota's conservative knee-jerk reaction to Molly's tender memories of their past sexual encounter, incites Molly's anger and hostility. When Leota insists that Molly will one day find the right person and settle down so that she can be taken care of in her old age, Molly's reaction is swift and devastating: "I'm going to be arrested for throwing an orgy at ninety-nine and I'm not growing old with anybody. What a gruesome thought. Christ, you're twenty-four and you're worried about being fifty. . . . I love women. I'll never marry a man and I'll never marry a woman either. That's not my way. I'm a devil-may-care lesbian" (*Rubyfruit*, 219–20). Leota's conventionality and hypocritical heterosexual righteousness send Molly hurrying back to New York City with new resolve to become successful to escape the destiny of being a "breeder of the next generation" (*Rubyfruit*, 221). Molly's visit with Leroy produces similar results. Since they had been close friends as children, Leroy is better able than Leota to sympathize with Molly and understand her, even in his limited way. His frustrations with the boring aspect of marriage and with his work as a mechanic add to the overall negative portrait of heterosexual marriage in the novel. After seeing the unhappiness of her two childhood lovers, Molly can progress toward her goal of filmmaking and confirm her sexual identity, to be "the hottest fifty-year-old this side of the Mississippi" (*Rubyfruit*, 246).

As Molly had told Polina in her critique of modern society, "People have no selves anymore (maybe they never had them in the first place) so their home base is their sex—their genitals, who they fuck" (*Rubyfruit*, 200). Molly does not want to be defined by her sexuality alone; true selfhood includes so much more of the individual that to limit oneself to this one primary definition is a travesty of human multiplicity and freedom. As strong as her lesbian identity becomes, neither Molly nor Brown herself wants to be limited to this one way of looking at life. As

Brown has commented: "If I thought I could only respond to half the human race, I'd jump off the Golden Gate Bridge. I love women. I love men. I love everybody. My assumption is that until proven otherwise, people are pan-sexual" (Mansfield, C8).

Molly's Feminist Quest. Molly's identity as a sexual being, of course, is bound to her female identity as a woman in a sexist society. *Rubyfruit Jungle* both parallels and counterpoints Molly's sexual adventures with her struggles to succeed as a woman in a traditional society dominated by men and their values. Molly shares with other female protagonists the conflict of her desires with the standards of traditional society: "The novel of development portrays a world in which the young woman hero is destined for disappointment. . . . Every element of her desired world—freedom to come and go, allegiance to nature, meaningful work, exercise of the intellect, and use of her own erotic capabilities—inevitably clashes with patriarchal norms" (Pratt, 29).

Although Molly, in effect, declares herself free of original sin, she is unfairly cast out of childhood by the false issue of legitimacy, which is the patriarchal society's attempt to define the child by her father. In order to succeed, Molly is forced to define herself by her actions instead of her heritage. Brown revolutionizes the Horatio Alger myth of American success by portraying woman as the true inheritor of the dream. Molly has absorbed all of the lessons of American success: ingenuity, education, hard work, individuality, life, liberty, and the pursuit of happiness. Through her experience with Broccoli Detwiler, Molly learns that money is power, demystifying male power and proving her business acumen in the process. In her revenge against Earl Stambach for telling her secrets, young Molly manipulates the less intelligent Earl into eating the rabbit turds by a combination of "masculine" dealmaking ("I won't beat you up if you don't tell on me when we go back to school") and "feminine" flattery ("Why you must be the fastest eater in all of York County") (*Rubyfruit*, 15). Her mental superiority over Leroy, Earl, Broccoli, and the other school children that she maneuvers into doing her bidding, along with her ability to use whatever method is expedient, makes her well suited for her defiance of conventional roles and for success in a competitive society.

Molly is clearly contrasted with the other girls, as epitomized by her rival Cheryl Spiegelglass, whose Shirley Temple looks and feminine behavior (she wears dresses even if she does not have to) endear her to adults, including Carrie. In their childhood games the two girls reveal their different values. Cheryl believes that only men can be doctors, while

Molly not only wants to be the doctor so that she can give the orders, but she also secretly wants to be president. Carrie's plan to domesticate young Molly ends in dismal failure when Carl (Molly's adoptive father) defends the girl's right to be different, to use her mind to lead to success. Though Carl is male and technically part of the patriarchy that Molly struggles against, his gentle nature, his lower social status, and his own lack of success, ironically, make him a successful mentor for her. He wants her to be a lawyer or even the next governor, to be anything she wants to be, regardless of traditional gender associations with those jobs. Unfortunately, he leaves her few resources to help her achieve those ambitions he instills.

Her career plans are threatened at times by women in service of patriarchy as well as by overtly sexist men. After discovery of Molly's affair with Faye in college, Molly is sent to the dean of women for a counselling session that turns into a bitter battle of the individual against the educational system. Molly baffles the repressed Miss Marne with her honest confession of love for Faye and her refusal to see anything wrong with their relationship. Miss Marne's amateur psychoanalysis enrages Molly, who turns the tables on her and accuses the dean of being "a goddamn fucking closet fairy, that's what you are. . . . You're running this whole number on me to make yourself look good. Hell, at least I'm honest about what I am" (*Rubyfruit*, 128). Molly is able to outwit the system by agreeing with the psychiatrists who would label her as dangerous or crazy for her honesty. Unlike Faye and other women who are defeated by the power of the status quo, Molly plays the game and convinces the psychiatrists of her new mental stability. The institution, however, has the final say when Molly is expelled from school despite her good grades and obvious intelligence.

Like Molly, Dean Marne is a single career woman who had to struggle to get to her position, but unlike Molly she is willing to hurt other women to hold on to her own job and hypocritical values. Molly's encounter with Marne is foreshadowed by a somewhat similar high-school incident. When Connie and Molly are driving home drunk one night, they spy an illicit romantic rendezvous between the principal Mr. Beers and the dean of women Mrs. Silver. In this encounter with the dean, Molly has the upper hand because of the couple's desire to hide their adultery, but Molly so sympathizes with the pathetic fear of her victim that she almost refuses to capitalize on the bribes she is promised. She can tolerate the heterosexual hypocrisy but not the closeted lesbian hypocrisy. She sets high standards for herself as her moral and sexual identity evolves and will accept no less of others similar to her (as her friend Holly later discovers).

The detrimental sexist behavior of men is mentioned throughout the novel as a reminder of the male-dominated world in which Molly exists: the ambulance workers who stare at her like a sex object as they remove her father's body from home; the construction workers ogling women as they pass down the street; the office co-workers who try to look up her skirt as she sits; the man at the restaurant who fondles Holly's breast in front of his wife and leads to Holly's being fired; the man in the bar who grabs at Molly when she is dancing and causes her to lose her job; the unseen boy who impregnates Faye and leaves her to face the abortion alone. But the dominant source of patriarchal power that threatens Molly's ambitions is the film world. For her artistic spiritual "fathers" Molly must look to Griffith and Eisenstein since few women role models existed or were well known.

The sixties were a time of artistic rebellion for many filmmakers because the old studio system was crumbling and the locus of power was moving from Hollywood to other parts of the country. These power shifts did not, however, open up many opportunities for women behind the cameras. Not only were film schools dominated by male students and male teachers, but the relaxation of the censorship codes led to the depiction of more sex and violence, often to the detriment of the portrayal of women. Brown reflects these shifts in her presentation of the film school students, teachers, and projects. Molly laments the sexism of the males who control the equipment, who do not like to take orders from a woman, and who make sexist comments about women in class. Even the head of the film department, a "fake-hippie, middle-aged washout," refuses to treat her fairly: "All through his lectures he makes rotten cracks about women. You know, the stud routine about the reason there haven't been any great women directors is because we have brains the size of peas—and he looks right at me when he says that. Makes me want to cram a can of *Triumph of the Will* right down his throat" (*Rubyfruit*, 223, 193).

It will take a triumph of Molly's will to overcome the kind of sexism that so arrogantly oppresses her. Her teacher is unimpressed by her idea to do a documentary about Carrie's life: "Pornoviolence was in this year and all the men were busy shooting bizarre fuck scenes with cuts of pigs beating up people at the Chicago convention spliced between the sexual encounters. My film was not in that vein" (*Rubyfruit*, 222–23). Molly's hostility against the men is increased by their pseudo-revolutionary poses; as Brown laments in many of her political essays, the college radicals had very little commitment to the women's movement. After Molly illegally appropriates a camera to do her film and returns for the final screening, the downwardly mobile filmmakers bring their "chicks" and "old ladies" to cheer their efforts, which include the prize-winning film about a Martian gang rape. Molly's simple, honest film is treated with silence. Despite her credentials, she is offered only secretarial work or hermaphroditic acting roles by the film industry. The education that she hoped would be the answer to her ambition is ignored: "I kept hoping against hope that I'd be the bright exception, the talented token that smashed sex and class barriers" (*Rubyfruit*, 245). Here as throughout her development in the novel, she reveals her deep faith in the American educational system as the way to escape the limits of her social class.

Class, Education, and the American Dream.   As a lower-class child, Molly depends upon education to assist her in her ambitions. A voracious and early reader, Molly is quick to learn, though she rebels against the authoritarian nature of the educational system. To help her endure the boredom of school routine as well as to capture the allegiance of her schoolmates (who might resent her if she were openly bookish), Molly develops her sense of humor. She soon learns the importance of couching controversial opinions and ideas in humorous terms. In high school the social/intellectual strata are more noticeable, and Molly astutely evaluates her marginality. In order to go to college she must identify with the upper-class college bound kids. Though economically she is classified with the redneck/greaser class, Molly defies the stereotype by making good grades, improving her grammar, buying quality clothes, and, of course, being funny. Still, she could not have realized her ambition to be student council president had it not been for her fortuitous spying on Mrs. Silver and her subsequent bribe. Without money for the campaign against the richest boy in school, Molly would have little chance, regardless of her political savvy. Talent can take her only so far; money prescribes the limits of success in our society. Without money and status, she, like the picaro hero, must rely on luck and good fortune.[14]

Molly's struggles against the social system are accelerated at the college level. Her desire to go to certain schools is frustrated by lack of adequate scholarship funds. Her education and ability can take her only so far; it takes money to go to the really good schools. Even in school, money becomes a serious problem. Molly is forced to pledge a sorority so that she can pursue a campus political career with their funds. Her generous roommate Faye must buy her a new wardrobe so that she will not be embarrassed to be seen with Molly in their friendly adventures. Idyllic as their relationship is in some ways, Molly experiences the basic difference between herself and Faye after their lesbian affair is discovered by the authorities. Like a Fitzgerald character, Molly learns that the rich are, indeed, different from the rest of us. At first, Faye is not disturbed by the situation: "Who the hell wants to rot in this institution of miseducation?" (*Rubyfruit*, 125). Molly cannot be so frivolous in her reaction even though she does not love the school either: "It's my one chance to get out of the boondocks. I've got to get my degree" (*Rubyfruit*, 125). Faye may be able to afford a private school with her father's wealth, but Molly must survive on her own. Though clearly Miss Marne and the forces of totalitarian authority are at fault for their hypocrisy, it is partly the irresponsibility of the wealthy that gets Molly into this precarious position of losing her scholarship when Faye carelessly tells the sorority girl of their lesbian affair. How can she achieve the American dream of success if the means of education are so systematically taken from her? She undertakes the same frustrating battle in film school as the patriarchal system again tries to deny her claim to the American ideals.

Because she has never had money, Molly is very sensitive to status symbols. In high school and college, she carefully uses clothes to create an appropriate image. In New York she is just as conscious of her navy pea coat around Holly's high-class friends. Yet when she borrows clothes for her lunch with Chryssa, she feels like an impostor, trying to be someone she is not. Her ambivalence is intensified as she is confronted with the possibility of achieving wealth through liaison with a successful woman. She is proud of her heritage as a working-class woman, with its concomitant prejudice against the wealthy, but she is tempted by the upper class that she would join. She does not want to make a religion of poverty, and severely criticizes those who are consciously downwardly mobile, but she does achieve a sort of moral righteousness, especially in her debates with Holly about being a kept woman. Fighting the temptation of Chryssa's "enticing money," instead of using her "ass to save [her] head," Molly must employ her brains to save her body from poverty and her soul from corruption (*Rubyfruit*, 167). Struggling to define herself in a stratified society, Molly wants her personality, her intelligence, her humor to be considered before her sex or her sexual preference.

Family Dynamics. Molly's attitudes about wealth, social class, education, and ambition can be traced back to the influence of her parents. Part of her evolution in the novel is her understanding of her place in her family, her reconciliation with her mother, and her construction of her role as daughter. Idealizing her father and arguing with her mother, Molly must come to terms with her love for both adopted parents. Unlike many orphans who would seek to know their biological parents, Molly wants to accept Carl and Carrie as her real parents, in that socially defined role. Because Carl sides with her against her mother, fosters her ambitions, and lavishes praise upon her, Molly absorbs many of his values about education and life. He counsels her that she can do what she wants as long as she does not get caught. As we later learn from Carrie, Carl had tried to live by this advice but had been discovered in an adulterous affair with another woman; this attempt to express himself emotionally eventually led to discord and misery in his life with Carrie. His ease with his own body and his ability as a secure male to offer a physical embrace and tears to another man who has lost his wife provide young Molly with a non-traditional masculine role model. The depth of Molly's passion for Carl is revealed in Brown's sentimental handling of his sudden death. After a poignant father-daughter discussion of Molly's problems and her future, Molly is awakened by the hysterical Carrie with the news of her father's death. Molly sees his tragedy as a sort of conspiracy against his goodness: "A whole human life is gone. A wonderful, laughing life and all that's left is this handful of used-up goods, and they're not even quality stuff" (*Rubyfruit*, 96). His last words to her echo through the novel: "Don't listen to nobody but your own self" (*Rubyfruit*, 92).

Molly's relationship with her mother, on the other hand, is fraught with tensions throughout the novel. Perhaps because the women share their volatile tempers and strong values, they do not get along with each other. Unfortunately for them, their values do not coincide as Carl's do with Molly's. While Molly wants to be accepted on her own terms as an autonomous individual, Carrie has trouble seeing beyond stereotypical sexual roles. Most of their early conflicts arise when Molly refuses to submit to Carrie's notion of what is proper behavior for a young girl. Carrie wants Molly to wear dresses, but Molly insists on wearing pants (this preference continues to be a visible symbol both of Molly's rebellion and of her modernity). When Carrie embarks on emergency remedial housewife lessons for the young tomboy, Molly locks her in the root cellar. Carrie would rather see Molly as prom queen than as student council president.

Because she believes that biological motherhood is the only true parenthood, Carrie never accepts Molly as a real daughter or as a real individual. She wants Molly to follow in her own limited footsteps, accepting her inferior status as a woman in a sexist society. Part of Carrie's insistence on Molly's fulfilling a traditional woman's role can be attributed to her jealousy of Molly's advantages. Instead of being glad that Molly can have more opportunities than she had (as Carl wants the girl to succeed where he has failed), Carrie is threatened by Molly's desire to improve herself. She constantly refers to Molly's ambitions as a form of snobbery, of thinking that she is better than Carrie. The repressed hostility created by her own unhappiness is taken out on the girl, who reminds her of her failure as a wife and mother. Because she cannot have children of her own, Carrie wants Molly to feel shame at her illegitimate status. Though she herself was a sort of a rebel as a young cigar-smoking woman about town, Carrie cannot accept Molly's rebellion against tradition. To Carrie, Molly's lesbianism is not a question of sexual identity but a form of teenage rebellion, like not wearing dresses, learning to cook, or trying to get a husband.

Despite their fundamentally different views of life, Molly cannot escape her mother totally. Though Carrie's cruel rejection sends her off to New York City in search of her future, Molly has inherited from her mother a strong sense of value and a dislike of class pretense, among other things. When Molly is faced with the possibility of becoming a "kept" woman, her memory of Carrie's pride prevents her from accepting Chryssa's offer: "Maybe I'm hung up on false pride. Carrie don't even make $1500 a year, and she won't take welfare or anything, not even from the church. Maybe it runs in the family. Family, now that's a fat laugh. What family? All I had was room and board. Well, some of it rubbed off, I guess. . . . Shit, I wish I'd stop thinking about Carrie" (*Rubyfruit*, 167–68). Without yet fully realizing it, Molly must reconcile herself to her past, to an acceptance of her heritage, if she is to progress as an individual. That is why when she chooses her film project she decides to film one woman's life, Carrie's. After witnessing Polina's control over her daughter Alice, perhaps Molly realizes the wisdom in Carrie's rejection. At least she was forced to become independent, to find her own way in the world.

Their long separation has caused changes not only in Carrie's appearance and health but in her attitude toward Molly. Though she is still skeptical about Molly's education, she is proud to find out that "those snotty-nosed, Jew-brats up there ain't smarter than you" (*Rubyfruit*, 225). Time has also affected her memory. She recalls Molly as a quiet child and reveals a different account of their angry separation: "You misunderstood me. You're a little hothead. You flew outa here before I could talk to you. I never said no such thing [about Molly not being her child] and don't you try to tell me I did. You're my baby. . . . Why I love you. You're all I got left in this world" (*Rubyfruit*, 229–30). Unlike the dramatic sentimentality with which Brown treats Molly's relationship with her father, this reunion of mother and daughter is revealed somewhat casually. Carrie's acceptance of Molly as her own daughter, something she had been unable to do throughout the girl's life, is stated matter-of-factly, without a tearful reunion or even a little emotion on Molly's part: "Yeah, okay, Mom" (*Rubyfruit*, 230). Their relationship remains tense during Molly's visit. For the first time, Carrie reveals details of Molly's true parentage and her suffering over Carl's infidelity with another woman. Neither of these revelations has much effect on Molly; she has never wanted to know much about her biological parents and she sympathizes with Carl's affair. Just as Quentin Compson eventually decides that he does not hate the South in William Faulkner's *Absalom! Absalom!*, Molly realizes that she does not hate Carrie: "Mom, I don't hate you. We're different people, strongwilled people. We don't always see eye to eye. That's why we fought so much. I don't hate you" (*Rubyfruit*, 241). An uneasy alliance is established as Molly is returning to New York. Again, a confession of love, this time for her mother, leads to a separation, but not a permanent parting as the other separations had been. Molly learns a lesson that every child must one day accept: "Even when I hated her, I loved her. Maybe all kids love their mothers, and she's the only mother I've ever known. Or maybe underneath her crabshell of prejudice and fear there's a human being that's loving. I don't know but either way I love her" (*Rubyfruit*, 242). Molly is finally able to accept her mother as a real person, the way she has always wanted Carrie to accept her. Now Molly is ready to face her future with this reconciliation with her past.

For Brown, this mother-daughter theme has multiple significance in her work. On a romantic level, the relationship between an older woman and a younger woman is often a means to compare different generations. As we saw her in political essays, the mother-daughter relationship reflects Brown's view of sisterhood, an acceptance of one's kinship to all women throughout history. On a personal level, the reunion with the estranged mother asserts the young woman's female identity and establishes the orphan's place in a new community. In *Rubyfruit Jungle*, Molly must overcome her youthful prejudice against age before she can accept herself and her mother. Molly and Holly first make fun of the older women they court. Holly admits that her actress lover is "okay even if she's over forty" (*Rubyfruit*, 156). Chryssa's lechery is ridiculed by Molly mainly because of her age: "What does she do, sleep in an alcohol bath? I get pursued by the human pickle. Some friend you are, fixing me up with the geriatric ward" (*Rubyfruit*, 157). As she actually meets these "old" women (who are 40 something), Molly likes aspects of their personality, but dislikes their pitiful attempts to hide their age with makeup. To enhance the sense of age associated with these women, Brown gives Chryssa and Polina careers in archaeology and history. Yet Molly is able to overcome her prejudice in her initial affection for Polina, whom she considers beautiful despite her years. Once she is able to accept the older woman, she can even love Carrie's prune face and white hair and envision herself as a hot 50-year-old woman.

The portrait of an artist.   In addition to her evolution as a daughter and woman, Molly experiences a transformation as an artist through the course of the novel. Her struggles to become an autonomous individual are expressed in her career as an actress, both on and off of the stage. The theme of role playing is important as Brown defies traditional modes of behavior and attempts to define herself through her actions. Brown excels in creating theatrical set pieces that descend into comic chaos. In *Rubyfruit Jungle*, several of these actually take place on stage as Molly explores the boundaries between art and reality. Her childhood rivalry with Cheryl is dramatized on stage for the whole town as they battle each other in the school's Nativity play. Ironically, Molly is cast as the Virgin Mary, even though at this time she is madly in love with Leota Bisland. The play degenerates into a marital squabble, not unlike those that Molly has been hearing in her own home between Carrie and Carl, for both Molly and Baby Jesus share the problems of illegitimacy. In high school, Molly and her girlfriends are cast as the three witches in *Macbeth*. It is during rehearsal that Connie discovers Molly's affair with Carolyn, which leads to the jealousy and prejudice that break the weird sisters apart. In both of these episodes, the staged drama seems to bring out the truth that might have remained hidden from others. In college, Molly meets the greatest challenge of her young acting career: "I beat out Bette Davis for acting awards," Molly claims as she invents dreams for the psychiatrists and convinces them that she is "normal" enough to be released after being hospitalized for her lesbianism and her attack on Dean Marne (*Rubyfruit*, 129).

Her involvement in the lesbian subculture involves a degree of role playing for Molly. At the gay bar with Faye, she pretends to be Faye's lover before they actually make love that night (again, acting can lead to truth); but in New York she soundly rejects the butch-femme and the "kept" woman roles that would deny her individuality and force her to submit to stereotypical sexual behaviors. In her affairs with Polina, Paul, and Alice, she learns the dangers of submitting to inauthentic role playing. She refuses to lie through her art or through the roles she assumes. When she finally can be in control of the creation of the images, not just a pawn in someone else's show, Molly chooses to portray the reality of one woman's life. Throughout the novel Molly struggles to lead an undivided existence, to be herself without the intervention of roles, labels, conventions, restraints. Experiencing life from many different perspectives, Molly is ready to assume her role as artist.

In her quest for selfhood on these various levels, Molly reflects the ideology of the radical gay liberation movements of the sixties. Old closeted gay lifestyles involved role playing to protect one's private life from exposure in one's public life. Molly chooses to redefine gender expectations by avoiding such role playing, by being openly gay. Her homosexuality is not just sexual behavior but the central nexus of her identity.[15] This lesbian novel of development deals with the process of coming out as the search for an already existing identity that goes beyond mere sexuality. Basing his theories concerning the end of homosexuality on the theories of Herbert Marcuse and Norman O. Brown, social critic Dennis Altman interprets the goals of the gay liberation movement as the eventual eradication of traditional sex roles, not just the provision of another alternative: "One hopes that the answer lies in the creation of a new human for whom such distinctions no longer are necessary for the establishment of identity."[16] Through Molly Bolt, Brown seems on the verge of the creation of such a "new human." Without rejecting her biology (as woman) and without adopting particularly masculine modes of behavior, Molly above all wants to be accepted for being herself, without having to define her identity further. Pratt describes *Rubyfruit Jungle* as a novel that "emerge[s] into the new space" of Jill Johnston's lesbian nation, where traditional patterns of romance no longer apply (Pratt, 106). But Bonnie Zimmerman is probably more accurate in her understanding of Molly's evolution; Molly does not reach that goal of creating a lesbian nation (which Zimmerman considers to be the end of lesbian coming-out stories). Instead, Molly escapes integration into traditional society by the continuation of her journey (Abel, 254). At the end of the novel Molly is still battling the patriarchy, still seeking her space for existence, but she does not plan to sacrifice her personal life for her career in film as many single women / protagonists are forced to do in order to succeed. As Pratt discovers, many modern women writers "portray romantic love and personal self-sufficiency as incompatible" (Pratt, 119). She will fight to live her life the way that she wants to live it, determined to have it all.

In Her Day: Daughter of *Rubyfruit Jungle*

While *Rubyfruit Jungle* emphasizes the growth of the individual in society, *In Her Day* focuses on the network of relationships that bind individual women to each other. Criticized in her first novel for neglecting the emotional bonds between women (by concentrating only on Molly's sexual adventures), Brown addresses the complex nature of sisterhood in this second book. She describes communities of women and explores how they relate to each other politically, socially, and sexually. Although Brown assesses her achievement in this work as "a technical improvement on *Rubyfruit*," most of the critics were very harsh on the strained humor, the weak characterizations, the inconsistent point of view, and the poorly written descriptions, all in all a disappointing successor to *Rubyfruit Jungle* (*Starting from Scratch*, 13). Janet Wiehe in *Library Journal* groups *In Her Day* with several other feminist novels to illustrate the struggle of women writers to convey their political ideas in an artistic prose style: "Brown's style is so literal and humorless, and her objectives so apparent, that one will read this novel for information rather than enjoyment."[17] Even a sympathetic critic like Deborah Core in the feminist journal *Sinister Wisdom* is aware of the serious stylistic shortcomings of this "flawed" but "brave book": "The novel depends on dialogue; when the dialogue is weak or the narrator must take over, serious stylistic flaws occur. Too often the narrator tells us things that should be left for us to infer from the action. . . . The novel would be more convincing if the narrator were more consistent. . . . The book is also marred by several spelling mistakes and a curious disregard for commas."[18] Brown's pride in her achievement in this book is predicated upon what she considers her success in jumping "the Grand Canyon between first-person narrative and third-person narrative" and her ability to handle several subplots feeding into the main storyline (*Starting from Scratch*, 14). In this sense, despite its many stylistic shortcomings, *In Her Day* is an important transitional phase from the single-story autobiographical *Rubyfruit Jungle* to the multiple narratives of *Six of One*.

In Her Day is also autobiographical, but in a different way than *Rubyfruit Jungle*. Relying on her experiences in the women's movement and lesbian organizations, Brown recreates the political turmoil and arguments that she describes in her essays in *A Plain Brown Rapper*. This emphasis on the ideology of the feminist struggle may detract somewhat from the aesthetic pleasure of fiction, but it reveals a spiritual autobiography that is as important to Brown as her adventures growing up as a lesbian in a homophobic America. Whereas *Rubyfruit* shows the evolution of Molly's individual lesbian identity, *In Her Day* takes lesbianism as a given that does not need to be explained or justified for her characters. Their sexual identities are firmly established and are not criticized or questioned, though the issue of whether or not one should "come out" is dramatized in one section. The two leading characters provide interesting political contrasts and reveal contradictory impulses within Brown's own feminist identity. In the affair between Ilse James, an ardent young feminist organizer, and Carole Hanratty, a much older woman and an established art historian, one would assume from Brown's biography an absolute identification between herself and Ilse. On the contrary, Brown shows a great deal of sympathy for Carole's point of view and the novel ultimately admits that "both [women] have a place in the feminist world" (Core, 88). Though they are unsuccessful in maintaining their relationship, each woman has a powerful effect on the other's political development as they take different paths to achieve the common goals of a feminist society.

In some ways Carole Hanratty reveals what Molly Bolt might have become some twenty years after *Rubyfruit*. Carole is a Southerner by birth and her heritage becomes increasingly important to her during the course of the novel. Using an image that Molly had used to describe Leota and her children, Carole envisions the elevators at New York University where she is a professor of art history as "mother possums, swaying under the weight of clutching children while backing down a tree."[19] Memories of her Virginia childhood fill her as she goes from her classroom to her office. Though she has gone to school in the North (Vassar) and worked there for many years, she still feels herself to be an outsider. Like Molly, Carole is prejudiced against Northerners, who seem to have lost perspective on their own lives, like the cyclist that she watches hit a traffic sign, spill his groceries, and ride away as if nothing had happened (*In Her Day*, 34). She detests people who make fun of her Southern accent, yet she has been forced to hide her accent so that people will not make the standard assumption that she is a country bumpkin. "Sometimes when something's close to the bone I fall into it [her Southern accent]," she admits to Ilse, revealing that her most important thoughts and ideas call up her Southern heritage (*In Her Day*, 80). It is her insistence on "Southern champagne" (or Coca-Cola) that leads directly to her first meeting with Ilse at the restaurant Mother Courage (*In Her Day*, 7).

When Carole returns to Richmond for the funeral of her sister, who was tragically killed in an automobile accident, her own pain is paralleled to the suffering of the Confederate South: "Generations later the scars intertwined with new roads, new buildings, but Richmond's wounds were never completely healed. The South was and remains a battered nation. Richmond will always rest next to the deepest of these wounds. As Carole walked the platform toward her waiting brother, Luke, Richmond filled her, opened her own very personal wound. It was as though she had never left this place and yet it was different" (*In Her Day*, 56). Though she disapproves of the extravagances of the traditional Southern funeral ritual, Carole admires her mother's strength, helps her brother overcome his alcohol problem, and vows to let her sister live through her. This important theme of sisterhood takes on a new dimension with Carole's Southern heritage, for the death of her real sister solidifies her spiritual sisterhood with her black friend Adele, who is a central character and a counterpoint to young Ilse, in the novel.[20] Like Molly and Brown, Carole has no racial prejudices. Adele is introduced as a character through her actions and dialogue, long before the narration reveals that she is a black woman. Their deep friendship signals the existence of the new South after the devastation of the Civil War and the civil rights movement. At the end of the novel Carole determines to leave New York to return to the land, to the South, to home, where she feels that her life and work can make a difference: "I know this sounds silly but somehow it's hitting me that I want to go back where I came from. Not in time and not back to the slums but back to the area, the land. . . . I want to go somewhere where my voice isn't so small. Back to my roots" (*In Her Day*, 174). Not returning to Tara for strength after she has been defeated by circumstances, this new Southern woman wants to take feminism back to the grass roots, to bring about change in the places that most need it, to reintegrate herself into the home community rather than hiding safely in the big city.

Carole is comparable to Molly in her concern for her lower-class background and her struggle to overcome it through talent, effort, and education. In her argument with Ilse, who rejects her Boston upper-class background in her radicalism, Carole justifies her own "beyond bourgeois" apartment and comfortable lifestyle by attributing her success to hard work: "I worked for everything I have. I didn't come from money.

Honey, I grew up in the Depression. . . . You walk into someone's life and assume their life is static. I worked for this. I've hurt no one in the process and I've helped those closest to me. Why should I be made to feel guilty?" (*In Her Day*, 68–69). Her use of the typically Southern appellation "Honey" shows how strongly she feels about this issue. She attacks Ilse for stereotyping poor people as "stupid, insensitive, inarticulate" without any real knowledge about poverty herself (*In Her Day*, 69). Like Brown she expresses hostility toward the downwardly mobile college radicals who wear jeans and work shirts as testimony to their revolutionary zeal. Yet her ambivalence is revealed in her strong attraction to both Ilse and Adele, who come from privileged backgrounds. Carole is more accepting of Adele than she is of Ilse, however, because Adele comes from a hardworking black family; she did not have everything given to her. Adele understands Carole's attraction to Ilse: "I think Ilse is in some way connected to Carole's background. Ilse comes from money as you know. Carole has always been fascinated and repelled by people who had it easy. Here is this Boston rich kid repudiating her own past and calling it a revolution. A potent combination for Ms. Hanratty" (*In Her Day*, 92–93). Ultimately, however, it is the class difference that triggers Ilse and Carole's breakup. Ilse cannot understand why Carole would ride around town in a Rolls Royce on a lark with her tacky friends, and Carole cannot accept Ilse's rejection of her background: "You can't be what you aren't. You're not a poor woman. You weren't raised in poverty. You can't go around pretending" (*In Her Day*, 121). Though they both couch their philosophical arguments in terms of what is best for the women's movement, this fundamental socioeconomic barrier ultimately keeps them apart. As Brown knew in her essays, class informs one's sensibilities in numerous unconscious ways, making it next to impossible to bridge the gap between classes: "Class is much more than the Left's definition of relationship to the means of production. Class involves your behavior, your basic assumptions about life, your experiences (determined by your class) which validate those assumptions, how you are taught to behave, what you expect from yourself and others, your concept of a future, how you understand problems and solve them, how you think, feel, act" (*Rapper*, 98–99).

In order to succeed, Carole has had to battle sexism in academia, not unlike Molly's own struggles in the film department and publishing house office. Carole is quite bitter in her descriptions of the department head who likes to sit by the elevator so that he can look up the women's skirts and who stares at Carole's breasts when he talks to her. She laments the fact that being a woman has prevented her from becoming a department head and from being promoted to full professor, yet she believes in her work and is very good at what she does. Like Molly she wants to be accepted on her own terms, not as a representative of a gender. Brown writes in the introduction to the reprint edition of *In Her Day*: "My spirit is informed by my gender but unencumbered by it," a manifesto that could apply to all of her major characters (*In Her Day*, xii). Lesbianism is not an overt issue in the novel except in the scene where Carole is forced to come out of the closet after one of Ilse's angry co-workers insinuates Carole's homosexuality in a local newspaper. Though Molly would not have hidden her sexuality for so long, she would have been proud of Carole's angry response to her department heads innuendo. When he tries to weasel the truth out of Carole, she explodes in feminist rage at his hypocrisy and threatens to reveal his affairs with coeds if he attempts to use her sexual preference to wreck her career. After she comes out to Fowler and to another colleague (who is very supportive), Carole feels much better about herself, a feeling that Brown would definitely endorse.

Since lesbianism is not treated as an issue in the novel, Brown can explore the significance of personal female sexuality in her characters without emphasizing sex as a political act. As in *Rubyfruit Jungle,* sex is a liberating experience in which the body overcomes the influence of the mind, bringing one into closer contact with the "root self." Again, physical attraction is the basis for the initial response of Carole and Ilse to each other as long passages describe the beauty of the two women. On their first date, Carole quickly overcomes her mental objection to kissing a woman in public and yields to her passions: "Without one more word of internal monologue Carole bent over and kissed her. It was one of the few times in her life since age twelve that she acted like a true animal. The freedom was intoxicating" (*In Her Day*, 15). Though she has always believed herself to be above emotions ("brains transcend genitals") in many ways, Carole succumbs to Ilse's sexual appeal while at the same time she is seduced by her feelings of community with all women (*In Her Day*, 19). The irrationality of their affair ("love is the wildcard of existence") actually appeals to the rational Carole, for after her first night with Ilse, she realizes how intellectual she has become: "When was the last time something unexpected happened or that I let something unexpected happen? I've lost my sense of play. When I laugh it's over words. Wit. Intellect. I remember—I remember when I was a kid we'd get into scrapes like this. Where did that go? When did it leave me? I want it back. I want it all back" (*In Her Day*, 34). Like Molly, Carole desires to reclaim a lost innocence that involves a spontaneous and direct response to experience.

   Humor: "I laugh, therefore I am."   Humor as a political strategy is proposed by Brown in both her fiction and non-fiction. In her introduction to *In Her Day*, Brown reiterates the significance of humor in her work: "We've become hagridden by facts, obsessed with product instead of process. Where's the energetic wit, the looney outlook, the frivolity, the lightness of comforting laughter? It has become fashionable to know and unfashionable to feel, and you can't really laugh if you can't feel" (*In Her Day*, xii). Instead of the Cartesian theorem for existence, Brown proposes, *"Rideo, ergo sum"*: "I laugh, therefore I am" (*In Her Day*, xii). The novel presents Brown's intended "glimmer of absurdity" both in its verbal wit and slapstick physical humor. Though Carole seems to prefer the slapstick style as being more authentic than wit, she eventually uses both. She and Adele have verbal battles that demonstrate their sympathetic natures as well as their adeptness at language and a mutual sense of the absurd. At first Ilse is attracted to Carole's wit because she has lost her sense of humor after two years of hard work in the women's movement; later she is disturbed by Carole's sarcasm about the movement and her inability to take Ilse seriously when she needs the support. Yet when Ilse finally responds to the allegations brought against her group by a vindictive Olive and the media, she creates a slapstick scene that illustrates the silliness of the situation.

   Realizing that verbal wit can degenerate into dry intellectual banter or mere cleverness, Carole needs physical, "pure" comedy to revive her spirit. Brown creates several visual puns to show this transformation of humor in Carole. She and Ilse literally "run into each other" at the restaurant as customer collides with the salad-laden waitress. In the "Candid Camera" style episode where Ilse and Carole hide in Ilse's old dresser to frighten passersby, a man tries "to pick up" Carole as he steals the supposedly abandoned furniture. Remembering her sister's death, Carole recalls how physical humor brings her brother out of his alcoholic depression and draws them closer together when they use his truck's loudspeaker system to impersonate the voice of God and frighten a poor woman on the street. Carole enjoys her rediscovered humor when she taunts a fastidious gentleman about the string hanging out of his poodle's rectum. Ilse brings out this playfulness in Carole but she cannot control this liberation. She believes Carole takes the humor too far when she accepts Adele's adventure in the Rolls Royce. Adele explains her reasons for this playful jab at social pretension in terms that Carole would accept: "I came to the conclusion that most people give up their dreams by calling them fantasies. All that's left of their lives is a dusty survival in old telephone directories. Once in a great while we have to let fly or we atrophy. So I'm making one evening the way I want it. . . . The unexpected keeps the human race from stagnation" (*In Her Day*, 132). Brown clearly identifies with this philosophy in her writing, as she pushes the limits of humor in this novel. In *Rubyfruit*, humor is a spontaneous outgrowth of Molly's character and social perceptions; here, the humor is much more strained as Brown seems determined to make the conversations and episodes hilarious to support her political uses of humor. If you do not find cursing birds, pratfalls, and stories about lesbian strippers to be funny, then you are not yet truly liberated. There is an uncomfortable, unintentional darkness beneath the self-consciously frenetic humor of *In Her Day*.

Personal and social history.   Humor and playfulness allow a return to the primacy of the physical over the intellectual and put one in touch with one's emotions. A sense of connectedness to the past is also involved in Brown's use of humor. This theme of personal history as a reflection of social history is demonstrated frequently in *In Her Day*. Both Carole and Adele are historians who recognize the value of understanding the past, while Ilse and LaVerne (Adele's lover) are much more involved in the present. Originally choosing the Renaissance as her field of study, Carole takes the advice of a wise professor to become a medieval scholar in order to succeed in the male-dominated art world. But she comes to love the period because of its mystery: "gradually another vision of lusty, violent, pious, contradictory people emerged" (*In Her Day*, 40). Like Adele, who studies pre-Columbian culture, Carole is fascinated by her discovery that "once, seven hundred years ago, the dead were flesh and her flesh depended on their prior existence" (*In Her Day*, 40). To Carole, continuity with the past generations in ancient history as well as in her own family history is essential to an understanding of life and of change. Adele expresses for Brown and for Carole the intense significance of history: "We're a human chain. The dead give to the living and the living must give to each other and we must secure the future for the unborn. The thought comforts me. If I get torn apart in my own time or confused, I at least know I have my place in time. I'm part of this chain" (*In Her Day*, 143).

This appreciation of history as a means to connect humanity causes strife between Carole and Ilse. As a representative of the younger generation, Ilse suffers the curse of all youth, "innocence laced with ignorance" (*In Her Day*, 50). Ilse reminds both Adele and Carole of their own youth as she is discovering things that they have both already experienced: "Here she is saying something that's absolutely a new thought to her but it's the same thing we said or went through twenty years ago" (*In Her Day*, 46). Seeing Carole as a "protofeminist," Ilse begins to learn the significance of history in her relationship with Carole as they discuss their different views of the women's movement. Ilse first believes women should forget the past and begin a new revolutionary cycle of history. On the other hand, Carole believes that one must remember the past in order to avoid making the same mistakes over again. Despite the failure of their romantic relationship, the women do influence each other's views of life and history. After her group's attack on the scandal sheet, Ilse expresses her awareness of the history of the women's movement, "I know what in this movement is right out of 1789 and what is ours" (*In Her Day*, 164). But history does not have to paralyze one; consciousness of the past and activism for the future can co-exist. Carole combines those lessons too when she decides to write a history of the women of the Middle Ages as her contribution to the movement. Though Ilse at times is made to appear young and foolish, she does effect a change in the lives of Adele and Carole. Her infectious idealism and commitment inspire the two apolitical women to reconsider their own ideals and contribute what they can to the movement.

Brown seems to have arrived at the conclusion that these very different women "both have a place in the feminist world" (Core, 88). With her intimate knowledge of the politics of revolution and her personal involvement with activism, Brown clearly knew the pitfalls of group tactics. Her snide characterizations of Olive and her followers reveal Brown's frustration with organized efforts toward revolution. They also caricature Brown's experiences with the Furies Collective. Brown even pokes fun at her own youthful idealism when she has Ilse give Carole and Adele a copy of "Woman Identified Woman" to read. They critique this document as being too much about biology and not enough about the human spirit. They agree that most feminist literature is "so badly written or run off so fuzzy I can't make it out" (*In Her Day*, 47). But she does not reject Ilse's position outright though her preference is definitely for the wisdom of age and individuality. *In Her Day* provides a transition for Brown from the group activist politics of her youthful revolutionary days to her personal, individualistic approach to reform. She makes the transition through an acceptance of her personal history—a return to the South—and the history of women (a shift from autobiographical narrative to historical fiction). Though Brown claims the significance of this novel to be in the shift from the first-person to the third-person voice, perhaps even more important is the movement from the present to the past, as her subsequent works (*Six of One, Southern Discomfort,* and *High Hearts*) explore the past and its connection to the present and the future.

Chapter Four
Six of One and *Bingo*:
The Hunsenmeir Saga

The main difficulty that Rita Mae Brown admits encountering during the writing of *Six of One* was financial. Since *In Her Day* was not particularly successful (although she received a larger advance for it than she had for *Rubyfruit Jungle*), she had to struggle to support herself while she worked on her third novel until grant assistance from the Massachusetts Council of the Arts and the National Endowment for the Arts allowed her to complete the manuscript. Her gratitude to these organizations is expressed in her special thanks preceding the text: "American artists are a national resource and critical to our spiritual/cultural life. There is no rebirth without art."[1] Harper and Row bought the novel in 1977, the same year that Bantam reprinted *Rubyfruit Jungle*, bringing acclaim and recognition to this "Southern, poor, and rebellious" woman (*Starting from Scratch*, 14). Not published until 1978, *Six of One* was the Literary Guild of America's Alternate Selection, Macmillan Book Club Alternate, and Woman Today Book Club Alternate. Dedicated to her mother, who is the inspiration for one of the main characters, the novel employs a complex narrative structure, glorious slapstick humor, and a wide array of characters to convey Brown's understanding of history, women, and community. As Brown comments, "the whole book is about relationships, making connections, whether sisters or friends or lovers or—husbands."[2]

History and Narrative Structure in *Six of One*

For *Six of One*, Brown abandons the contemporary landscape in favor of an excursion into the past, a fascination that will continue to intrigue her through *Southern Discomfort* and *High Hearts*. Her revisionist look at history and her exploration of the conventions of the historical novel express through fiction many of her political, personal, and social theories. As we see in her essays and poetry, Brown strongly believes that the understanding of history is necessary to the definition and progress of the human race. As in a conventional historical novel, *Six of One* sees individual struggles in light of larger historical movements. Brown takes on the male domains of war and labor relations to look at these important activities from a uniquely female point of view. In Brown's fictional landscape the childhood battle over a hair ribbon can take on as much significance as World War I or the battle between the sexes. Focusing her action almost exclusively in the female community within the small fictional town of Runnymede, named for the historic site where the Magna Carta was signed in 1215, Brown establishes a convincing moral base from which to view and comment upon the political changes of this century. History has traditionally been the domain of men, for they are the actors and initiators of the actions—the wars, the elections, the work—that have been recorded and revered as human history. Disenfranchised and powerless, women have always been on the fringes of male history, often indirectly the victims of male actions. Brown attempts to correct that imbalance by looking at how women's lives are affected by the history that men create and by giving a voice to the unrecorded history that women themselves create in the course of their daily lives.

The structure of the novel subtly conveys many of Brown's assumptions about history. Instead of chapters, Brown divides her book with dates, randomly alternating events from 6 March 1909 (the date of the infamous hair ribbon battle between the sisters Julia Ellen and Louise Hunsenmeir) and 21 September 1980 (a date slightly in the future, since the novel's publication occurred in 1978). The more or less contemporary story in 1980 serves as an anchor to which the other story lines are tethered, afloat in the sea of time. The sections in the past follow a roughly chronological pattern with many unfilled gaps and a rather hurried treatment of time from the fifties to the eighties (the period of the narrator Nickel's childhood). These numerous segments from the past, however, do not really seem like flashbacks. Brown is able to create a sense of equality between all of the characters and time periods, more like a type of crosscutting montage than a rigid flashback-flashforward system. Because there are so many mutual echoes of character, theme, and action between the past and the future (ironically there is no true present, except in the reading), the past seems continually alive, simultaneous. This peaceful co-existence of the past and the future stresses Brown's theme of the continuity of human history. As John Berger succinctly states: "History always constitutes the relation between a present and its past. . . . The past is not for living in; it is a well of conclusions from which we draw in order to act."[3] Through her characters and narrative structure Brown also hints at a belief in reincarnation as a historical force; the life force continues though the shapes and manifestations of life may change. The history of these and of other women is kept alive through individual and collective memory, through an oral tradition of storytelling, which is necessary since no one will write their stories in the history books.

The unusual point of view created by Brown for the presentation of her fictional history makes further statements about what history means to women. The book begins with an "I" that is quickly submerged into a limited omniscient perspective and does not resurface. That "I" is initially associated with Nickel (Nichole), the lesbian-feminist, college-graduate, adopted daughter who seems at first to be Brown's alter ego for another autobiographical excursion into fiction. But as we discovered in *In Her Day*, such simplistic autobiographical identifications are misleading, for Brown in that novel expresses a multiple point of view, revealing her identification with several key characters. The same is true here. Though Nickel in the very first sentence of the novel asserts her actions ("I bought Mother a new car"; *Six of One*, 1), she recedes slowly into the background as the actions and conversations of her mother Julia and her aunt Louise come to the foreground. Nickel is transformed from an active participant (turning cartwheels on the lawn with her mother), to an observer of the actions, to a reporter of actions that she does not witness, to a pawn in the rival sisters' battles. Thus, as she becomes more and more involved in the life of her family, she is absorbed into the fiction that she initially creates, becoming a third person character two-thirds of the way into the novel. Appropriately, the plot surrounding her involves her attempt to buy her grandmother's family homestead so that Nickel can return to Runnymede and reintegrate herself into her childhood environment. Through this shift in narrative perspective, Brown defines the role of the writer as a conduit through which others begin to speak and act; she demonstrates in her fiction that difficult leap over the Grand Canyon of first-person to third-person narration that she had attempted with limited success in *In Her Day*. In contrast to the polemical style of *In Her Day*, Brown lets the characters define themselves by their actions and words, rather than by an intrusive narrator. By allowing the other characters in the book to speak for themselves, Nickel creates an environment of equality and openness; since she too becomes a third-person character, she puts herself on a par with the others rather than claiming a position of privilege as first-person narrator.

As the 1980 narrative line suggests, Nickel must not only use her powers of observation to create fiction but she must also recreate imaginatively events that she does not witness. To do this we assume that she learns to listen to Julia and Louise to gather important details, then she employs her deep understanding of their characters to imagine how things might have happened. For example, though Nickel is not party to Julia and Ev's plot to sneak into Louise's house to find incriminating evidence for blackmail, the detailed descriptions of the disguises and the comic actions are believable even if things never happened in quite that comic way. We can imagine Julia bragging about her exploits to Nickel on the front porch one evening, relishing and exaggerating every detail, after which Nickel retires to her room to translate the stories and incorporate them into her narrative. The strong Southern storytelling tradition is evident in Brown's style and technique. This oral tradition also is responsible for the bulk of the novel, the historical narrative about Celeste Chalfonte, Cora Hunsenmeir, and the rest of the Runnymede inhabitants.

The interaction between the past and present/future sections suggests that the historical narrative that dominates the book is a result of Nickel's research and provides a means for her reintegration into the community after her absence. In the 1980 sections, Louise and Julia often comment on Nickel's books. Louise complains about being misrepresented but is actually more afraid that she might be left out of the next book. At first, Julia and Louise try to keep their mother's romance with Aimes Rankin a secret from Nickel so that Nickel cannot write about it, but they eventually reveal this secret, which is, of course, incorporated into the historical narrative of the family. This and other evidence point to the historical narrative as Nickel's fiction, constructed from family legends transmitted over the generations but filtered through a modern consciousness. The sisters do not want Aimes to be mentioned because they are ashamed of his illegitimate relationship to the married (but deserted) Cora; Nickel, who could not care less about this old-fashioned morality, is more interested in his unionizing activities, so the narrative reveals this bias in the sections about him.

Not understanding the modern consciousness of the narration, some critics have complained about the idealism with which Brown treats the past, especially Celeste's lesbian relationship with Ramelle. They feel that all of the women of this era would have faced more prejudice and social rejection in reality, that they would have been more closeted about their behavior. But as critic Cynthia MacDonald writes in her enthusi-

astic review of *Six of One*: "Brown uses a kind of revisionist history to
support her conviction that what was seen in the first half of the
twentieth century as the life of women was only what was on the surface,
not what was underneath. She opens the seams to give her vision of what
was really there. We are shown not the seamy side of life, but a body
ready for anything, especially celebration."[4] Similarly, if we were to see
the narrative as Nickel's selective recreation of the past, we would realize
that she is not concerned with the pettiness of homophobia. She, like
Brown, is interested in much larger issues. Also, neither is really interested in writing history in a strictly factual sense. The novel is about the
process of fictionalization, about how the artist interacts creatively with
her sources. As Nickel admits early, the truth about the past is elusive.
When she first tells the story about the hair ribbon, having heard it from
different points of view at different times of her life, Nickel realizes, "In
May of 1980 I still can't untangle victor from victim. It changes
regularly like night and day as each sister revolves around the other" (*Six
of One*, 1). Truth is a fluid not a fixed quantity. All history involves
mythologizing, including Nickel's own narrative.

Spiritual Foremothers.   Like her attempt to buy the house of her
ancestress, Nickel's fictional account of her family's past is an attempt to
reclaim her own history as much as it is a recording for posterity the
fascinating lives of a diverse community of women. Nickel's personal
connection to the historical narrative is revealed through her intense
identification with the character of Celeste Chalfonte. Nickel may be
Brown's alter ego in factual detail but Celeste is the author's spiritual
ancestress. While Nickel represents Brown's appreciation of the working
class, Celeste is admired for the grace and power that only wealth and
social status can bring. Her wit, generosity, pride, loyalty, courage, and
open-mindedness are praised throughout the narrative. Though Brown
continually espouses the values of the middle class, part of her longs for
the comfort and class of the wealthy, a dichotomy for which many of her
fans have criticized her.[5] Because of the autobiographical similarities
between Nickel and Brown in fact and between Celeste and Brown in
spiritual wish-fulfillment, it is only appropriate that there should be
significant parallels between Nickel and Celeste. Many of the older
characters comment that Nickel reminds them of Celeste. Most important, however, are Celeste's repeated statements of belief in reincarnation. Portrayed through the novel as a natural force (her first introduction
in the novel is as a "fragrant tornado"), Celeste dies on the eve of her own
birthday when Nickel is born illegitimately to a young girl who even-

tually abandons her baby to adoption by Julia (*Six of One*, 3). Right before she takes her fatal horseback ride, Celeste thinks with excitement about the expected child: "She was tired of sharing her birthday with William Blake and Friedrich Engels. Celebrating earthly renewal with a new person might be fun" (*Six of One*, 271). She assures her friend Fannie Jump that all their friends will return through reincarnation. Celeste's death leads to her spirit's rebirth in Nichole and the continuation of her soul's quest for perfection and nirvana. Even Fannie Jump's suggestion that Celeste should have been a writer seems to be fulfilled by Nichole's future. Martha Chew has noticed this tendency in Brown's fiction, her repeated creation of an "aristocratic double," for the autobiographical narrator/character; in *Rubyfruit*, Molly is paired with Polina, and in *In Her Day*, Carole is paired with Ilse. This technique in *Six of One* reveals Brown's attempt to resolve class differences symbolically: "Although attempts to break through class barriers are only partially successful on the literal level of the novel, on a symbolic level the two classes are brought together through the identification of Nickel with her 'aristrocratic' double, Celeste, an identification that is underlined by the complex paralleling of Celeste's two families" (Chew, 208).

If Nichole is indeed the spiritual descendant of Celeste, Brown suggests that eternity is possible through life and through fiction. Though men are obsessed with time and its demarcations (as Brown depicted in her poetry), women represent an eternal, natural principle. Time divisions, as the chapter headings indicate, do not have to be destructive; the past can exist simultaneously, harmoniously, with the present. Celeste will continue to exist through the memories of the other characters, the legacy that a loving life leaves behind. As Ramelle remembers her beloved, "She's in my mind every day, every hour. . . . I mean, even dead, Celeste fills the room" (*Six of One*, 308). The wise and earthy Cora knows that "when one falls out, one steps in," that life continues in an unbroken chain (*Six of One*, 308). Living a life in harmony with nature, the women do not fear death but embrace it as part of a natural cycle. They experience traditionally religious comforting visions of loved ones greeting them in the next world, happy that they have lived their lives fully. Their comic tombstone epitaphs laugh at the idea that death is serious.

Nickel's portrait of herself as a young artist cannot begin, as most such books begin, with her own birth, but must encompass her entire heritage, the generations that went before her, the extended community that nurtured her. Celeste, as her elegant alter ego, represents an ideal that has been transmitted to Nichole. The story of how Celeste created and nourished a community of women around her, how she and the other women lived satisfying and rich lives, is essential to understand as Nickel is trying to reenter that community of her past and face her own uncertain future. In her poetry, essays, and early novels, Brown explores the forces that separate and divide people from each other—class, race, background, politics; here, she turns her attention to showing how women can live in harmony together in true sisterhood. Friendships abound in the novel. Triangular relationships defy the traditional notion of couples. Surrogate families are formed and reformed. Each life touches many. And all of these complex permutations are contrasted against the larger social turmoils of war, infidelity, conflict, and change.

Celeste is the apex of several of the intersecting triangular relationships in the novel. Celeste balances her love for the beautiful and graceful Ramelle with her devotion to the down-to-earth Cora. Celeste and Ramelle share the ideal lesbian relationship, combining passionate sexual fulfillment with total spiritual communion in an environment that accepts their non-traditional relationship. So perfect is their union that the formation of another triangle does not upset Celeste's bond to Ramelle. When Ramelle meets and falls in love with Celeste's brother Curtis, Celeste is completely understanding and without jealousy of their love, which Ramelle reveals does not in any way compete with the depth of her feelings for Celeste. Ramelle recognizes that their personal history of love have bound them together forever: "Our lives are woven together like a braid. If I left I'd unravel everything that was dear to me, including myself" (Six of One, 109). Celeste's solitary bent is not enough to isolate Ramelle from her feelings when they share so much of their lives. They both discover that love is not the force that separates people (as it often does in jealous, possessive situations); as Ramelle exclaims to Curtis: "Loving you makes me love her more and loving her makes me love you. Do you think it's possible that love multiplies? We're taught to think it divides. There's only so much to go around, like diamonds. It multiplies" (Six of One, 108). The astounding truthful simplicity of "love multiplies" echoes through the novel, embodying Brown's mature concern for "marathon love," the love that "deepens experience and makes all life exquisite and valuable" ("Another Time," Poems).

Just as Celeste accepts Ramelle's love for Curtis and adores the resulting child of that union, Ramelle refuses to be jealous over Celeste's deep relationship with Cora, who in many ways is the opposite of Celeste. Like Brown, Celeste finds solace in the study of Greek and Latin, in mental pursuits; Cora can neither read nor write. As her name suggests, Celeste is in many ways ethereal and elusive; Cora is all common sense and traditional human values. Brown chose the name "Cora" to represent the large heart of this, her favorite character, whom she patterned on her own very strong grandmother (Turner, 60). Their oppositions in personality as well as physical circumstances balance their relationship: "Cora's wisdom and endurance, her ability to find joy in the simplest of events, grounded Celeste. . . . For all her wit and cool distance, she needed to be included in humanity. Cora included her as an equal" (*Six of One*, 19). On her side, Cora sees beneath Celeste's glittering facade to her essential goodness and appreciates her for what she is, not for what power and wealth she possesses: "Even when I'm mad at you I love you no end," Cora confesses to Celeste after the fiasco with the piano that Celeste out of pride refused to give to Louise (*Six of One*, 29). The two women endure the traumas of their lives with each other's help. Celeste finds Aimes's murdered body for Cora and later murders the responsible villain (Brutus Rife) in cold blood to achieve a primitive justice for Cora and herself. In one of the most touching moments in the novel, Celeste experiences insomnia and a reaction that might best be called an anxiety attack. In the middle of the night she heads for Cora's house for comfort, awkward at their sleeping nude together but in desperate need of human affection. Cora takes her in unquestioningly, like a sister.

Celeste is surrounded by other surrogate sisters, her two childhood Vassar friends, Fannie Jump Creighton and Fairy Thatcher. The three women are known in school as Hic, Haec, Hoc, and later as the Furies. Together, they spend endless hours in Celeste's mansion, talking, eating, and playing gin. Here, as later in *Bingo*, a competitive but leisurely game is used to draw people closer through friendly rivalry. The gin game harkens back to antebellum customs of the nobility as the women try to preserve some of their heritage through this civilized pastime. Brown undercuts the elegance of the card playing tradition, however, by using it as a setting for outrageous modern conversations and by having Celeste cheat constantly at the game through a secret code system with Cora (Cora arranges the tea sandwiches on the tray in certain ways to reveal what cards the other players possess). The friends' habitual gin game is contrasted later with the cutthroat play of the newfangled board game Monopoly. In gin, the skills of mathematics, strategy, and memory are essential to the excellent player; winning money is really not the object of the game as in poker and other gambling card games. Like the capitalistic society it reflects, Monopoly depends heavily on luck and ruthlessness; an accumulation of wealth and property is the goal. Julia Ellen convinces Celeste and her friends to play the game against a rival trio of sisters, La Squandras—Ruby, Rachel, and Rose Rife—so that she can earn real money at their expense.

At first Fannie Jump and Fairy are portrayed almost exclusively as adjuncts to Celeste; their married lives outside of the circle of friendship seem irrelevant. Fannie Jump is a lecherous seducer of young men, but eventually proves her talent and worth when she is abandoned by her husband after the stock market crash. With Celeste's help, she turns her house into a fashionable speakeasy during the prohibition era. Her personal love of drinking, talking, and flirting becomes the key to her professional success; in the process, she gains a new sense of self-worth and competence. On the other hand, Fairy struggles morally with her social position of privilege, revealing in her dialogue a nascent political consciousness. Beginning to read Marx and other radical theorists, she eventually turns her back on wealth and status, making the difficult decision to go to Europe to work for the revolution of the proletariat. Caught in Germany during the rise of the Nazis, Fairy dies heroically in a concentration camp. Through these two minor characters, Brown shows how different women successfully faced the challenges and changes of the twentieth century, as active participants, not merely passive pawns. In doing so, they also reveal their independence from the dominant force of Celeste; she nurtures and strengthens them to the point that they assert their own identities and determine their own destinies, in Fairy's case, against Celeste's better judgment.

These surrogate sisters are contrasted to Celeste's own family. She is one of triplets with two different siblings, her beloved brother Spottis-wood and her detested sister Carlotta, or La Sermonetta as she is known to Celeste. Carlotta proves that blood alone does not create true sister-hood. She is criticized, like most of the Catholics in Brown's books, for her religious fanaticism, subtle hypocrisy, and idolatry. The simple faith of Cora rooted in true moral principles contrasts sharply with Carlotta's showy religion of expediency. Carlotta's alliance with the dreaded Rifes, who are responsible for much of the tragedy in the book, reveals how the church prefers to align itself with wealth and power rather than making difficult moral choices. The battle between simple personal ethics and organized religion is unwittingly perpetuated by Celeste when she pays for Louise to attend La Sermonetta's school; the impressionable girl is in essence corrupted by the feelings of moral and social superiority im-parted by Catholic piety, creating a constant source of tension between the sisters Louise and Julia. Spottiswood, on the other hand, is truly Celeste's male counterpart. Not only do they look like each other, but they also share values, a similar sense of humor, and a strong sibling bond. It is his violent death in battle that troubles Celeste through the novel and solidifies her anti-war attitudes. When his memory is threatened by Brutus's hypocritical offer to build a war memorial to Spotts, Celeste harbors an undying resentment that leads to her murder of Brutus.

The wealthy Chalfonte family is contrasted with the poor but proud Hunsenmeir family, as the communal action of the novel shifts from Celeste's garden and card parties to the informal family celebrations on Cora's front porch on Bumblebee Hill. The female triumvirate of Cora and her daughters Julia and Louise supersedes and survives any of the different male-female relationships that are brought into the story. Although these women are lucky to have good men to share their lives, they not only dominate their men but they long outlive them as well, showing the strength associated with the female principle in Brown's fictional world. This female strength is also touted in the real women who inspired these characters, Brown's mother Julia Ellen Brown and her sister Mary: "I grew up with these to almost mythical figures around me, my mother and my aunt, who didn't give a rat's a _ _ what anybody thought. They'd say anything to anybody, and they did as as they damn well pleased. . . . The people closest to me were all very dominating characters. The men weren't weak, but somehow the women. . . . they were the ones you paid attention to" (Fleischer, E2). Abandoned by her first husband Hansford, whom we never see in the novel, Cora is befriended by Aimes Rankin, with whom she finds a satisfying sexual and emotional relationship: "When Aimes made love it was as though he was trying to tell her something with his body. Cora felt the same way toward him. There were places words couldn't go but bodies could" (*Six of One*, 56). Here, as in other Brown works, the best sex is communication, a purely physical experience where self is lost in sensation and language (the mind) is transcended. To Julia, Aimes is "more my daddy than my daddy," reinforcing Brown's notion that a family is not created by blood but by love (*Six of One*, 71). But his gentleness makes him vulnerable to the powerful machinery of the Rifes. Rife may win the short-term victory by having Aimes killed to stop his unionizing activities, but Aimes wins the long-term battle with the rightness of his principles.

As his nickname "Pearlie" suggests, Louise's husband Paul also dem-

onstrates a non-macho sensitivity, one that is taken advantage of by the
domineering Louise until he is totally confused about his masculinity:
"If I show my feelings I'm a sissy. If I don't I'm a brute. If I tell my wife
what to do, I'm ugly. If I don't, I'm henpecked. What the hell" (*Six of
One*, 221). Warped by her religious fanaticism, Louise is implicitly
criticized for her treatment of her good-hearted but not too enlightened
husband. Denying her own sexuality, she sees his demands (for rouged
nipples) as being perverse and cannot understand how Julia has such a
friendly, relaxed relationship with her husband Chester (Chessy) Smith.
Julia experiences the perfect romantic relationship with Chessy. She falls
in love with him at first sight as they stare in amazement at each other
through the kitchen screen door. They work closely together on all of
their projects, sharing every aspect of their lives. The depth of their bond
is comically revealed when Chessy teaches Julia to drive his truck; after
Julia careens through the yard, frightens all the guests, and plows into
the porch, Chessy admits that he loves Julia more than his now-damaged
truck, the ultimate compliment for the Southern male.

Though these very different male-female relationships are important
to the plot, the real emotional center of the novel is the relationship of the
sisters. Celeste has a key role in their drama as well, for the young girls
idolize her. More importantly she is responsible for initiating the infamous hair ribbon incident and later for separating the sisters by providing for Louise's but not for Julia's education. Thus she becomes a
determining agent in how their lives and relationship with each other
evolve. Her beneficence in each incident leads to conflict, creating a
snake in their childhood gardens. When Celeste casually gives Julia a
beautiful ribbon for her birthday, she arouses Louise's jealous, competitive instincts. Their ensuing mock heroic battle takes on Christian
dimensions as both Louise and Cora use the wisdom of Solomon to help
argue their cases. Louise cuts the ribbon in half because Christians are
supposed to share; Cora retaliates by threatening to give half of all of
Louise's toys to Julia as punishment for Louise's selfishness. Julia com-
plicates the situation by giving Louise her half of the ribbon and
"logically" claiming all of Louise's toys. Theology, we learn, can be used
to prove any point. This often remembered event represents a fall from
innocence for the girls (though they were hardly angels before this); it
seems to be the episode to which they trace back all of their sibling
rivalry, the main motivating factor in their long and turbulent love-hate
relationship. Similarly, Celeste's gift of education, this time to Louise,
sets the sisters out on different paths in life. Louise is allowed to pursue

her musical talents, but in the process of going to La Sermonetta's school, she is also transformed by Carlotta's religious program and is instilled with a feeling of social superiority by going to private school: "Louise would look back on these days as the happiest of her life. Julia would remember them as when Louise got religion and piss elegance at the same time" (*Six of One*, 31). Despite their increasing differences in personality and education (nature and nurture), the sisters achieve a kind of equilibrium in their battles, an uneasy alliance that speaks as much for their love as for their hatred.

The main elements of humor in *Six of One* are the continuing antics of the sisters, from these childhood episodes into their seventies. In Brown's typically theatrical scenes, for instance, the two sisters disrupt the solemnities of the annual Independence Day parade. Julia, a lowly tugboat, gets even with Louise, who is dressed as the Statue of Liberty, by battering her on the float, starting a fire, and unleashing total chaos on the town. Through this stunt, Julia enacts her jealousy about Louise's growth into an older, more sophisticated woman. When young Julia feels shut out by Louise's elaborate preparation for a date with Pearlie, she assaults her sister's rejection and pretensions to beauty by putting blue dye in the shampoo water. Louise's retaliation, cutting off half of Julia's hair, backfires when Ramelle turns the shaggy hair into a fashionable bob to usher in the twenties. This plot-counterplot pattern continues into the novel's present, culminating in their elaborate battle over Nickel's purchase of the family homestead. Louise always tries to assert her superiority (in taste, righteousness, status), but Julia denies her pretensions and tries to knock her off her high horse.

Their comic hostilities, however, cannot mask their deep understanding of each other, their underlying loyalty and affection. They might fight with each other, but they will not allow anyone else to hurt the other. Despite her disapproval of adoption, Louise will not allow Julia's hopes for a child to be disappointed by the irresponsibility of Nickel's biological mother; she overcomes her moral objections and accompanies Chessy on the arduous journey to reclaim the infant from an orphanage where the young mother had abandoned her.[6] They are described as "fried eggs in a pan, separate but together" (*Six of One*, 198), "six of one, half dozen of the other" (*Six of One*, 47), or as Aimes observes, "for all their feuding, one couldn't get by without the other" (*Six of One*, 57). They need each other to create the tension necessary to keep them young and lively. When they are plotting against each other in the competition over the house, Julia and Ev in their foolish costumes are like children playing dress up or preparing for Halloween; Louise and Orrie Tadia behave "like two girls at a slumber party minus the slumber" (*Six of One*, 177). Brown stresses the youthfulness of all of her women characters; they remain active right up to their deaths. Julia especially keeps up with the current fashions (granny glasses and hotpants) and accepts the new behavior of the younger generation (smoking marijuana is not that far removed from running whiskey during Prohibition). Brown also introduces the subject of the sexuality of the older generation, which she will develop in *Bingo*.

Social Criticism in *Six of One*. The sisters' comic battles take on another dimension in the context of the historical changes that the novel depicts. As Aimes notices, "Those two bicker over hair and overseas men die over not much more" (*Six of One*, 57). Clearly, Brown uses the silly rivalries of the two sisters to criticize the politics and senseless reality of war, one of her major themes in the novel. The ever-present background of the Civil War in this town divided by the Mason-Dixon line with its competing Yankee and Confederate statues provides a perfect environment for the family bickering. The traditional patriotic causes of war are completely ignored in the discussion of World War I and II, as these international events invade the peaceful community of Runnymede. Ramelle compares war to two schoolboys fighting over marbles in the playground, only on a larger scale. Julia's tugboat demolition of the Statue of Liberty is prophetic as the munitions contractors, personified by Brutus Rife, lead the politicians into war to enhance the profit and strength of the military-industrial complex and fill their coffers with wealth. The war interferes with the life of the community indirectly when Brutus breaks up the strike that would unionize his factory. As Spottiswood discovers during his time in Washington, Brutus uses the country's need for weapons to force federal agents to break up the labor union, which leads of course to his own increased profits. Spotts identifies the three musketeers of war as steel, railroads, and munitions; these industries are actually responsible for encouraging the conflicts and making warfare possible.

When Spotts is shipped out to battle, Celeste recreates a battle station in her house, replete with maps and flag markers, so that she can chart the progress of the war. The women put war into perspective in a way that Brown approves. Fairy, the budding Marxist, perceives the truth in the old saying that "old men start wars and young men fight them. . . . You'd think after all these thousands of years fellows would catch the hint" (*Six of One*, 86). The women seem to agree that if their own land were attacked, "when war intruded on their personal sphere," they might follow their Southern female ancestors into battle (*Six of One*, 89). But, as Celeste says, "Men must prove they are men. We don't need to prove anything" (*Six of One*, 89). War is just another manifestation of the "kingdom that kills"; the cycle of violence begins in the food chain with animals eating plants and other animals (*Six of One*, 90). Brown recognizes the excitement and allure of violence for humans, though she does not necessarily approve of its outlet in wars: "I'm no stranger to violence. I fought all the time. And it is extraordinarily exciting. Your adrenaline level gets so high that it's an excitement rarely repeated by other events. And until the human animal recognizes that it's in all of us, and finds outlets for violence, I don't think we're going to stop killing each other and beating up on each other" (Ball, 9).

The abstract discussions of war by the people at home are counterbalanced by a very graphic depiction of battle as Spotts charges to a brutal death. Before he dies he perceives the social injustice of his battalion of immigrant Americans, a group that would not be treated fairly and with respect in the States, here being sacrificed in a futile charge against the Germans. An even more graphic passage describes the jungle warfare in World War II that engulfs Extra Billy Bitters, the wild youth who impregnated and married Louise's daughter Mary despite Louise's prejudices against him. The maggots and the stench of the soldiers' rotting bodies Brown describes were never acknowledged in John Wayne's patriotic versions of war. Brown shifts perspective to the Japanese commander on the attacking side, revealing him as an equally scared youth with a family that he does not want to lose. Billy learns a bitter lesson that haunts him the rest of his years, preventing the Southern good old boy from enjoying his former favorite pastime of hunting animals. In these battles scenes Brown invades traditionally male territory and avoids the glorification of actual battle, though Spotts and Billy achieve a personal heroism beyond the bounds of patriotism. The grotesque details of combat and the shift of place outside of the familiar terrain of Runnymede, where all of the other scenes (except the trip to the orphanage to retrieve Nickel) take place, make war seem doubly strange. The terrifying experiences of these two soldiers reveal another similarity. Though they different in backgrounds and status, both men turn physically to other men for comfort as they face imminent death. As Spotts lies broken and bleeding on the ground, his Irish companion stretches out full length beside him; after Spotts confesses, "Sergeant, I love you," the sergeant holds and kisses him as he dies. Similarly, Billy Bitters overcomes his initial prejudice toward his Jewish compatriot in battle, finally holding the wounded boy's body and kissing him on the lips before he leaves for a medic. These moments are treated very tenderly by Brown, implying her regret that it takes such extreme violence for men to be able to show affection toward each other. Perhaps if men could be more emotional with other men in their daily lives, there would be no need for war.

Much of Brown's anti-war fervor is directed at Brutus Rife, who represents the fundamental human greed that causes governments to declare war. As his name suggests, Brutus is the descendant of a long line of cruel and corrupt men. He is the personification of Brown's criticism against male culture. An attractive, smooth-talking villain, Brutus is the cause of most of the misery and death depicted in the town of Runnymede. But when he kills, he kills by proxy, through hired thugs or through the government that he controls, because he is not man enough to face an opponent openly and directly. He cannot see Celeste Chalfonte without dreaming of raping her, for sex, like everything else in his life, is conquest and possession. Celeste's constitutional dislike of Brutus evolves into open hostility after the deaths of Aimes and Spotts, which she blames on Brutus and his kind. When he delivers the graduation address for Carlotta, hypocritically praising the men who fell in battle (while he himself stayed safely at home and profited on their misery), Celeste must speak out. Women must get the right to vote so that they can save civilization from the destruction caused by such powerful men as Brutus Rife. Adding insult to injury, Brutus wants to erect a war memorial to Spottiswood and the other Runnymede heroes, not out of sincere honor for the dead but to improve his social status in the town and suggest his connection to the powerful Chalfonte family. A product of the old Southern code of honor, Celeste cannot allow such injustice to prevail: "Celeste thought of justice, or more precisely, the lack of it. The law allows what honor forbids" (Six of One, 102).

The confrontation between Brutus and Celeste reveals the clash of the new, industrial, Northern, male culture with the old, pastoral, Southern, female culture. Brutus describes this contrast when Celeste visits his office during a storm: "You live in another world, a world of cavaliers, courtliness and romance. You don't understand how the world really works . . ." (Six of One, 120). After Celeste shoots Brutus for honor, for "simple morality and simple responsibility," she feels no guilt for her actions and no retribution is demanded by society: "What she did feel was pride tainted with disgust, disgust for the human race for producing such machines as Brutus and disgust for the rest of us for allowing them to flourish unmolested" (Six of One, 121). Honorable, well-meaning citizens are chided for allowing evil to exist by their inaction. Brown gets to exact her fictional revenge upon the wicked through Celeste's bold action, knowing full well that in the real world such men not only survive but prosper. As Celeste awaits the birth of Ramelle's baby and prepares for parenthood, she seizes this opportunity to rid the world of a Rife, not only in respect for the people who have already suffered, but also to free the next generation of his evil influence. Justice prevails: "right is wrong and wrong is right. And who can tell it all by sight?" (*Six of One*, 123).

Landscape as character. The Northern/Southern contrasts of Brutus and Celeste are just one of the many references in the novel to the importance of region and place, a typical Brown theme. As she evaluates her settings, Brown is pleased by "learning how to use my environment both as another character in the book and as a counterpart to the human characters" (*Starting from Scratch*, 15–16). The fictional town of Runnymede, placed on the Mason-Dixon line, with half of the town in Pennsylvania and half in Maryland, provides ample opportunity for Brown to contrast landscapes. The competing Civil War memorials show basic differences in Northern and Southern attitudes. The Daughters of Gettysburg's statue is a Yankee general on a horse; the Daughters of the Confederacy's memorial has three footsoldiers in battle. The North emphasizes authority, power, domination; the South reveals a community of shared suffering. Since most of the action is localized on the Chalfonte/Hunsenmeir properties on the Southern side of the line, Brown's sympathies are clear. Her South is dominated by a community of women, with a few "gentle" men, who respect and love each other despite differences in social class and background. Aware of the modern realities of the Yankee world, they prefer a romantic world of honor, loyalty, faith. Instead of exploiting the land for its resources as Rifes would, the land is nurtured and nurtures the inhabitants in turn in a symbiotic relationship. Instead of factories, homes are the center of their life and work. Portrayed as a traditional earth mother, Cora best states the power that the land holds: "I don't want no money. I know this earth. I know when my morning glories will come up and I can feel the sap rising in the apple trees. Why, land that's yours is like your kin, your mate, sort of. Money can't buy that" (*Six of One*, 125–26). Ramelle attributes to Celeste her understanding of the importance of "place and the life of the mind" (*Six of One*, 107). One must have a secure home, a sense of belonging to lead a rich and fulfilling life. Danger stalks those who leave that security—Fairy to Germany, Spottiswood to Europe, Billy Bitters to the South Sea islands. Even a visit to the outskirts of town, to Dead Man's Curve, is dangerous (to Aimes and Cora's father Hans Zepp). Runnymede is a self-sufficient microcosm, the center of existence for all its inhabitants in this novel. Though they might fight among themselves, they have their own system of justice as well as a strong sense of loyalty to the town, divided though it is: "It's one thing to fight among your own kind. It's quite another to have some outsider come in and do it for you" (*Six of One*, 12). This description of the town, of course, parallels the relationship of Julia and Louise. It is little wonder that Nickel must return here to recuperate from her life outside. By purchasing Bumblebee Hill she has a chance to reenter the past, to reclaim her lost childhood, to recapture the lost paradise, to prove that one can go home again. As Ramelle senses about the Chalfonte mansion: "Inanimate objects can exert an influence just as people can" (*Six of One*, 225). The Hunsenmeir house, a magnet for Celeste and her friends when Cora was alive, draws Nickel back home.

Birth, Rebirth, and Family.   *Six of One* is a novel about rebirth; Celeste is reborn into Nickel, and Nickel's return to Runnymede signals her chance for rebirth on Bumblebee Hill. The importance of rebirth is stressed by Brown's treatment of birth and parenthood. Celeste's two spiritual children are honored by special scenes surrounding their entry into the world. Ramelle and Curtis's child is adopted by Celeste before its birth, as Celeste jokingly plays the role of the father during Ramelle's pregnancy. She insists on naming the child Spottiswood, in honor of her dead brother, so that his spirit might live on in the child, whether the baby is a boy or a girl. As mentioned, Celeste's murder of Brutus may be seen as a sort of ritualized sacrifice to prepare the world for her newborn, the next generation. Spottiswood's birthday is celebrated by the entire community on Magna Carta day on Bumblebee Hill. Settling all the old scores, Celeste finally brings Louise the upright piano that rightfully belonged to her from her previous promise. The baby's celebration becomes a means of integration to bring the men Curtis and Pearlie into the extended surrogate family. Brown heightens this effect by focusing on each person's reaction to dancing with the infant as she is passed around among the guests. Father Curtis's response summarizes the significance of this new life: "Maybe there was joy in this confusing world. Maybe people's basic instinct was to love rather than to hate. . . . here, for this moment on Cora's simple porch filled with laughing people and with this dear baby in his arms, he wanted to live forever. He wanted to love unto eternity's echo" (*Six of One*, 135). The child promises salvation, love, rejuvenation, and immortality for everyone.

Similarly, the anticipated birth of Nichole brings hope to Celeste, Julia, Chessy, and Cora. When Julia learns that Chessy is unable to father a child, Cora advises them to adopt, for "the world's full of children that need somebody to love and care for them. . . . It ain't birthing that makes a mother. It's the raising up of the child" (*Six of One*, 265). Though Louise insists that biological motherhood is the only true motherhood, her position is undercut by her own disappointment in her two daughters (one marries beneath her and later dies in a fire set by one of the Rifes; the other goes crazy). Initially protesting the genealogy of the illegitimate child, even the pious and hypocritical Louise is eventually brought into the scheme to procure the child for Julia and Chessy. The extended family of Chalfontes and Hunsenmeirs surround the sickly child and nurse it to health together as a child again creates harmony among a band of disparate individuals. Born on the day of Celeste's death and on the eve of the end of World War II, Nickel translates the spirit of the old South into the postwar era, a world disillusioned by the concentration camps and the atomic bomb. With her return as an adult to the old family homestead, with all of its memories and associations, Nickel is infused with hope for the future. In the last passage of the novel, as Nickel is beginning her repair of the barn, she experiences peace: "The sun poured into Nickel's body, she felt an incredible euphoria. She felt lifted, inspired. She suddenly trusted the future. She had always trusted herself, but now she trusted the future. Hearing the comments, catcalls and laughter from the ground, she knew in her heart she could trust the future because those two women [Julia and Louise] had given it to her. She opened her arms wide like a bird and gathered the sunlight" (*Six of One*, 336). When Julia and Louise warn her about falling off the roof in her ecstasy, Nickel responds, "Everything is possible. Pass the word" (*Six of One*, 336).

This ending echoes the optimistic conclusions of Brown's previous two novels. After returning home for reconciliation with her mother, Molly is ready to face and conquer the world; Carole prepares to go back to Virginia to make her contribution to feminist change. As with those two novels, Brown in *Six of One* faces the critical charge that her characters lack development, that they are the same at the end of the novel as they began: "No one is particularly likeable and—greatly weakening the novel's credibility—none of the characters develop one iota from the moment she is introduced to the reader," laments one critic.[7] As we have seen, this notion of character development has not traditionally been part of the fictions of female development. Brown is profoundly ambivalent about this notion of human change. On the one hand, she says that she is attracted in life to people who change as well as to fictional characters who do: "I'm interested in people who are able to change and grow. I find that in very few people. Most people get locked into a pattern of behavior, and they just don't get out of it. They just keep repeating that pattern all through their lives, and wondering why they're not living fulfilled lives" (Ball, 9). On the other hand, Brown often expresses belief in "root self," and sees herself as a person who has not experienced the kind of change that she says leads to a fulfilled life, yet she does not view herself as being unfulfilled or unhappy: "I don't see that I've gone through any changes at all. To me, my life is a total, organic straight line that I laid out when I was teeny. It started when I was 4 or 5. I've always been doing what I wanted to do" (Ranson, 1B). In a sort of compromise position, Brown writes in her introduction to the 1988 reprint of *In Her Day*: "I accept that as I change I also remain the same in fundamental respects"; however, her spirit, "will never change" though some of her behavior and thoughts may be modified through time (*In Her Day*, xii).

Brown's characters are encouraged to be true to their root selves; thus they should not change to fit societal expectations but should follow their natural impulses. Women in particular are portrayed as eternal forces, hence beyond the concept of temporal change or adaptation. Celeste, as Ramelle frequently notes, does not need to change; she is fully and perfectly formed: "You are complete. You have always been complete" (*Six of One*, 226). Conversely, Ramelle herself has always been "unformed," which is her essential nature. Growth in Brown's world involves understanding one's true or root self before awareness of socially determined differences. Survival, endurance, the living of life is what is ultimately important. Celeste comes to admire the Amish faith (Brown's father was a Dunkard) for its adherence to the principle of living life: "They insist upon living their lives, defining their lives, by their standards. . . . We've concentrated on the means to life and forgotten about life itself" (*Six of One*, 275). Instead of character development, which implies that individual life is a process of change, of evolution toward something better, Brown emphasizes rebirth, rediscovery, the continuity of the life force through reincarnation. Hence, the central character transformation that occurs in *Six of One* is the infusion of Celeste's spirit into the soul of Nichole, the transformation of history into fiction. As Brown knows, change is rare but possible. In the novel, the callow youth Billy Bitters can and does learn something about death and prejudice from his experience in battle. There is no attempt to change Brutus, however; he will always be dominated by his greed. Celeste approaches perfection and therefore needs no change.

Beneath Brown's vision of history is the wisdom of Ecclesiastes that there is nothing new under the sun: "Every day I hit on some fantastic idea full 2000 years old" (*Rapper*, 12). The attitude toward war in the novel, that history repeats itself, that men will always find an "other" to fight, informs her view of other historical and personal events. Prohibition changes none of the characters's behaviors toward alcohol. Smoking marijuana is not really that different from drinking illegal whiskey during Prohibition. The stock market crash occurs during Julia and Chessy's first argument; Cora's advice, "you'll live through it," applies equally to both events. Julia and Louise enact the same sibling rivalries as children and as adults. Brown thinks that it is wonderful that these two women have preserved their sense of the absurd, that they are able to partake of their childhood innocence, that they do not fully become "adults" since that usually means that the rational overpowers the irrational. It is the irrational that makes life worth living: "The entire affair was absurd, but you have to be absurd sometimes. Nothing is more deadly than routine rationality," Ramelle notes, with Brown's full approval (*Six of One*, 54). Julia's disguise as the long-dead Patience uses such absurdity to defy logic and point out the continuity of life. She knows that no one will penetrate her disguise if she behaves as the crazy Patience always behaved; they will simply think that Patience is still alive. And she *is* alive as long as Julia remembers and reenacts her life.

The characters' reliance upon folk wisdom proves that the advice of previous generations is still applicable to modern times. Like fellow-Southerner and author Flannery O'Connor, Brown finds not only verbal delight in the colorful homilies but also a degree of enduring truth. Brown's use of anachronism, her placing of modern concepts into the mouths of the past, also reveals her belief that people are basically alike, no matter what their social class, personal past, or historical context. In contrast to this view of the continuity of history, however, is Brown's conviction that the human race can change the course of history: "My job [as a writer] is to reveal us to ourselves. . . . I suppose underneath is still that Protestant belief that we can improve, that there is such a thing as progress, and that it's our duty to try" (Fleischer, E2). In this novel as in her other works, harsh reality keeps brushing up against a resurgent optimism as Brown carefully balances these oppositions. By the end of each novel, optimism about the future wins out over the realities of prejudice, social injustice, and personal depression. As Brown defines her fiction: "I try to write books that will stretch me. Most will be funny, at least partly, and about people surviving, and sometimes triumphing" (Horn, C13).

Bingo as Sequel to *Six of One*

With the publication of *Six of One*, Brown announced her intention to write a sequel to the story at some point in the future, a goal she accomplished in 1988 with the publication of *Bingo* by Bantam. Though there are superficial similarities of location, themes, structure, and characters, the sequel lacks the sparkle and exuberance of the original. Since ten years passed between the two novels, Brown does not allude too specifically to events of the first. Thus, while it is not necessary to read *Six of One* in order to understand *Bingo*, one's appreciation of Brown's development of her historical themes is enhanced by knowledge of the earlier work. The dominant force of Celeste is mentioned only in passing at several points in *Bingo* as she and her wonderful circle of women recede into the haze of memory and lose their potency. Subtle references to the details of the original, however, make current actions more comprehensible for the knowing reader. For instance, Julia gives Louise a subscription to *Playboy* magazine for her eighty-sixth birthday. We appreciate the scandal of such a gift even without knowing that Julia is taunting her sister with this allusion to Julia's discovery of the porno magazines hidden in Louise's bed, a key episode from the end of the first novel. Brown also adds stories that could appeared in *Six of One*, like the story of Dante the amazing fire horse, but retells only one anecdote in great detail, the story of Nickel's rescue from the orphanage.

Instead of the crosscutting technique of *Six of One*, *Bingo* has a circular structure, covering the events of the one year from Louise's eighty-sixth to her eighty-seventh birthday. The image of Nickel flying a kite in both the opening and closing chapters reinforces this sense of cycle. The chapter headings have become much more elaborate, with numbers, titles, dates and days indicated. The sense of timelessness and eternity generated in *Six of One* has in this modern world been bound to earthly fact. As a reflection of Nickel's newspaper career, specificity has become increasingly important. Brown includes a diagram of the town and sample bingo game cards to illustrate and concretize her action in a way unthinkable in *Six of One*. The chapter headings seem at first like the technique used by a prisoner counting off the days to keep control over his sanity, but as Nickel's character changes, the details ultimately show how precious each day can be and how much difference a year can make in someone's life.

As her chapter titles indicate, Brown's vision of history differs somewhat from her earlier works' emphasis on the continuity of human existence through the centuries. *Bingo* takes place almost exclusively in the present. Rather than finding comfort in exploring her heritage from such strong women as Celeste, the Nickel of *Bingo* has only the tawdry Jim Bakker and Gary Hart scandals by which to measure her life. These contemporary news stories have none of the passion and power of the cataclysmic events that engulfed the historical characters in *Six of One*. The main history that is still alive for the citizens of Runnymede is the Civil War. The North-South rivalries in this divided town, like the constant battles of the Hunsenmeir sisters, help to keep the town alert and alive. Outsider Michelle cannot understand why people still refight those old battles, but Nickel thinks this cultural heritage is just as important to preserve for future generations as the Hopi Indian dances. Traditions, especially Southern traditions, are valued in Runnymede. The rituals of the beauty salon, the horse shoes, the bingo parlor, the Easter parade, cemetery visitation, and the Sunday promenade are faithfully upheld.

Six of One ends with Nickel optimistically facing the future after she has returned to her birthplace, bought her grandmother's house, and recorded the history of the community. After ten years, she is badly in need of rebirth, again. She has done little to improve the house as she had planned; she has gone from imaginatively reconstructing epic events to reporting facts and recording opinions (although she loves the newspaper business). Unlike Ramelle's joyous affair with Celeste's brother and their successful, open, romantic arrangement, Nickel is involved in a furtive, desperate affair with her best friend's husband. A workaholic, she is in danger of losing her cherished sense of humor and her identity as a lesbian. In both novels it is the birth of a child (Nickel in *Six of One* and Nickel's baby twins in *Bingo*) that rejuvenates the community and offers the possibility of spiritual rebirth. Nickel has to relearn the lesson that love multiplies, that people can change, that "life is too important to be serious."[8] A shadowy figure in *Six of One*, submerging herself in the narrative, Nickel is maddeningly present in *Bingo*, dominating the narration with her insistent "I." She speaks with such authority that it is hard not to believe her; yet it is impossible to ignore the contradictions and confusions that her words and actions demonstrate. Concentrating on her own predicament, she is actually alienated from her emotions and generally unsympathetic to the problems of others. Seeking in *Six of One* to integrate herself into the community, Nickel has yet to realize where she belongs in her environment. As Brown comments in interviews, we must know where we are in order to understand who we are; we must not distance ourselves from our environment or from nature.[9] Through the course of events in *Bingo*, Nickel gradually develops sympathy for others, begins to see beyond her own problems, and becomes a full member of the community, not just someone who performs a necessary function, but one who shares her true self with others.

Nickel as heroine.   Nickel possesses many of the trademarks of the usual Brown semi-autobiographical narrator/character. A witty, educated, Southern, openly gay artist, Nickel spouts out many of Brown's firmly held beliefs about class, society, family, and sexuality. But the contradictions in her words and actions suggest a growing chasm between belief and reality. She criticizes Ursula for her social pretensions, while justifying her own membership in the Tennis and Racquet Club by de-emphasizing its elitist connotations. She twice describes Liz Rife's ostentatious display of diamonds, yet she admits wanting to possess a sable fur coat. She detests how Americans define people by their sexuality, while she confesses to being ruled by her hormones in her affair with Jackson Frost. She notes with condescending approval how Ursie's high-handed daughters mistreat the mother who spoiled them, but her own treatment of her mother is similar at times. She gleefully enjoys knowledge of the illicit sexual scandals of Gary Hart and Jim Bakker as she bears the illegitimate offspring of her best friend's husband. She believes that there should be no stigma to the birth of a child out of wedlock, but she marries the town's gay hairdresser so her child will have a father (even though everyone in town knows that he is not the real father). She espouses the journalistic code of truth, while she participates in the community lie about the cannon "accident." She thinks the country should abide by the same rules for rich and poor alike, but she seems to have one morality for herself and one for others. She celebrates the liberating power of humor, yet she actually uses her sarcasm to detach herself from her experience and values. Nickel, however, is not to be dismissed simply as a hypocrite; she is learning the complexity of life, that one cannot neatly pigeonhole people in conveniently prescribed categories. Just when she thinks she has everything figured out, the unpredictable, the human element, forces her to re-evaluate her perspective and offers her the possibility of redemption.

Her relationship with Michelle reveals this dilemma for Brown and for Nickel. Nickel has a difficult time trying to understand and accept Michelle, whom she tries to stereotype as an elitist, aristocratic snob. But the facts show us a different person, one who is honestly attempting to do a good job as a fledgling reporter, who is adjusting to a very different culture, but who seems genuinely concerned about the feelings of others, including Nickel. Interestingly, Brown presents Nickel with an intelligent and sensitive woman who could be her friend, but Nickel cannot see through the superficial barriers of clothes and class habits. Always better at analyzing other people's problems than at noticing her own, Nickel complains that Michelle would be okay if she would lighten up her outlook on life; ironically, this is precisely Nickel's own problem. Michelle is paralleled by Nickel's childhood friend Regina as the "aristocratic double" that Brown often employs in her novels. Regina is obviously more of the aristocrat that Michelle is, yet because she has known Regina for so many years, Nickel does not analyze her motives and actions as severely as she does Michelle's. Although Regina is her dearest friend, Nickel pursues a futile relationship with Regina's husband, partly as an attempt to alleviate her loneliness but also perhaps as a way to get closer to Regina. This notion of loving someone through an intermediary is a recurrent feature of Brown's characterizations, present especially in many of the triangular combinations of friends and lovers.

By focusing so much of her affection and attention on Regina and Jackson, Nickel misses the obvious pairing of herself with Michelle, though the reader constantly suspects that Nickel and Michelle will eventually get together. Molly Bolt would not have let such a possibility go unnoticed as Nickel does. It takes Mr. Pierre, the gay hairdresser whom she marries for convenience, to point out the obvious to her: "Pierre swears Michelle has a crush on me. He can be wicked that way because he knows he'll make me self-conscious. I don't think that she does, but if she does, I wouldn't know what to do about it. I've banished romantic love from my mind. It seems like such an overrated emotion. If I had to choose between a great, overpowering passion and the love of good friends, I'd choose the love of good friends" (*Bingo*, 289). Nickel comes to this conclusion, however, after she has endangered the love of her good friend Regina by her overpowering passion for Jackson; only Regina's love and open-mindedness allow Nickel to be able to make such a broad claim. Once again, Brown coyly avoids having to portray a mature intimate relationship between two women.

Avoidance, it seems, is part of Brown's strategy here. Nickel's lesbian identity is dangerously submerged as she struggles for economic and emotional survival. Openly out of the closet for many years, Nickel is an accepted part of her community, not having to endure the cruelties or curiosities of homophobia. She can even get away with some risqué comments in front of her co-workers about lesbian sex. Since she is not actively involved in a lesbian relationship, Nickel is a lesbian in name only and as such, ironically, becomes invisible to others; no one suspects her of having an affair with Jackson because of her lesbianism, an unusual twist to the homosexual's usual problem of invisibility in American culture. Having had an unsuccessful relationship with a woman several years prior to the events of this novel, Nickel uses the pain of that loss and her obsessive work as a buffer against recommitment; she humorously refers to herself as an "infomaniac." Determined to stay in an environment that is not conducive to lesbian singles, Nickel ignores the advice that Mr. Pierre, her mother, and others give her throughout the novel, to leave Runnymede. They both want her to have another relationship so that she will not be left alone in life (Julia) and so that she will be someone's number one instead of always being second (Pierre). Despite her better judgment, she lets herself fall into traditional gender roles and expectations in her affair with Jackson, who is portrayed as the new, sensitive, post-women's liberation man of the eighties. Nickel uses him for physical comfort in her loneliness. During their weekly Tuesday night trysts, he complains that she does not take his emotions seriously because he is a man instead of a woman in a role reversal that could be deliciously humorous if Nickel (and Brown) did not take everything so seriously in this novel. Trying to end the affair, Nickel finds herself prey to petty jealousies when she discovers that she is not his first affair, though he tries to convince her that he did not love the others.

In contrast to the melodrama of their doomed relationship is the comic courtship and competition of Julia (Juts) and Louise for the new man in town, Ed Tutweiler Walters. Their antics amuse Nickel as well as the rest of the town, but Nickel does not see the parallel between her definition of love and her mother's pursuit of a new lover. Julia, like Molly Bolt at the end of *Rubyfruit Jungle*, appears to be trying to be the hottest 50-plus woman this side of the Mississippi. Not expecting to find a replacement in her heart for her dead husband Chessy, she does not close herself off from sexuality and emotions as Nickel seems to have done.

Thinking it disrespectful to the dead if one gives up on life, she could have married other men, but she holds out for a stimulating emotional romantic adventure. In fact, she could have married a gay man, which of course Nickel later does, but she wants and gets "love at first sight." Flirting outrageously with Ed, Juts even stoops to wearing falsies to impress him: "Better a girl has tits than brains, because boys see better than they think," she advises Nickel in her traditional wisdom about male-female relationships (*Bingo*, 68). As it should, love sparks other aspects of her life: she redecorates her house, dyes her hair magenta, devours fudge sundaes, and prances about town in wild fashions. Her techniques of entrapping a man might be a bit old-fashioned, but her decision to let him move in with her without the benefit of marriage shows that Julia is able to be an individual, to use what is appropriate for her from any custom or culture, as long as she is comfortable with herself, not alienated like Nickel.

Sexual self-definition and the nature of human change. Working again with triangular patterns as the model for new relationships, Brown balances Regina and Michelle, then Jackson and Pierre, as catalysts for Nickel's transformation. Since Regina and Jackson are straight, Pierre is openly gay and Michelle is potentially a lesbian, Brown gives Nickel a range of options to explore in her search for contentment. She is in love with both Regina and Jackson, who are understanding and supportive of her behavior, while tensions run high in her inexplicably strained friendship with Michelle. She is more comfortable with heterosexuals than with a potential challenge to her self-definition as gay. Her friendship with Mr. Pierre confirms this opinion. His queenly presence is totally non-threatening to Nickel as well as to all the townspeople who allow him to live peacefully in their community because he fits their stereotype of a "faggot"—a foppish hairdresser with interior decorating skills who spends most of his time with the blue-haired ladies of the town. Like Nickel, Pierre has given up on romance after the death of his longtime partner. This loyalty to his mate endears him to Julia and Louise because they admire his fidelity and perceive him, like themselves, as a grieving widow. Florence King in her witty exposé of Southern stereotypes, *Southern Ladies and Gentlemen*, devotes a chapter to the delineation of the Southern homosexual. According to her description, the "Town Fairy" is adored by the women of the town "because he behaves like the classic belle every Southern woman wants to be. . . . Town Fairy's greatest allies are the little old ladies in the garden club—he adores flowers and can talk about the finer points of horticulture for hours on end. . . . he is the only male they [the blue-haired ladies] know who actually talks to them" (King 1975, 157–58).

Brown and Nickel see Mr. Pierre as a product of a particular period in gay history, a stereotype that today's politically correct generation has a difficult time embracing as one of its own. Nickel provides an interesting interpretation of Pierre's "faggot" dress and behavior. She sees it as a form of rebellion, a direct response to the prejudices of the majority. As Pierre states it, "If I'm going to be hung for a sheep I might as well be hung for a wolf" (*Bingo*, 131). His lilac-tinted hair and flamboyant mannerisms are not only an expression of his creativity and difference but also part of his sense of humor. Like Nickel, Pierre tends to use humor (in his case, the humor of his stereotypical identity) to create a buffer between himself and potential pain. His life is transformed by his marriage to Nickel and especially by his sense of duty as a father to the twins. He tones down his mannerisms, changes his style of dressing, and tastefully redecorates the house, all in the process of what Nickel calls becoming a "real man."

In one of the most controversial aspects of the book (along with the birth of the babies and the subsequent marriage of convenience), Brown risks alienating the gay audience for her work. If Pierre becomes a "real man" through his sense of responsibility toward marriage and family, is Nickel simply relying on the unfortunate stereotype of homosexual men as irresponsible and incomplete? She seems to be saying that one cannot be a real man if one is gay. Brown seems to revert to the oldest of gender roles and gay stereotypes when what is really happening is that Nickel is finally seeing the real person behind her own conception of Pierre as a queen. After he tells her about his experiences in the Korean War (proving that men are not sissies just to get out of combat), Nickel glimpses Pierre's humanity and passion outside of his visible role playing: "His face, impassioned, changed before my eyes. His protective, queenie mannerisms melted away. Mr. Pierre was a man, a real man. I'd never seen him that way before" (*Bingo*, 254). She later starts calling him "Pierre" instead of "Mr. Pierre" to indicated this shift in her perception.

The reason that Nickel had not seen him as a real person, of course, is that she is too busy concentrating on her own problems to connect with people on a human, individual, personal level. Michelle, Jackson, Julia, and others point this out to her throughout the novel, but she thinks she is too smart, too self-aware, to listen to other people's advice and perceptions. Nickel's rebirth in the novel is charted by such moments of acknowledgment: when she finally perceives someone as a real human being; when she transcends her isolation to become part of the human race. Louise becomes more than just an annoying, gossipy old relative; at one point Nickel actually understands Louise's pain, what it must have been like to have experienced the death of her husband and two daughters. Such awareness leads to restraint; Nickel actually passes up the opportunity to be sarcastic at her aunt's expense: "Tempted as I was to tell her I was changing my life, I would become Shirley of Nazareth, specializing in foot washings, I bit my tongue. The charge I would get from her outrage would be vitiated by the subsequent lecture. Was I growing up at last?" (*Bingo*, 181). Here her humor would have been the type to distance herself from others, to deflect involvement, but humor can also lead Nickel out of her personal focus into the world at large, for instance, in the popcorn episode (when Louise's auto accident coats her and Ed with popcorn): "She started to laugh and then he laughed and I laughed and for a few moments I forgot about the paper and remembered to be glad I was alive on this spring day with my loony old aunt and her boyfriend—well, kind of her boyfriend" (*Bingo*, 137).

The last episode of the novel reinforces the power of humor to liberate the individual in a typically exuberant and optimistic proclamation by Brown. Nickel sends up a kite with a message for her father, announcing the birth of his grandchildren and confirming his advice to her: "You were right. Life is too important to be serious" (*Bingo*, 291). To reinforce this idea of humor, Brown creates her usual farcical scenes where individual and social pretentions are publicly deflated: Ursie's elegantly formal horse show is reduced to comic chaos through the antics of an indecorous skunk; the long-anticipated blackout bingo game degenerates into a riot with howling dogs, exploding cannons, and attempted robbery; Louise is exploited in a series of joke vignettes about bad driving; the drunken sheriff attacks his Northern counterpart with the town cannon and convinces the town to join a conspiracy of silence about the "accident." Brown claims that in *Bingo* she was "aspiring to be silly," in the manner of Aristophane's comedies (*Starting From Scratch*, 18). Though many of the book's episodes are funny, Brown's humor seems more strained and predictable than usual, partly because of Nickel's own perspective. Nickel defends the value of a sense of humor but often in a humorless way; she relies on sarcasm and dry wit instead of the pure belly-laugh humor of slapstick antics. This style of verbal, reactive wit is symptomatic of her emotional detachment. Only when she becomes the focus of a joke herself (the center of attention during Julia's public announcement of Nickel's pregnancy and marriage plans at the bingo game) can she begin to defeat the seriousness that plagues her life. Her gesture of flying the kite is the kind of whimsical act that Brown approves; only such unpredictable and nonsensical behavior can free one's spirit as humor is meant to do.

Nickel has mixed feelings about the subtle process of change that she is undergoing. As she knows, people sometimes change without its being noticed by others. Certainly she questions whether her new self-control over her sarcasm is a sign of her maturity. Though she says that she wants to live and learn, she at times believes that such evolution is the hope of the immature. She thinks that Julia and Louise might be better off if they did not change since they so perfectly balance and complement each other. But she also realizes that her mother, in her relationship with Ed and especially in her acceptance of Nickel's predicament, is "growing up," even in her eighties. In fact, in *Bingo* all the major characters undergo considerable change, or as Brown prefers to label it, discovery of the root self. In her eighties, Louise finds a new career, as a columnist and local commentator, finally putting her love of gossip to productive use. One of the dreaded Rifes who villainized in *Six of One*, Diz Rife proves himself not to be such a bad guy; though he buys out the *Clarion* for financial reasons, he becomes part of the Runnymede community as Nickel makes him godfather to her twins. Pierre discovers new strength and resources as he drops his homosexual mannerisms and becomes a father.

Constantly touting Easter as her favorite holiday, and describing the events that occur in the spring, from one spring to the next, Nickel seems to believe in the concept of rebirth, in the possibility of renewal and growth. Chessy, who was a slight character in *Six of One*, in death becomes a major force in Nickel's view of life, death, and immortality. Her visit to his grave inspires intimations of immortality: "How fitting that this cemetery should be a scene of renewed life. And how fitting that the robins, deer, raccoons, and other animals erected no monuments to their dead. They were too busy living. Only humans hid away their dead so the remains couldn't replenish the earth, so the flesh could not go to keep alive another animal" (*Bingo*, 184). Death is part of the natural cycle despite man's selfish and unnatural attempts to deny his animal nature. This is quite a critique of humankind in a novel where animals are introduced before human characters and where people are evaluated according to how pets respond to them. The spirit and memory of the dead are what survive and flourish, as Nickel knows from her expanding love for her father: "Love doesn't die. It keeps growing. Perhaps someone you love has to die before you can believe that" (*Bingo*, 182).

Extended families and the creation of community. Chessy's strong presence in the novel is more than Brown's usual idealization of the father. It is also indicative of her focus on the family and a new definition of community. Most of Brown's novels have attempted to demonstrate in some fashion how people can bond together in makeshift families and in communities of kindred spirits. *Bingo* balances family ties with other loyalties in its portrait of the individual's place in society. Nickel's need to be part of a nuclear family is stressed by her rebellion against her status as bastard. Her romanticization of her dead father, his omnipresence, the parallels between Chessy and Jackson (with their similar personalities and their heart attacks), and her insistence that her child must have a father—all point to her defense of a traditional family structure, the kind of family that she herself did not fully have because she was adopted. Again, Nickel's maddening contradictions cloud her perceptions and our interpretation of her actions. She reminisces positively about her childhood as she remembers feeling herself to be the center of a large family. Yet she bitterly remembers her constant awareness of being adopted and her frustration at how Julia and Louise battle over this issue of blood kin: "For three decades I had heard variations on that theme. It still felt like a wasp sting on tender flesh. I don't know why I never fought back. Why did Mother and Aunt Louise have to tell me repeatedly that I was not related by blood, that I was adopted? Tell me once and I'll remember. I guess I never fought back because I don't know how. What can you say when your mother, or the only mother you've ever known, tells you you aren't hers" (*Bingo*, 14).

In chapter Twenty, Nickel begins to fight back when she explodes irrationally over a childhood memory of Julia taking away her paint set because it reminded Julia of Nickel's real mother, who was an artist. As she contemplates becoming a mother herself, she defines that role in a lengthy litany: "Mothers invent our idea of love. Mother feeds us. Cleans us. Puts us to bed at night. . . . Mother not only tells you right from wrong, she shows you. . . . Mother teaches you sympathy for others and responsibility. She scolds, chides, and whacks you when she has to but she's there. She's always there. . . . Dad is beloved and in my case even worshipped but he's not there the way Mom is" (*Bingo*, 233). After her own children are born, Nickel is able as a real mother herself to express finally what had bothered her about her own childhood: "To be loved but never to belong. It's a form of punishment" (*Bingo*, 284). Not conscious of how much pain her own disappointment at not being a "real" mother had caused young Nickel, Julia does what she rarely ever does, apologizes to her daughter about the paint set: "I knew I'd won, at long last," Nickel remarks after her mother leaves the hospital room (*Bingo*, 286). Brown's problems with her own adoption and her concomitant tension with her mother come closer to the surface of this book than in her other works. It was adoption, the labeling as "bastard," that sent Molly off on her quest for success and a place to belong. The repetition in *Bingo* of the story of Nickel's adoption from *Six of One*, using the same details of Brown's own adoption, affirms the biographical inspiration for this theme of adoption.

Neither Brown nor Nickel would deny that families can be formed from people unrelated by blood, if the adoption is handled correctly and the child given the truth when she is ready for it emotionally. Through the influence of Julia and Louise, Nickel defines the family as "a bizarre combination of people with conflicting interests by blood" (*Bingo*, 114). But Pierre's definition is actually more in concert with her stated philosophy in other parts of the book and with Brown's views on the subject: "Fate—the Fates—are kind. They saw two alone people—and note I said alone, not lonely—and they gave us a baby, a reason to make a family. Someone to worry over and dream about. Two someones. You and the baby. People don't have to sleep together to be a family. They only have to love one another . . ." (*Bingo*, 255). Jackson too wants to defy the traditional family by including Nickel with Regina in a full and open friendship. In effect, he gets part of his wish by the end of the novel since Regina knows of his affair with Nickel and he is godfather (with Diz Rife) to his own children. Mr. Pierre becomes the real father to the twins in Nickel's plan as their young lives help him to discover his true self. The children, likewise, have a positive effect on the lives of everyone in the story as they become the center of attention, just as Nickel had been in *Six of One*. Love had indeed multiplied, with two new lives (male and female) instead of one to solidify the bonds of the community. Ironically, and perhaps subversively, the children of the town's future will be reared by gay parents.

The family extends beyond the boundary of one household as the whole community of Runnymede embraces Nickel and later her children. Just as she considers what will happen to the town when the paper is taken over by a big company, so the townspeople worry about Nickel's future, much to her own surprise. Despite her high-sounding ideals about community, Nickel is so alienated from her home in some ways that she is amazed when the locals give up their bingo profits to contribute to her coffers to buy the newspaper or when they comfort her after the newspaper is sold to her rival, Diz Rife. As in *Six of One*, Cora's house again becomes the center of spontaneous communal activity that suggests that the human race is part of one big family. On this level, the conflict is not between parent and child, but between men and women. The open competition between Julia and Louise over Ed reminds the reader of traditional relationships, while Regina's lack of jealousy of Nickel shows not only a modern liberalism but illustrates Jackson's point that women and men relate to each other differently. He feels that Nickel will not take him seriously because he is a man. Regina is not as surprised by Jackson's infidelity as she is disappointed by Nickel's dishonesty: "Men are different from women and I know that and I know Jack. This is going to sound odd but I expect less of men than of women" (*Bingo*, 279).

Nickel too seems aware of the incompatibility of men and women in our society, and is openly sensitive to the fact that men are denied emotional expression. Her experience has taught her that she can go only so far in an emotional relationship with a man and that her straight women friends feel basically the same: "We feel much closer to women than to men" (*Bingo*, 107). Nickel speaks not with the anger of a radical separatist here but as a sympathetic observer of male behavior: "I was beginning to half-believe that men's deepest emotions were inaccessible to them. . . . we do something terrible to men in our culture. We take away from themselves and we substitute money, power, and toys" (*Bingo*, 107–8). She comes closer to understanding this situation when she discusses how mothers and fathers influence the evolution of their children: "A man grows up and expects to find some of this mother-love in his wife. A woman has to transfer her affections to a man. She doesn't expect a man to love her as her mother did. Already, we expect less" (*Bingo*, 233). This revisionist psychology reveals a fundamental difference between the sexes, one that cannot be breached by simple affirmative action or comparable pay schemes.

Like ripples on still water, Brown portrays life as a series of concentric circles spreading outward from the individual, to the family (nuclear and extended), to the community, to the human race. Sixties radical that she is, however, Brown does not neglect the political and economic pond in which all people exist. The repeated reference to the sex scandals of Hart and Bakker along with comment on the struggle of the individual old-fashioned business against the modern corporate giant form a backdrop for the novel's events, reminding us of the outside world that filters via the Associated Press into this small, comparatively isolated, and unique community. The professional and the personal are paralleled throughout the novel, as gossip is compared to the reception of "news," as personal detachment is compared to news objectivity. Nickel does not want to lose the local, the personal perspective in the newspaper; neither does she want to lose her ties to community in her own life as she battles to stay in Runnymede in defiance of the advice she receives from Julia and Pierre. The newspaper should reflect the townspeople's unique perspective on life, not what some three-piece-suited businessman from New York City thinks about events. When she tries to negotiate with Diz about the *Clarion*, Nickel realizes how incompatible their ideas are. She likes the old printing press, as inefficient as it is, and does not want to modernize the equipment since it will put loyal workers out of work. While Diz wants to maximize profits, Nickel states her idealism about the freedom of the press: "A newspaper is more than a business. It's a community resource. If we don't guard that resource, the press will soon become indistinguishable from General Motors or any other industry. We're the life blood of a free country. No press, no democracy. Profit is secondary to that function" (*Bingo*, 135). Refusing to take a chance on Nickel, the banks, like all modern businesses, are threatening to homogenize society since they see only the bottom line of profit without individual considerations. Eventually the free-enterprise system of American democracy helps Nickel achieve victory for her idealism. As editor of a competing newspaper, Nickel preserves the local element, making a celebrity of Louise through her gossip column. Friendly competition, like the tennis matches between Nickel and Diz, turns out to be good for the health of both newspapers and, in turn, for the whole region.

The sex scandals of Jim Bakker and Gary Hart that punctuate the action of the novel not only inform us about the hypocrisy of modern public leaders, but ironically parallel Nickel's own frustrating affair with Jackson. In both cases public confession seems to be the only solution to the corruption. Nickel writes a harsh editorial in defense of public exposure of the private details of the lives of political figures, even as she is hiding her own infidelity from her best friend. Just as she had urged Hart to be honest in his confession of pleasurable sex with Donna Rice, Nickel bows to circumstances that disclose her own private life to the inspection of the community. Honesty, it seems, is the best policy on all levels of endeavor. *Bingo* leads Nickel out of her private prison of self into communion with family and friends. This "coming out" is different in kind from her coming out as a lesbian and assumes religious and social implications. Though she does not agree with the forms of organized religion and attends church mainly as a social activity to spend time with Julia and listen to classical music, Nickel expresses belief in the primitive tenets of Christianity. While the Ten Commandments may be harder to follow in this modern age of mass transit and mass communication that multiply the possibilities of temptation, Nickel believes in Easter's promise of renewal and in the power of one's actions: "What you do in this life will save you" (*Bingo*, 247). Despite their illegitimacy, the twins are her means to salvation; she enters the flow of humanity through public confession and through motherhood. Through the course of the novel, she breaks out of her isolation to realize the importance of community, of friends: "Whenever I entertain doubts about the existence of the Almighty, I remember that through my friends God has loved me" (*Bingo*, 204). *Bingo* projects the reconciliation of opposites, the creation of harmony from disparate elements in what is ultimately a positive outlook on life.

Chapter Five

Southern Discomfort: "Form Is as Important as Content"

Southern Discomfort was Brown's first book not to emphasize a lesbian relationship, although it included a number of other fairly shocking sexual pairings (as one reviewer noted, everything except zooerasty).[1] This omission of lesbianism is particularly ironic since, when she was writing the novel, Brown was romantically involved with Martina Navratilova, admittedly one of the two great loves in her life. Around this time Brown was quoted as expressing her desire to be considered more than simply a lesbian author: "I hope people get over calling me 'Rite Mae Brown, the lesbian author.' I want them to remember me as 'Rite Mae Brown, author'" (Jackovich, 81). Published by Harper and Row in 1982 and issued in paperback by Bantam, *Southern Discomfort* continued Brown's bid for acceptance by a mainstream audience. With her humor and outrageousness intact, Brown manages in this romp through Southern history at the turn of the century to maintain her assault on social hypocrisy and sexual restrictions without direct reference to her lesbian identity. A more important aspect of her consciousness in this book seems to be her quest for belonging (a variation of her theme of adoption) and her championing of individual freedom (albeit within certain boundaries). While many of her usual concerns arise—the lessons of history, race relations, the Southern landscape, the transforming power of love—she sees as her major accomplishment in this novel the fulfillment of her desire to "use my environment both as another character in the book and as a counterpoint to the human characters" (*Starting from Scratch*, 16).

Narrative Structure and the Limits of Freedom

Like *Six of One*, *Southern Discomfort* intercuts the plots of many different groups of characters, but instead of using time as the governing principle of this crosscutting, Brown uses social strata, showing how actions and attitudes reverberate through every level of the society in Montgomery, Alabama. The train station is the center of the town, a site of fascination for Brown the author (according to Navratilova, Brown spent much time there as part of her two years of research for the novel) and a gathering place for characters of all social classes (*Martina*, 212). A melting pot of cultures and a place of general movement and excitement in the early part of the century, the station also links the characters to the modern world. As one character notes, "The ricochet of massed voices in the various waiting chambers made her feel a part of the movement, of the future."[2] This industrial symbol of travel, escape, progress, and industrialization, however, only provides the illusion of the freedom it seems to offer. The train tracks divide the community and perpetuate artificial social barriers. The prostitutes and blacks live on the "wrong" side of the tracks, and the wealthy socialites like Hortensia Banastre live on the "right" side. This ambivalence toward the locomotive's promise of progress is revealed when Hortensia takes her husband to the station: "Trains meant progress, speed, and end to provincialism. Few people questioned the fact that it forever altered humans' conception of time as well as distance. The sun gave way to the clock. Between timetables and industrial whistle, humankind would never again feel time as did their ancestors or the beasts in the field. A grid dropped over the human race; the hours bound one as securely as a cell" (*Discomfort*, 110). As in her political poetry, Brown criticizes the patriarchal society (represented by the phallic train) for the disruption of natural harmony by the creation of arbitrary barriers of time and space. The image of the grid, like the tracks themselves on the landscape, is the central metaphor of the novel. Examples of barriers, borders, and boundaries, of all types—physical, social, and emotional—permeate the novel.

In fact, the structure of the novel itself is the starting point for a discussion of boundaries. The zigzagging of the subplots interrupts the smooth flow of narrative and like Soviet film montage forces the audience to make intellectual connections between the segments that are spliced together. *Southern Discomfort* is divided into two large and separate blocks of time. Half the novel takes place in 1918, partly so that Brown can express her usual anti-war sentiments, but mainly because it was a time when society was on the verge of radical social change, when the traditions of the past would be questioned and challenged by the roaring twenties. The turmoil caused by the war forever changed the way people would look at life. For the South, which had lagged behind the North in modernization, this change was even more significant and drastic. The novel's second half take place 10 years later in 1928, during the Prohibition era that followed the surge of freedom. Some general details are supplied about what happened to the characters during that decade, but part two explores primarily the implications of the actions and changes in attitudes that were generated in part one. What the characters find in this time of reaction is that the external rules may change but inner human nature cannot so easily adjust to restraint and deprivation after the experience of freedom. Unlike *Six of One*, whose montage was structured to investigate the nature of time, *Southern Discomfort*'s structure explores the implications of actions. The carefully plotted strands intersect to demonstrate Brown's notion of community, that no man or woman is an island, that each person is woven into the social fabric by visible and invisible threads.

The novel's prologue and epilogue encompass the two large divisions and provide a frame that reinforces Brown's notion of individual freedom within bounds. These brief sections establish many of Brown's themes, giving a context in which what follows can be understood. They also underscore a big joke of mistaken identity that creates the belly laugh that Brown desires while at the same time subtly undercutting what happens in the majority of the novel. The story of prostitute Blue Rhonda Latrec is introduced in the prologue and her secret sexual identity uncovered in the epilogue. A foul-mouthed, cocaine snorting whore with a heart of gold, Blue Rhonda is applauded for her honesty. Though to everyone else's estimation she lives on the wrong side of the railroad tracks, Blue Rhonda feels herself to be fortunate to be so close to new customers, proving the dictum that "each resident views a city with a particular set of references" ("Prologue," *Discomfort*). Those "references" are, in effect, blinders that limit one's perception of the truth, as the novel proceeds to illustrate for each of the main characters. The Prologue also hints at the topsy-turvy world that Montgomery will become as these perceptions are challenged, rejected, and revised.

The prostitutes are praised for their honesty because they do not possess the usual hypocrisy that surrounds sex in our society: "In this world, lying, fornicating and thieving are prerogatives of the sane. Small wonder that the two women, or any prostitutes, for that matter, were regarded as nuts" ("Prologue," *Discomfort*). In a favorite theme of the sixties, the notion of sanity is questioned. If the so-called normal people are really mad, repressed beyond repair by restrictive social codes, and the people outside the fringe of respectable society are really the only happy and free people, then everyone would be much better off in a lunatic asylum.

Sometimes, insanity is the only sane course. The novel's action reinforces this questioning of conventions, proposing to a degree the uninhibited actions of the human spirit. The epilogue, however, undercuts the basic themes of independence and honesty, when her fellow prostitutes discover along with the reader that Blue Rhonda has been lying all along. She is not what she has seemed. Instead of a sexually open and honest prostitute, she confesses to having been born a man, feeling herself to be a woman trapped in a male body.[3] Brown does not condemn "her" for her deception partly because this transsexual who specializes in "oral flourishes" is a particularly appropriate punishment for the "righteous" men of Montgomery who frequent her establishment ("Prologue," *Discomfort*). Their hypocrisy is cleverly mocked by her sexual deception. Although she does not believe in closeted behavior or fundamental dishonesty about identity, Brown can perceive the underlying social and psychological forces that drove Blue Rhonda to this ruse and can celebrate in a perverse way the power that this "woman" gained.

Blue Rhonda can also be seen as a rebel, someone who defied the sexual stereotypes dictated not only by convention but by biology. Through the courage of his conviction that he is really a she, Blue Rhonda fulfills her true female nature, ignoring the physical reality that conspires to limit her to a particular set of sexual roles. This brazen creation of her individual identity is not without its problematic symbolism in the context of the novel and of Brown's works. If Blue Rhonda is masquerading as a female, then is she really attempting to experience the emotions of a woman, or is she actually fulfilling some homosexual fantasies in her safe disguise as a prostitute? Brown does not really bother herself with such fine psychological distinctions. She is so accepting of divergent behavior that she leaves the reader to ponder any such questions on her own. What is important is that Blue Rhonda has a good heart; she is entrusted with the weighty secret of Hortensia Banastre's scandalous affair with the young black fighter Hercules Jinks and, after his tragic death, she comforts her partner Banana Mae Parker with an act of sexual compassion (which brings up even stranger questions of whether Blue Rhonda is expressing heterosexual or lesbian impulses). With the sexual confusion created by Blue Rhonda's experiences, Brown confirms her view that one's sexual expression is ultimately not essential in one's social or personal definition.

Sexual and Social Rebellion

Framed within the story of Blue Rhonda Latrec is the main plot of beautiful, rich, but unhappy Hortensia Banastre, one of Brown's elegant and wise social rebels. A clear descendant of the wealthy and rebellious Celeste in *Six of One*, Hortensia is often compared to Blue Rhonda as her spiritual double. The secrets that they share with each other and that they attempt to keep hidden from the town bind them together in sisterhood despite the obvious differences in class, status, and biology. They are both rebels who have defied the social codes that would restrain their sexuality. Hortensia feels that she can trust and communicate with Blue Rhonda "because there was a curious quality of pain, of understanding, of being outside" that draws them together (*Discomfort*, 140). While Blue Rhonda has defied her biological limits to express the woman that is trapped in her male body, Hortensia breaks the social code of respectable marriage by having a passionate, primarily sexual, affair (thus becoming on one level, in the eyes of society, a prostitute like Blue Rhonda) and breaks the racial barrier by falling in love with a young black man and secretly bearing his child. Later, after Hercules's tragic death, in order to protect his child, Hortensia permits an incestuous liaison with her degenerate son Paris, breaking the oldest sexual taboo in our culture. The novel charts her development as she explores through chance, choice, and necessity the various social boundaries of traditional Southern upper-class white society.

Hortensia's marriage is a brilliant social match between two influential families, but it totally lacks passion. Her husband Carwyn's attentions to her are described in terms of forceable rape, and his open dalliance with prostitutes is part of the hypocritical double standard that allows men a degree of sexual freedom while forbidding women any outlet for their desires. He is not condemned for his visits to the local whorehouse but for taking Banana Mae out in his carriage for the whole town, including Hortensia, to see. Hortensia is left to find comfort in her possessions and her social status, which she does enjoy. Passion is illogical, a form of "madness" that does not fit into her scheme. She has neatly divided and defined people by the suits found in a deck of cards; only later, after she had experienced passion and love does she realize the limitation of this rigid schematization. Her son describes the system: "Clubs are when you use force, so the lowest people are clubs. . . . Spades are when people work for a living. A man digs a ditch. That's next. Diamonds are smart and rich, but the best, the very best people in the world, are the hearts" (*Discomfort*, 7). Hortensia is originally portrayed as the ace of diamonds and her cold and brittle qualities are emphasized. Because of his boxing skills and physical strength, Hercules is at first classified as the ace of spades, but love reveals that he is truly the king of hearts. Though the system is seductive in its simplicity, it ultimately limits one's perception of the complexities of life. One can appear to be one thing on the surface and a very different nature may exist underneath the facade (as Blue Rhonda can attest). Such artificial boundaries in this child's game parallel the even more destructive social and racial restrictions that keep people apart. Blue Rhonda explains to Hortensia her Buddhist view of spirituality that perceives the soul in everything: "So maybe we aren't the same outside, maybe we are unequal, but inside, the soul is pure. All souls are equal. If only we could see the soul" (*Discomfort*, 142).

Hortensia is first seen playing a game of cards with her two sons Paris and Edward. Her desire to win what the children perceive as yet another "round of humiliation" is concomitant with her "obsession for power" in the social realms of Montgomery (*Discomfort*, 3). Her cold nature fosters only "facsimiles of affection" from her children, those "two strangers masquerading as sons." Playing the role of wife and mother, Hortensia is a failure; she is acting without emotion, distanced from her inner feelings. Emotions are crystallized into manners as one climbs the social ladder, fulfilling the mere forms without experiencing true emotions. This internal division of head versus heart/body, of emotion versus reason, is demonstrated in many aspects of the novel. The elaborate sexual masquerades that are required by many of the customers of the new whorehouse show how alienated people have become from their true selves and how dependent they are upon socially defined roles for identity. The judge who dies "in the saddle" while pretending to be Napoleon conquering various territories tries to extend his legal/social authority into the sexual realm with disastrous results. Brown criticizes his inauthenticity and his hypocrisy by having his corpse wrapped in a rug full of mouse turds. The visitors to Bunny's establishment are seeking "simple relief from a confusing sexual code" (*Discomfort*, 60). With characteristic honesty, Blue Rhonda sees through the facades of the "respectable" wealthy clients: they are magnolias upstairs and skunk cabbage downstairs.

Hortensia too lives a divided existence, "from the neck up," until her affair with Hercules awakens her to love's liberating power (*Discomfort*, 6). Even after that passion, however, she still struggles to overcome her sense of alienation, a feeling she shares with Blue Rhonda. When Blue Rhonda questions her about her soul, "Do you ever feel like your body is a blouse? . . . . I mean, that you put on flesh like a blouse, like you're a stranger in your own body? Your spirit is different?" Hortensia expresses a similar sense of alienation: "Sometimes I feel like a pair of giant eyes, watching" (*Discomfort*, 141). From unawakened socialite to passionate woman, Hortensia learns what her rebellious Aunt Narcissa already knows, that great love is always at odds with society. Society by its very definition demands adherence to certain rules and roles, while true love is too expansive to be bound within rigid codes.

Brown ups the ante by having Hortensia fall in love at first sight with a black man. The Southern stereotypical fear of the delicate white woman being raped by a brutal black, one of the traditional justifications of enforced slavery that led to the Civil War, is subverted by Hortensia's willing seduction, her sexual experience in educating the virginal Hercules. He seems her opposite in almost every way, yet they perceive spiritual qualities in each other that allow love to blossom. Hortensia fosters his love of architecture and literature; Hercules sees beneath the social facade that others, not even her husband, care to penetrate. When his brother criticizes Hortensia for being shallow and unthinking, Hercules defends her: "People are one way on the outside and sometimes another on the inside" (*Discomfort*, 72).

In order to overcome the tremendous social stigma of their illicit relationship (even she refers to "sin" when they first kiss), Hortensia must surrender to her instincts, to her sexual longings, without the restraint of logical thought: "Hortensia, as if outside herself, did what she couldn't think of. She could act but not think. She knew she was wrong to do it but she couldn't stop herself. She also knew she wanted Hercules and she'd never wanted a man before in her life" (*Discomfort*, 78). While others are assuming roles to enjoy sexual fantasies, *Hortensia* strips herself of all pretense and role, lapsing into pure physical, animal pleasure. Before her final seduction of Hercules, she warns him, "This could ruin both of us" (*Discomfort*, 78). Here, Brown flirts with the powerful sexual myth that all women need is sex to subdue them, that women secretly want to be raped and possessed. What prevents these stereotypes from surfacing, however, is Hortensia's active role in the sexual encounter. She gains confidence and power through her actions, aware of consequences but determined to take risks. Brown also reveals the redemptive power of love in the subsequent actions of the novel.

With the experience of her first passionate love, Hortensia is transformed; as her mother notes, she "behaved like a different person, affectionate and easy to please" (*Discomfort*, 79). As in *Six of One*, love multiplies: "It was not until she had accepted and given love that she could see who else loved her" (*Discomfort*, 80); "Hortensia was so in

love with Hercules that her abundance of goodwill spilled over. . . .
The passionate lovemaking with Hercules enabled her to experience
every moment as special" (*Discomfort*, 101). She even becomes sympathetic and attentive to Carwyn as her whole outlook on life is changed.[4]
As we learn in the sections dealing with the prostitutes in the novel, most
extramarital sexual activity is motivated by lack of communication; Blue
Rhonda wisely notes about her customers, "Sometimes I think people
need to be listened to more than they need to fuck" (*Discomfort*, 76).
Similarly, Hortensia's affair helps to open channels of communication
and areas of thought that she had never anticipated: "Hortensia absolutely never carried on conversations like this, but with Hercules she
talked about everything and anything. She asked questions of herself
she'd never asked, and together the two of them laughed over the silliest
things" (*Discomfort*, 94). Realizing how her materialism had filled her
emotional emptiness, Hortensia now can exist simply in her cottage with
Hercules.

But the danger of their relationship cannot be forever ignored. When
Hercules tries to persuade her to leave with him for their safety and for a
new life in the North, Hortensia realizes that despite the revolution in
her emotions and her worldview she is still bound to Montgomery, partly
by her responsibilities to her sons. But perhaps even more telling is her
inability to surrender her social power. She would lose not only the
privilege accorded her by her wealth and family name but also the
superiority provided by her white race. Hortensia's resolve is never fully
tested, however, because Hercules is abruptly killed in an accident. His
leg is amputated on the tracks as he saves his father from a runaway
boxcar; when the white ambulance refuses to take him to the hospital, he
dies waiting for the black ambulance. Perhaps it is fitting that he is
crippled as he tries to cross the tracks that, as we have noted, divide the
social classes in the town. Emblematic of the future, the train ironically
robs both Hercules and Hortensia of future happiness together. For some
critics, this accident is all too convenient a plot device. Hortensia can
become noble in her tragedy and suffering without having to challenge
the social order or to relinquish any of her privilege; since her affair was
secret, her closet rebellion lacks conviction. But the fact that Hercules's
death is directly attributable to racial prejudice certainly makes Hortensia's burden more difficult to bear, considering her own underlying racial
attitudes. She also must deal with the consequences of her actions, the
child Catherine, born of their doomed union: "Hercules' grave was a
fixed point in her emotional life. The other coordinate, the point moving

into the future, was Catherine" (*Discomfort*, 138). Using the image of the graph, Brown suggests how subtly the social order has reimposed itself after the slight disruption caused by their potentially revolutionary affair.

The Limits of Family

The second half of the novel deals with Hortensia's relationship with this new child (whom she raises as the daughter of her black maid), with Catherine's quest for identity, and with the impact of Hortensia's actions on her own two sons. The romantic love of the 1918 section is transposed to the story of Grace Deltaven and Payson Thorpe, which will be considered shortly. Although it is tempting to see Brown fully in the Hortensia character, the social rebel who defies racial boundaries (as Brown herself did at the University of Florida, getting herself into trouble with the dean of women), Brown must also identify strongly with the character of Catherine. As a youth wondering about her own parentage, suspecting that she was part black, Brown must have felt some of the same sense of alienation that Catherine experiences. Like Nickel in *Six of One*, Catherine helps heal the wounds of the past as she reincarnates traits of Hercules to keep his memory alive for Hortensia. She blends the blood of the races that in the past have supposedly been kept separate and thus indicates a way for future generations. She is such a symbolic child (Brown also makes her annoyingly precocious), that she seems less than real, not unlike Pearl in *The Scarlet Letter*. Her symbolism is most fully exploited when she illegally enters the all-white Great Witch Hunt and leads her team to victory with her astute intelligence in answering the riddle-like clues. The traditional Halloween game was described in detail in section one as Paris and Edward play and Hortensia's mother Lila serves as the Great Witch. This central social ritual (like bingo or gin in her other novels) allows Brown to swirl her action and subplots in a bubbling cauldron of delight. Beneath the banter, however, is the significance of the particular sport. According to Brown, this game teaches the children at an early age to learn boundaries and to cooperate with others in their social peer group rather than to rely on siblings. The second version of the game, played a generation later, reveals changing social implications. Disguised as a white ghost, Catherine can participate surreptitiously in the game. When she is unmasked and revealed to be black, the children are perplexed about how to react. Their traditional upbringing tells them that "niggers" are inferior and should be excluded from their activities; their observations tell them that Catherine deserves a medal for her participation: "Something had been violated and they were entangled in a web not of their own making" (*Discomfort*, 254). This web of traditional racial prejudices (like those responsible for Hercules' death) is challenged by the actions of the individual, but the net stays in place. A grim reminder of vigilante violence is discovered by the children during the hunt—a lynched rum runner dressed in a witch's costume. Prohibition, whether through laws controlling the selling of alcohol or the social customs regulating racial contact, results in the destruction of the individual.

The child Catherine also plays a role in the drama between Hortensia and her son Paris. As the classical name suggests, the Paris subplot contains elements of Greek tragedy, this time played out against a less than mythic background. The tense mother-son relationship, born out of the neglect witnessed in the first section, bears evil fruit in the second section. It seems that the sins of the mothers are visited on the children. Paris and Edward do not benefit from Hortensia's expansive love during her relationship with Hercules, and once Catherine is born, her attentions are taken even further away by the love child. Brown attempts to demystify traditional maternal love: "For Edward she felt some warmth, but toward Paris she was curiously empty. She felt estranged from him even when he was in the womb. If she'd wanted to discuss this with anyone, she never did; there was no one she could or would talk to anyway" (*Discomfort*, 58).

Part of her distance from the child could be linked to her perception that he is like her; later her guilt increases as she sees in his behavior a pitiful attempt to win the affection that she could never feel for him. His sexual irresponsibility seems an extension of her own disregard of sexual regulations, his raging libido a comment on her own illicit sexual passions. When Paris begins his assault on her, he comments before the act of incest that "laws are made to be broken." The narrator interjects, "Had anyone seen them, they would have looked to be carbon copies of one another, an artistic tableau" (*Discomfort*, 218). Thus when he confronts her with the truth of her own "sin" and threatens to harm the only thing she loves, sensing a "logic" in his madness, Hortensia finds she must yield to his pleas. Since she has not loved him emotionally, he demands that she love him physically. But as in her marriage to Carwyn, she denies him possession by giving only her body and not her spirit, leaving him even more distraught than before: "She gathered into herself like some creature retracting into a density higher than our own and therefore impenetrable. . . . He'd possessed his mother but she'd never belong to him. The act by which he'd sought to bind her to him only drove her further away" (*Discomfort*, 230).

When he attacks Catherine, however, Hortensia must destroy the monster that she has, in effect, created—her son, her lawless double. Her discussions with the dark side that Paris represents lead her to revelations about her own lingering racial barriers and the problem of motherhood. In trying to protect Catherine from the prejudices of the upper-class whites, Hortensia has relegated the child to second-class citizenship as a black. Even more importantly, she had denied Catherine the dignity of the truth. Selfishly, Hortensia wants to be able to enjoy the presence of the child without the full responsibility of motherhood. After Paris's murder is covered up by the sheriff (in reparation of his debt to Hercules), Hortensia can be honest with Catherine and accept her role as mother despite the social inconvenience that it will cause. Ironically, it is not Hortensia's decision to make; representative of the new generation, the blending of the best of the two races, Catherine exerts her own independence: "I don't feel like I belong to anybody but myself" (*Discomfort*, 273). Her manifesto "I like myself" reminds us of Brown's other heroines coming to terms with their identity.

Brown's concern for motherhood is reflected in her portrait of Hortensia's relationship with her mother Lila Reedmuller. While Hortensia sees her parents' marriage as an ideal friendship/romance between equal partners, Lila is sympathetic to Hortensia's marital problems, feeling somewhat responsible for her daughter's unhappiness. Lila fosters Hortensia's surrender to her passion while at the same time wisely warning her not to lose her head, her rationality, in her romance (which, of course, she must do in order to experience pure passion). Brown confirms that parents can influence children but that ultimate accountability rests with the individual. Neither nature nor nurture controls destiny; we each define ourselves through our actions. Lila connects the main plot to the subplot of Grace Deltaven through her friendship with Grace's mother. She witnesses Icellee's problems when Grace wants to become an actress: "Lila wondered why you make all your mistakes on your own children when you can so clearly see how to help other people's children" (*Discomfort*, 55).

Like Hortensia, Grace Deltaven has to break social rules in order to pursue her happiness. She scandalizes her high-class family by her decision to pursue the disreputable profession of acting, in Hollywood no less. Whereas Hortensia represents the past, the South's struggle with family and racial issues, Grace is associated with the present and the future, partly through her travels on the train and her success (à la Tallulah Bankhead) in the movie industry. She seems in tune with her times. Her aristocratic background gives her the strength not to be devoured by Hollywood as so many actresses were. In one of her most astute passages on Southern culture, Brown comments, "The security of her heritage sustained her no matter how remote or antiquated it might seem to someone else. She knew her place, she knew her people and she knew what was expected of her. Southerners always had the wisdom to realize that form is as important as content" (*Discomfort*, 238).

Grace becomes involved in a "modern" romance with another screen idol and Southern (Savannah, not Montgomery) aristocrat, Payson Thorpe, whose drinking, homosexuality, and anti-Semitism make him vulnerable to the powers that control the Hollywood studio system. The lovers forge an interesting relationship together, allowing each other freedom to express their bisexual longings, but accepting the responsibility of their professional and personal commitments. Together they test the boundaries of marriage. Their attempts to battle the studio powers, however, prove fatal. Although they experiment with new collaborative production techniques, the patriarchal Jewish studio system, as they see it, conspires to ruin Payson by preventing his successful transition from silent to sound films. He literally becomes the Man in the Iron Mask, the character of his greatest film role, as he is locked out of the future by technology. Committing suicide in despair on the train, he writes to his wife Grace in a final note: "In chess it isn't the moves that kill the king; it's the rules by which the game is played" (*Discomfort*, 264).

Though Brown through this subplot is able to interject her knowledge of film history, it remains unresolved and only tangentially related to the rest of the novel's action. The insular town of Montgomery seems far more real and dramatic than the modern world outside. Characters either find themselves unable to leave the comfortable boundaries of the town or destroy themselves when they attempt to escape. Place defines the characters even more than they themselves are willing to admit.

Chapter Six
Sudden Death: "This Is Really Judy's Book"

No matter how vehemently Rita Mae Brown tries to deny participation in the composition of *Sudden Death*, critically one of her least successful novels, much about the novel recalls her earlier fictional interests, not to mention the many biographical similarities that exist. In her "Genesis" prologue to the book, Brown explains the promise to her dying friend that led to the creation of *Sudden Death*. When Judy Cook Lacy, a sportswriter for the *Boston Herald American* to whom the novel is dedicated, encouraged Brown to write a novel about the women's tennis circuit, Brown declined, suggesting that Lacy write her own first novel. Believing that writing empowers individuals and creativity improves society (as best expressed in her introduction to *Bingo*), Brown nonetheless eventually promised Lacy a few days before Lacy's death from cancer that she would write such a novel. Taking her promise seriously, Brown undertook the task more out of a sense of friendship and duty than one of inspiration and personal commitment to the project. As Brown admits in the prologue, "This is really Judy's book. Whatever virtues the novel possesses are more Judy Lacy's than my own. The faults, however, are mine alone and no reflection upon my inspiration."[1] As late as 1987 in her *Starting from Scratch* writer's manual, Brown sees *Sudden Death* as an aberration in her development as a novelist: "Each novel—with the single exception of *Sudden Death*, which was written as a promise to a dying friend—was more difficult than the previous novel" (*Starting from Scratch*, 16). One wonders whether this disclaimer was intended, as she wishes us to believe, merely to downplay Brown's role in order to confer credit on her friend, or to avoid lawsuits for the thinly veiled portraits of actual tennis stars, or else to deflect the anticipated criticisms of the work. Such modesty from the egotistical author who in the acknowledgments of this same book expects the readers to "swoon at regular intervals" at the sight of her photograph on the book cover is disturbing and uncharacteristic enough to give us pause (*Sudden*, x). Her protestations raise suspicions. How can she deny the work when it so clearly fits into her usual themes and concerns and when it clearly relates to her far from secret relationship with Martina Navratilova? Perhaps it was the pain from the memory of her friend's death, from the harsh criticism the book received, and from the aftermath of her relationship with Navratilova that forced Brown, against her normally honest and open impulses, to pretend almost that she never wrote the book.

The title itself gives us a clue about her intentions in the book. Not only does "sudden death" refer to the sports rule about how a tie is broken and a game is won, but it can also refer to the unfair and unpredictable death of her friend (upon whom a character in the book is modeled) and to the sudden demise of a relationship (which happened in Brown's own interpretation of her affair with Navratilova). Events conspire to tear apart Brown's seemingly secure world at the time: "This period of my work coincided with the sorrows that come to us all in time. I lost the love of my life, who unfortunately went to the press about it. Public humiliation is a special torture. . . . At this same time, 1981, I lost my money. . . . (divorce is savage; first you lose your love, then you lose your second seat of security—your house—and maybe you'll lose the car, the dishes, etc., too)" (*Starting from Scratch*, 16). With unexpected financial burdens from the "divorce," Brown was forced to move West to work in television (with Normal Lear) for a while. To add to her emotional stress, her cat Baby Jesus (her companion for over 17 years) died upon Brown's return to Charlottesville in October 1982. Her premonition of her mother's imminent death would be fulfilled the following summer, after the publication of *Sudden Death* in May of 1983. It is not surprising, then, that this book shows so little of her character-istic humor and so few of her outrageous situations; it takes itself far too seriously, but because of its clear connection to the events of her life at the time of its composition, it is in some ways a very personal book, more revealing than Brown would wish.

Most reviewers were aware of the connections of the novel to Brown's biography but were critical of its significance: "After all, of what great merit is it, really, to be the former lover of a professional tennis player? It is, I hasten to inform you, of not such great merit that it validates a book whose literary worth is comparable to, say, a work from Harold Robins or from the mistress of the fantasy roman à clef, Jackie Susann—though Brown's latest is not as readable as either."[2] This reviewer contends that Brown simply desires "to exploit an unearned—and uninteresting—celebrity." If the reviewers did not mention Brown's autobiographical interest in the subject, they did refer to the recent Billie Jean King lesbian palimony scandal as a possible source. The major problem with the novel for all of the reviewers, however, was not so much its subject matter as its weak style. Critical of Brown's shallow characters, the *Booklist* reviewer complains of the "cliché-riddled, cynical voice that is hard to recognize as hers," while realizing that the book will probably still be a "succès de scandale."[3] The style of the novel is similarly criticized in the *Best Sellers* review for its lack of depth in characterization: "Most of the gays are shown to be as cruel and perfidious as the straights. Brown's characters, whatever their age and sex, all have a way of sounding like gleefully naughty little girls. Why they love, suffer, and betray, is dealt with only superficially."[4] Another critic complains, "Brown's usual wit and flair for characterization are missing here: the characters are unsympathetic and one-dimensional."[5]

Sudden Death shares some of these same problems with the Brown novel that it most resembles, *In Her Day*. Both are based on Brown's real life romances between older and younger women; her relationship with the older actress Alexis Smith and the younger tennis champion Navratilova. The relationships that evolve in both of the novels suggest the difficulty of finding common territory between women who are very different, not only in age but in intellectual and social backgrounds. In *In Her Day*, Ilse comes from a privileged Boston family, while art historian Carole Hanratty comes to treasure her Southern hard-working background. In *Sudden Death*, Argentinian tennis star Carmen Semana, with her total absorption in the physical, contrasts significantly with the intellectual American college professor represented by Harriet Rawls. The novels share an academic setting, though that is weakly described in *Sudden Death*; to the chagrin of one critic, we never even find out what subject Harriet teaches (Wilenz, 35). The older woman's longtime friendship with a woman of her own age is a central concern in both novels. Carole's deep friendship with Adele in *In Her Day* reveals the power of true spiritual sisterhood. In *Sudden Death*, Brown sees that friendship subplot as the point of the book; in describing the plot of the novel to her friend Armistead Maupin in *Interview*, Brown admits: "It's about a woman in her thirties who's in love with a young woman on the women's tennis tour, but the real theme is the older woman's friendship with a female reporter who's also her age. These two women should have been lovers, but one's heterosexual and the other's gay, and they're both attached to other people. And they realize too late, when one of them is dying, that they made their mistake. There's the terrific loneliness of two right people who met at the wrong time, and missed" (Maupin, 50).

The important issue of closeted and open homosexuality appears, again with a reversal. Young feminist Ilse is very open about her sexual preferences, while the older academic is somewhat circumspect about her behavior; in *Sudden Death*, the young tennis star Carmen Semana believes she must not be openly gay or she will endanger her sports career, while professor Harriet Rawls refuses to be dishonest about her lesbianism though it does ruin her career. The fundamental difficulty of modern two-career relationships is revealed in both books, with the additional stress of the social taboo of lesbianism. In both novels, death of a loved one (Carole's sister in *In Her Day*, the sportswriter in *Sudden Death*) leads the heroine to important self-discovery. Since *In Her Day* has marked a transition from the first person to the third person for Brown, from autobiography to history, *Sudden Death*'s return to the personal might be seen as a throwback to an earlier style and perhaps justify Brown's attempts to deny its place in her oeuvre. Despite its stylistic shortcomings, however, it does develop certain themes and techniques that Brown had been concerned with throughout her writings—the use of a central game metaphor to comment on the action, the critique of patriarchal hierarchy, and the individual's battle against prejudice.

Sport as Symbol

Brown's ambivalence about tennis comes through in her writing about the pro tennis tournament circuit in *Sudden Death*. As a teenager in Fort Lauderdale, Brown remembers being followed around by a young Chris Evert on the tennis courts that she frequented, playing with young and old opponents (often in exchange for books from their libraries). She won awards for her athletic abilities and a degree of social acceptance for her skills and for her participation on the high school tennis team. Throughout her essays in the seventies, Brown lauded the physical development of women as essential to the feminist movement. Women could not afford to be passive creatures, to be closed out of the traditionally masculine areas of competition and sport. Physical fitness was as essential to woman's development and health as intellectual growth. In a section subtitled "The Body Politic" in her essay "The Good Fairy," Brown shows how physical changes in posture, body language in interpersonal communications, even in fashion can create a new sense of women's power and freedom. Since "the external reflects the internal," as women regain their physical strength, they will increase their political power (*Rapper*, 189). Women who develop their physical potential "are the most free from oppressed mannerisms and thus radiate an engaging sense of well-being" (*Rapper*, 188). In "The Lady's Not for Burning," Brown calls for a study of sport and its techniques to contribute "to a revelation or new perception of ourselves," as a "way to deal with the irrational and the suprarational" (*Rapper*, 212). Since sport mediates between mind and body, feminists could learn from coaches and athletes. In her conclusion to *A Plain Brown Rapper*, Brown calls for three programs to defeat patriarchy: feminist assemblies, feminist organizer's school, and sports leagues. The need of women for physical power is evident: "Women do not control the most basic geography of all, our own bodies. Submission is a product of physical weakness. Patriarchs like their women weak, soft, etc. Only recently have Americans begun to tolerate the concept of the woman athlete. As children our identity is tied into physical prowess. Little girls, discouraged from sports, grow into women incapable of defending themselves not because they can't but because they don't know how and because they perceive themselves as weak. A strong person is much less likely to be anyone's victim, personally or politically" (*Rapper*, 221).

Despite her personal love of tennis and her political belief in the power of sport to transform women, Brown can still be very critical of tennis in her book. It is difficult for her to reconcile her enjoyment of tennis with the image of the sport as an elitist entertainment. Though she insists that she learned tennis on "pockmarked clay courts at South Side," perhaps trying to downplay the country club aura of the sport, Brown eventually does play at the best tennis courts (*Starting from Scratch*, 8). When she was living with Navratilova, they had their own private court and installed $4000 worth of gym equipment in the basement of their large house (Mansfield, C1).

In *Sudden Death* the loss of the genteel tradition of the sport is lamented in comparison to the crass commercialization of professional tennis. This history is echoed even in the title, for "sudden death" was a tiebreaker innovation made to improve the sport for the spectator by speeding up the game, instead of allowing the sport to extend into theoretical infinity. In the old days, "the two of you could conceivably be there on the court until the Second Coming" (*Sudden*, 17). Nostalgia for the elegance of the past is expressed by Harriet Rawls in her response to the Paris Open setting: "Harriet imagined Edwardians strolling the grounds, a very different crowd from those who attended racetracks or tennis tournaments today" (*Sudden*, 162). Part of her preference for the history of the sport is associated with the beauty of the old courts; comparing the French Open to the now defunct Forest Hills, Harriet noticed that "each was covered in ivy, built to human scale so one was not overwhelméd by architecture and each bordered a city—accessible but not chokéd by the concrete octopus" (*Sudden*, 162). The personal and natural aspects of the game seem to have been destroyed by the intrusion of modern society, the expansion and exploitation of the sport.

But Brown does not have to go back to the origins of the sport for meaningful comparisons to show how the game has become overly professionalized. The recent history of tennis since it became a competitive sport instead of a leisure activity reveals significant change. In *Sudden Death*, Lavinia Sibley Archer represents the older champion who returns to help organize women's tennis into a professional activity, transforming it from a sport into a business. Ideally, as a former player, she should be able to preserve some of the old elegance of the sport (after all, she "remember(s) tennis when men wore white flannel trousers") and to bring some sensitivity to the women's side in her negotiations (*Sudden*, 93). However, she is so intent upon saving the sport and making it prosper that she is guilty in her altruistic greed of ignoring individuals; she has to place the good of the many over the good of the few (in this case, the lesbians). Like many of her fellow businessmen, she tries to sell the sport on its sex appeal while in the process unwittingly changing tennis from sport into entertainment. The stars must be young, pretty, and conventional. Brown satirizes Lavinia mercilessly in the early parts of the novel. Because of her social pretensions, she is the target of one of Brown's familiar acts of comic mayhem. In this case, Harriet and reporter Jane Fulton sabotage Lavinia's ceremonies by putting bras and jockstraps in the American flag. A manipulative lush, Lavinia can still be appreciated even by her critics for what she accomplished—she made it possible for women to earn a living by playing tennis, providing for a type of career dedication never before possible. Gradually, the fact that she is a victim of the sport as well, a past-her-prime athlete who inspires behind-the-back laughter, reveals a tragic dimension to her character.

The professionalization of tennis (and other sports), to Brown, is just another manifestation of the capitalistic system that conspires to repress the individual, especially women. The athletes are on the bottom, providing the talent and playing the sport. They are subject to a variety of controlling forces—parents who dictate their careers (illustrated by Rainey Rogers and her mother in the novel), coaches who manipulate their game, lovers and friends who make demands on them. On the next level are the managers, people who package and sell the athlete to the highest bidder. Carmen is at first handled by an agency that represents the top athletes in all sports: "Athletes Unlimited crept over the sports world like a wild vine. From a tiny seed, the corporation threatened to take over the whole forest" (*Sudden*, 22). The agent gets wealthy from commissions and kickbacks from the advertisers and event organizers, who wish to exploit the player's name, image, and person. Carmen yields to her brother Miguel's request to manage her affairs, thinking that he will protect her interests, when instead he forges her signature on disastrous contracts that lead to her financial doom and his own temporary profit. In the cutthroat world of business competition, even family ties are endangered.

Not only are the players controlled by their managers, but in the sport itself they must obey the rules of the Women's Tennis Guild and the Players Guild, which in the novel are run by Lavinia Sibley Archer. Ostensibly organizations to protect the athletes and to create a sense of democratic control over one's destiny, these organizations function as a "puppet show" to prevent unionization; the pension plans and insurance provided by the guild were inadequate to the players' needs and insensitive to the demands of the actual sport. The true power in this hierarchy, however, is the sponsor. Local sponsors and tournament sponsors had to be courted for their support. *Sudden Death* focuses on a mythical cosmetic company, Tomahawk, to show the interaction of the sponsor with the tennis tournament. Since the sponsor is mainly concerned with selling its products, the players become walking advertisements; what is good for the company must also be good for the players. Women's tennis has traditionally been sponsored by feminine products, which increases the problem for the athletes as they struggle for respect. Instead of being valued for their athletic skills and physical prowess, women are still being judged and rewarded for their physical appearance and beauty. The players themselves are products that represent majority cultural sterotypes: women's tennis stars should be young, pretty, white, and heterosexual.

These cultural biases are detailed throughout *Sudden Death* as factors that various players must confront sometime during their career. The overriding prejudice is sexism—male tennis stars make more money, have better publicity, are more sought after than female tennis champions; their tournaments are more established and prestigious than those for women. As the Athletes Unlimited manager understands, "The less the girls knew about the financial transactions of the men players, the better. Let sleeping dogs lie" (*Sudden*, 25). Siggy Wayne, Lavinia's cohort in attracting sponsors to women's tennis, cannot contain his own prejudices against the sport he is promoting: "He thought of women's tennis as his burlesque show with clothes. . . . Women's tennis couldn't compete with men's tennis. The men's game was faster, stronger, and longer. All the women had to sell was tits and ass. Plenty of them had neither, but the few that did, the Page Bartlett Campbells, the Rainey Rogerses, they were his aces" (*Sudden*, 47). Brown assumes that this inequity is so overt that she spends little time directly comparing male athletes to females.

Some of this sexual bias, however, surfaces in the controversy over homosexuality in the sport. Since there is the stereotype that women who compete in the male domain of sport cannot be true females, part of the hostility over lesbianism is a subtle attack on all women in sport. Just as lesbianism was used politically by some to attack and discredit the women's movement, so the charge of lesbianism in professional sports seems a way, to some, to discourage all women's participation in sports. The mental gymnastics of this "logic" is personified in the closeted behavior of the lesbians in *Sudden Death*, especially the character of Susan Reilly. Susan maintains a respectable heterosexual marriage as a cover for her lesbian behavior on the tour; she has a series of female lovers yet denies to them and to herself that she is a lesbian. She callously discards her lovers when they get too close or too demanding, in a way that Brown sees as "male" behavior: "If a person asked for equality, especially a lover, Susan unceremoniously terminated the relationship. She could not grant anyone equal status with herself. She resembled a lot of men in that respect" (*Sudden*, 96).

As long as lesbianism is not openly discussed or admitted, the players, coaches, managers, sponsors, and public can ignore its existence, can pretend that it does not exist: "The lesbian threat cowed the women. Each player over the age of twenty knew what it was like to be regarded as a freak because she liked sports. Lesbianism insinuated itself into the consciousness of women and frightened them. It frightened the lesbians most of all" (*Sudden*, 42). Brown refers to Carmen's closeted lesbianism as living in a demilitarized zone between lies and truth. The battle lines are drawn clearly, however, when rumor of her relationship with Harriet is leaked to the press by her tennis rival and ex-lover Susan Reilly. For a variety of reasons, none of which are satisfactory to Brown or to Harriet, Carmen retreats into lies, marrying an out-of-work actor who will

conveniently allow her to continue her new romance with Bonnie Marie:
"Bonnie Marie would never admit to being a lesbian. She was new. No
past. No problems. She was wonderful" (*Sudden*, 195).[6]

Sexism against women in general and lesbians in particular is not he
only problem faced by the professional athletes. Racial attitudes are
revealed in how Carmen and her brother Miguel (both South Americans)
are treated. Miguel especially notices how businesspeople respond more
favorably to him when he exaggerates stereotypical "gaucho" Spanish
traits. The lack of black women players is lamented by Lavinia not
because of the injustice that it represents and how it identifies tennis as
a rich white sport but because she is not able to exploit the black
middle-class audience that might be attracted to the sport. The cruelest
problem faced by the athletes, however, is the tyranny of age. Younger
and younger players appear each year to challenge the champions, while
"piece by piece, under repeated stress, the body unravels itself" playing
this demanding sport (*Sudden*, 45). To heighten this injustice, player
contracts, according to Brown, do not usually contain provisions to
protect players should they suffer career-ending injuries. As the body
fails and the competition gets stronger, each player has to face the
inevitable, yet the psychology of the sport does not allow one to prepare
for this natural aging and evolution. As the sportswriter astutely notes
about Carmen: "She's in a world that formalizes conflict and protects her
from everything except tennis. That's not exactly preparation for life's
continual assault on one's narcissism" (*Sudden*, 85). Like most stars, no
matter what the field, Carmen is sheltered from the real world so that she
can concentrate mentally and physically on her game, to the exclusion of
everything else. Harriet cannot criticize anything before a match because
it might affect Carmen's mood. She cannot be bothered with the mun-
dane details of daily life. As long as she has money to spend, she is not
concerned with Miguel's mismanagement of her affairs: "Carmen's in-
centive was to show off and get paid for it. Like a dancer, her time was
short, the applause was bracing, and the future was nonexistent except as
an extension of the present. The truth would set in later, like arthritis"
(*Sudden*, 125).

Though the physical metaphor is apt, Brown also sees the problem of
aging as a mental one, particularly in Susan Reilly's desperation. In
describing her attitude toward winning, Brown writes, "What was a
source of self-confidence and joy in her youth, became a contest for sanity
at thirty. She willed herself to win. She had to prove to herself that she
could win one more time" (*Sudden*, 171). Carmen, on the other hand, is

known as the "Ozone Cookie" because when she is bothered mentally she can "float off into her own world" and play "out of her head" (*Sudden*, 86–87). She frees herself mentally to enhance her physical game, while Susan struggles to use mind over matter. As the athlete seeks transcendence, either of the physical or the mental, however, the return to reality gets harder and harder to accomplish.

The tennis world's emphasis on physical appearance and performance confirms the player's status as entertainer. Throughout the book, Brown compares the sports figure to dancers, actors, and media celebrities. As a sports columnist, Judy Fulton seems most aware of the tragedy associated with the player's star status: "What happens to Carmen when the cheers are over, I mean, when real life sets in with a vengeance and all of its aches and pains" (*Sudden*, 39). The unreality fostered by these professions keeps the women from maturing; like willful children, temperamental stars, spoiled brats, they develop techniques to ignore truth and protect their egos. Carmen uses escapism to avoid conflict: "Take a drink, smoke a cigarette, or puff on the magic weed, but under no circumstances face the pain" (*Sudden*, 20). Instead of facing the lesbian scandal with Harriet, when their relationship is tested, she runs away to a less complex situation. Susan Reilly has "moral amnesia" to prevent the natural remorse that any normal person might feel for her cruelty to lovers and competitors alike (*Sudden*, 20). Like an actress, Carmen thrives in the spotlight on the court; she is "a creature of performance," feeling the effect of the audience on her game (*Sudden*, 33).

The cutthroat attention to winning as the only value in sport condemns it (in Brown's view of the political and social responsibility of the individual). As a manifestation of capitalism's struggle for material rewards, sport becomes "a symbol of the fragmentation of life" (*Sudden*, 92). Part of this fragmentation is explored in the rootlessness and alienation of the players. Not only do they exist in a protected, unreal environment, they are constantly on the move from one tournament to another. As she has striven to do in *Southern Discomfort*, Brown attempts to use architecture, in this novel, city planning, symbolically to show what is wrong with contemporary society. Many chapters open with a brief description of the city and the sports arena for the next competition. These cities share a landscape intersected by highways and surrounded by desolation; natural harmony has been disturbed by unnatural structures of concrete and steel that divide and destroy beauty. Brown slams the stadium off the Capitol Beltway in Washington, D.C., as a "hymn to the fact that urban planners don't know shit from shinola" (*Sudden*, 15). In the next breath she proclaims that the "beauty of the round robin format was that no one understood it," thereby paralleling the awkwardly located and physically ugly arena to the unintelligible format of the tennis tournament (*Sudden*, 15). Both designed by committees, neither the building nor the rules have much to do with ordinary humanity. The arena in Kansas City is built over a confusing labyrinth; Chicago is compared to a "glittering choker"; Los Angeles is "clinging to the Pacific" (*Sudden*, 59, 83). Though the passages attempt to establish a sense of place, the locations themselves seem unreal, unstable, and confusing. They serve as perfect counterparts to the sports intrigues and relationships that exist within the seemingly orderly structure of the tennis court. As a Southerner rooted in history, family, and tradition, Brown conveys the unreality of this precarious, artificial world, deploring the aimlessness of the lives and the disconnectedness of this insular world.

Despite the negative aspects of the sport—its commercialization, its sexism, racism, and ageism, its physical and mental exploitation of the players—tennis has those few moments of transcendence that promise eternal youth and adulation through the exhilaration of victory. Brown exults in those moments, which are comparable to the lack of self-consciousness that she associates with the primal "root self," that feeling of playing outside of one's self that athletes often try to describe. Sport also "strips away personality, letting the white bone of character shine through" (*Sudden*, 177). The idea that sports can lead to self-knowledge is a common enough truism of locker room journalism, but Brown extends it by comparing sports to art: "Sport, like a sonnet, forces beauty within its own system. Art, on the other hand, cyclically destroys boundaries and breaks free" (*Sudden*, 177). With its rigid demarcations and coffin-like shape, the tennis court becomes a classic testing ground for the soul. Even though commercialization threatens to transform the sport into pure capitalistic expression, "the human spirit occasionally slipped through" (*Sudden*, 178). The players become goddesses (Carmen/Artemis and Page/Athena) in a superhuman contest, where the best of the sport is revealed. Instead of "competition," which has aggressive connotations associated with the male, the match becomes "a sophisticated form of cooperation" between the two women (*Sudden*, 179). Subverting the classic metaphor of the competition as war/battlefield, Brown sees the potential of cooperation, that sport might be used to settle conflict: "Why didn't the leaders of bickering countries pick up tennis racquets and go settle it on the court?" (*Sudden*, 8). Thus despite her harsh critique of sport as emblematic of much that is wrong with modern society, Brown reveals the redeeming characteristics that draw her to this game and show what the ideal sport might be.

Against this backdrop of sport, Brown portrays a romance that contains within it the same flaws as the tennis world, one doomed to failure because of the very nature of the lovers. The relationship between Carmen and Harriet is described mainly in the present; there is very little information given about how and why they fell in love and how their relationship got to the point that it had in the novel. Thus, as characters, they seem alienated and disconnected from their own personal history; hence, their emotions seem shallow and unconvincing. The battle between their careers ends when Harriet agrees, in essence, to give up her teaching to follow Carmen on tour. Believing that Carmen needs "one true fan," Harriet goes against her better judgment and sacrifices her job (and some self-respect) to accompany Carmen and protect her from those who had "glad-handed, back-slapped, and star-fucked" her throughout her young career (*Sudden*, 28). A moment of perfect harmony is achieved as Carmen feels certain of her possession of Harriet's love: "She slept, as do all lovers, with one synchronized heartbeat, for she was one with another human being and the universe as well" (*Sudden*, 29).

But as any competitor knows, when victory is achieved, the sport is over. Carmen begins to think Harriet less exciting because she has given up the career that helped to make her appealing in the first place. Harriet becomes an "invisible wife" on the tour, with little identity of her own and certainly no support from the other tennis wives and lovers (*Sudden*, 39). As Brown does, Harriet believes that "love is a risk" and so accepts the challenge to love Carmen (*Sudden*, 39). When the lesbian scandal breaks, the game of love proves to be more difficult than either imagined. Harriet refuses to relinquish her last bit of dignity by lying about her sexuality, realizing the schism that is growing between her and Carmen and within her own feelings for Carmen: "Harriet tried not to pray her lover would be the woman she wanted her to be. She prayed instead that she would be able to love Carmen no matter what she did" (*Sudden*, 141). A product of the sport she plays, Carmen cannot leave her safe cocoon in order to face a painful reality; she denounces Harriet, accepts Lavinia's dishonest solution to the dilemma (by marrying a man), and initiates a new and uncomplicated relationship with Bonnie Marie. Her dealings with people are no less shady than Miguel's business ventures, but she will blind herself to self-knowledge just as she must block out problems in order to play a good game of tennis.

Chapter Seven
High Hearts: Fact, Fiction, and the Historical Novel

The personal turmoil that Brown underwent during the composition of *Sudden Death* continued during the research for and writing of *High Hearts*, her Civil War saga published by Bantam in 1986. Her mother's death in August 1983 followed by the death of a former lover and best friend Jerry Pfeiffer from AIDS in September 1985 forced Brown to confront issues of love, mortality, and the past. Through this four-year period, when Brown admittedly did not know whether she was "coming or going," she turned to her work to sustain her, often breaking down emotionally as she tried to write (*Starting from Scratch*, 17). The frequently bitter and violent tone of this historical novel reveals Brown's inner struggles during this difficult time of her life as she explores the physical and emotional devastation of war on inhabitants of Albemarle County in Virginia. Graphic descriptions of death, mutilation, and destruction fill the pages of her longest work to date. The Civil War years (specifically from 11 April 1861, to 24 August 1862) provide a superb setting for Brown's continued interest in history, in gender experimentation, and in the possibility of political and personal change. Like all Southerners, Brown is fascinated by this period, and her book comprises a revisionist look at its cataclysmic events.

Her "Acknowledgments" and "Foreword" reveal a commitment to historical research in her conception of the project. As she had noted about other research for her prior novels, Brown believes that details of daily life are the most important aspect of historical research. If an author knows how people eat, dress, talk, and live, then she can flesh out the rest of the details, assuming that fundamental human behavior has not really changed that much over the centuries. This is not to say that character is a function of exterior elements alone. Brown is sensitive to the class, race, and gender differences expressed in language and in human behavior, as her chapters on dialogue and character development in her writing manual discuss (see *Starting from Scratch*, 85–105). But in her view, characters reveal themselves through carefully selected traits of language, dress, and especially action: "To explain the inner life of characters, at length, is to cheat readers of their own intelligence and experience. Show them people as they would meet them if the reader were in the book" (*Starting from Scratch*, 99).

Although she credits a number of people for specific research assistance, claims to have spent about two years in research, and includes a bibliography of sources at the end of the text, Brown does not convince all of her readers that this is an accurate historical text. Southern author and critic Florence King points out in her review some of the flaws, claiming that Brown's research "sticks out" (as in using addresses and names instead of meaningful, insightful details and putting "jarringly modern phrases into the mouths of the 19th-century characters" and the narrator).[1] Indeed, much of her history appears as the names of important battle fields, but for the Southerner these names often have talismanic qualities, and when repeated often enough assume the effect of a litany that conjures intense emotions. Surrounded by war stories in her childhood (from books and from relatives), Brown admits, "I was not really learning anything but rather I was being reminded of something that I already knew."[2] Many of the unconscious assumptions that white Southerners absorb by the fact of living in the history-haunted South surface in her writing, often suggesting unfortunate stereotypes (especially when considering attitudes toward slavery and when creating the black characters of the book). She cannot seem to filter out the modern consciousness in her revisionist attempts; the book abounds with anachronisms in language and character that distract from many of the finely observed details. Her view of history, as being a continuum throughout eternity, is partly responsible for her reliance on anachronism. She wants to be true to human experience whether or not all of her surface details are true: "If you're setting your novel in a time different from your own, remember that emotional relationships are more important than facts" (*Starting from Scratch*, 109).

The factual starting point for *High Hearts* was Brown's desire to examine a woman who goes into battle, as many women had up until World War I when physical examinations were required for enlistment. She is then free to explore what repercussions this action would have on the woman's emotional development and social situation. Brown also wanted to consider women's overall contributions to war, not only in battle but in their unstated agreement with such orchestrated violence: "No nation or people can go to war without the tacit support of its

women" (*High Hearts*, xv). In the novel she refers to the women as a
"shadow army," fighting their own battles on the homefront as they run
the plantations in their husbands' absences, take care of the wounded
soldiers, and try to maintain a semblance of order in the face of overwhelming chaos. Not only did she want to revise views about women's
roles in the Civil War, but she also wanted to examine class and racial
differences, to answer the question of why so many poor whites and
blacks fought to preserve the privilege of a white male minority. Because
she intended to question traditional views of the Civil War and to
invade the male territory of battle as a woman writer as well as a female
protagonist, Brown deliberately chose the "conservative style" of the
historical novel (*Starting from Scratch*, 111). The more familiar, conventional form would disguise the revolutionary aspects of her content (just
as she often uses humor to mask controversy and make it more acceptable
to a general reading public).

"The Past Is Prologue"

Brown does not express her vision of history in *High Hearts* with the
device of alternating periods that she used in *Six of One*. Instead, she
chooses the more straightforward daily-diary approach to document the
progress of the war and its effects on a small group of related characters.
The novel is divided into three major sections followed by a brief
epilogue that leads into the historical records of the soldiers and her
bibliography. "The Deceptive Calm" denotes not only the calm before
the storm of real battle but also the seemingly normal individual lives
that are immediately challenged by the changes brought about in the
upheaval of war. The action begins with the marriage of Geneva Chalfonte Chatfield to Nash Hart on the eve of the battle of Fort Sumter that
began the hostilities in the Civil War. The parallels of the personal and
the political are developed through the novel as the marital squabbles of
several different couples are dramatized against the backdrop of battle in
a war that symbolized a national domestic dispute. Brown does not
pursue the Northern family/Southern family contrast that D. W. Griffith employed in *The Birth of a Nation* or John Jakes in *North and South* to
portray the war as an extended regional family altercation. Her focus is
definitely Southern and Virginian.

Section two, "The Anvil of God," interprets battle as a testing ground
with God as a blacksmith forging the weapons of war and challenging
the mettle of one's character by such bitter trials. "These Bloody Cards"

continues the emphasis on battle but looks at the futility of the South's cause, the disintegration of relationships, and the emergence of the true individual, stripped of all the false social constructions of gender, race, and class. The section's title comes from a comment by Geneva's cracker cohort Banjo about soldiers being bloody cards in a game of fate (*High Hearts*, 238). The notion of destiny and human history is integral, as we shall see, in Brown's evaluation of war in the novel as a whole. The final entry in this last section takes the action into the next century (11 June 1910), as the aged Geneva passes on her stories to her granddaughter, who is approaching her own wedding day. Thus, on the eve of World War I, the cycle of history seems complete as the characters are ready to begin another marital experiment. The action of the novel flows so smoothly, however, the artificial section divisions hardly seem necessary; the dated chapter headings would be sufficient to orient the readers to the evolution of the characters in battle.

In structure and theme the novel is most similar to *Six of One* and *Bingo* (especially in its use of chapter dates) and indeed can be seen as a sort of "prequel" to those related books. Not only is Geneva's mother a Chalfonte, the family that dominates *Six of One*, but Brown makes one reference to Cassius Rife and his munitions factory, as an example of profiteering during wartime, in a critique that is also an important part of the narrative in *Six of One* (in which Celeste Chalfonte murders Brutus Rife for his dishonorable activities). *High Hearts* ends in 1910, close to the time frame that begins the action in *Six of One*.

The guiding principle in this book is "the past is prologue," as Brown states in her foreword.[3] Parallels with the past are integrated through the continual references to the Old and New Testament daily scripture readings that bind all of the characters in their different locations and the repeated references to military history as the characters try to interpret and understand the political events that surround them. That Brown also intends for the readers to make connections between the Civil War and Vietnam is clear in her "Foreword." When analyzing the sources she consulted for her understanding of battle history, Brown notes that Union officers would not file a battle report if they lost the battle: "They habitually inflated Confederate numbers and then screeched to President Lincoln that they needed more men. Does this sound familiar? The more things change, the more they stay the same" (*High Hearts*, xii). She sees the Civil War, as many contemporary historians do, as a transitional phase in battle history, "the last of the old wars and the first of the new" (*High Hearts, xiv*). The chivalry and idealism of a "gentleman's war," however false the reality of this notion, tied the Civil War to the old ways of battle, of men flinging themselves against other men in brave charges across clearly defined battlefields. The war against a civilian population and the introduction of new long-distance, impersonal weapons of mass destruction heralded the new way of fighting that was perfected in that other civil war, North Vietnam against South Vietnam. As Geneva realizes at the end of her life, "What started out as a classic war became something new, something ugly, something that twisted everyone. No one was safe at the end. We all live in the dark shadow of Sherman."[4]

While demonstrating in her book that the past is prologue, that history does repeat itself in many ways, Brown supports the belief that war is inevitable, that humanity is destined because of its inherent violence and aggression to exist forever in conflict. The structure of her novel in its daily-report format shows the characters being swept along by events that seem out of their control. Constant references to fate and destiny also suggest that humans have little choice in the directions of their lives. Brown's gambling metaphor, that soldiers are bloody cards, that individuals are "dice thrown on the plains of destiny," projects the image of people as pawns in some cosmic game beyond their knowledge and control, an almost Greco-Roman view of whimsical gods playing with human destiny (*High Hearts*, 43). Geneva's mother Lutie interprets fate in a Christian context, as "God's will" for the individual, but she has difficulty accepting this principle on a larger social level: "I've felt desolation and grief. But those were personal sorrows, sorrows that come to everyone when God wills it. They test us, but this is different. This is the sorrow visited upon a people" (*High Hearts*, 28). The characters dimly perceive that the stated causes of war are not the real reasons, that "the reasons are only excuses. Events are moving at a tragic velocity" (*High Hearts*, 23). Once set into motion, events take on a life of their own with individuals having little control over their direction. Geneva takes a certain comfort in her belief in fate, for she feels she will die when it is her time; thus she is freed from fear in battle. Her mother Lutie struggles to "bear the yoke of fate" (*High Hearts*, 231), believing that "in highly intuitive beings, Fate and free will are the same thing" (*High Hearts*, 61). Geneva's black half-sister Di-Peachy sees through the sham of human excuses: "Fate was invoked to explain human stupidity. And then, too, it was always the weaker ones, the chattel of this earth, that believed in fate so as to explain their misery" (*High Hearts*, 61–2). Though the characters lament the role of destiny in determining their future and sense that they might be using fate as a rationalization of what they do not fully understand, inside they perceive that individuals can change, that they do have choices in their personal lives.

Religion, Superstition, and Myth as History

Brown, however, does not want people to settle for the easy answer that war is inevitable because that kind of thinking keeps people from questioning their government and allows them to accept horrors that they should never tolerate: "If this war were not taught as inevitable, it would force students of all ages to question methods of government, to question the morality of powerful lobbying groups forcing their will on the majority as well as to encourage the student to formulate strategies. . . . If we believe that great forces—first embryonic, then fully developed—move on a collision course, then nuclear war is inevitable, as inevitable as the War Between the States" (*High Hearts*, xiv). Throughout the novel, Brown strips away the excuses that people use to deny the truth; she refuses to let her characters blame fate for their misery, whether their definition of fate be based on religion, superstition, or historical determinism.

To accomplish this, Brown uses the Bible as an echo of events, one that should bring comfort, and would under normal circumstances, but that now only reinforces a depressing vision of violence. Brown selects passages that are particularly brutal in their violence and cruel in their sense of justice. The shared readings draw the characters closer together and reflect the common Judeo-Christian heritage of violence. The chapters selected by Brown form a running commentary and secondary bibliography for the reader (passages are mentioned but not described in every instance). As war becomes a reality, the Bible passages provide less and less comfort for the characters, and the number of readings decreases as battles progress. When Lutie first hears the cannons, she also hears "the voices of the Old Testament Yahweh calling for blood" (*High Hearts*, 143). Even when she tries to celebrate the victory of the first battle of Manassas by reading the prayer of the biblical Manasseh, Lutie is disillusioned by what she reads: "Manasses [sic] beat his breasts bragging on his sins. Lutie had hoped for something edifying" (*High Hearts*, 178). The trials of Job are "too depressing to contemplate" though she dutifully reads her lessons (*High Hearts*, 178). The most religious character in the book, Lutie eventually questions some of the disturbing stories that she reads. When King David ordered his soldiers to kill all of his enemies, including the crippled and blind, Lutie "thought he was horrid to be so cruel" (*High Hearts*, 276). As a nurse to mutilated and destitute men, Lutie cannot condone the horrors she finds in the Good Book. At church services, the people are bombarded with biblical battles from their religious leaders, who have joined the politicians to support the war: "The Bible was ransacked for examples appropriate to Manassas. Since the Old Testament was one long military interlude, the good pastor suffered an embarrassment of riches" (*High Hearts*, 180). Then as now, the Bible can be used to support almost any moral stance or political point of view.

The Old Testament verses not only describe the tribal warfare of the Israelites but also examine marriage and family relationships. They describe how kings possessed numerous wives and concubines, how the children murdered others for their inheritances, how a Levite allowed his wife to be gang raped by his hosts then dismembered her for her dishonor when he returned home, how Elisha watched "with satisfaction as two she-bears destroyed and devoured forty-two children who had made fun of his bald head" (*High Hearts*, 279). The reader wonders, along with Geneva, "what th[ese] gruesome stor[ies] had to do with her spiritual life" (*High Hearts*, 95). Along with the battle stories, these morality tales of family life reveal the cruelty of men in a patriarchal society; this brutality is not reserved for political warfare but visited upon the family as well.

The New Testament offers some solace to the characters, but Brown provides fewer references to these positive aspects of the New Testament, in which Yahweh is transformed into a merciful and forgiving god. After reading about Christ clearing the temple of the moneychangers, Lutie is still dissatisfied with the Bible: "it's so full of anger and violence. What a bloodthirsty book this is" (*High Hearts*, 47). While providing some comfort, the stories of resurrection question the validity of miracles; it is not difficult to believe the cruelty of man, especially during wartime, but it is hard to accept life after death, when one is surrounded by carnage. Geneva admires Saint Paul for his clever attempts to convince the Greeks to believe in God, but she sympathizes with their hesitancy to believe in resurrection: "Right now she was rather glad the dead stayed dead. Imagine if those rotting soldiers rose out of their mass graves to turn on one another anew, or worse, to turn on her?" (*High Hearts*, 314). Brown's use of the Bible as a record of human history reveals her ambivalence about destiny. The Bible provides a graphic reminder that society has not changed that much over the centuries; people still fight and commit unspeakable acts of cruelty. Yet, despite its shortcomings, the New

Testament holds out hope that individuals can change, can achieve grace, can find inner peace, can live instead of die, which is exactly what Brown's characters must do. Though she has little sympathy for organized religion and has serious qualms about original sin and resurrection, Brown does have faith in the spiritual and moral life of her characters. Christianity is not the only moral and spiritual system considered in this novel. Existing alongside this tradition is a world of superstition, magic, and omen primarily associated with the African heritage of the black house servants Sin-Sin and Ernie June. Though they are Christian, their interest in the Bible often reflects their own peculiar spiritualism. The stories or resurrection, for instance, puzzle Ernie June because of her knowledge of burial customs: How could Lazarus walk if his hands and feet were bound? Did he smell of rotting flesh if he had been in the tomb for several days? As happens when two different cultures collide, each culture appropriates what it wishes, what reflects its own initial beliefs, what meaningfully answers a particular emotional/spiritual need, just as Paul had grafted Christianity onto certain religious practices of the Greeks. Sin-Sin responds to the story of Jesus's expulsion of the money-changers from the temple, "I likes when Marse Jesus fluffs his feathers" (*High Hearts*, 47). Although Jesus is just another white master to her, she can appreciate his righteous indignation at the greed of supposedly religious men. As a slave in a free America, Sin-Sin is not unaware of hypocrisy.

While Christianity is a patriarchal religion, the slave superstitions presuppose an animistic world inhabited by active spirits that influence human life. Brown's research is rewarded as she unearths and records interesting slave customs. A kettle placed by the door will capture the sounds so that no white person can hear the blacks speaking. Babies are passed over the coffin at every funeral to prevent the soul of the dead from taking the child with it into the afterlife. Sin-Sin's magical pottery brings luck to the owners. Brown does not dismiss these customs as childish superstitions but places as much credence in them as she does in other mythologies, whether Christian, Greek, Roman, Norse, or Native American. Although Geneva never discovers that her original marriage pot had been broken, her first marriage does indeed fail, thereby providing justification for belief in the spirit world.

The whites have their own local legends and superstitions to provide commentary on their actions. At several key points in the story, Brown relates the ghost story of the Harkaway Hunt. The Harkaway men were cursed by an ancient Indian tribe for raping the chief's daughter, so they continue to ride at dusk to warn others to avoid the mistakes that they committed. Lutie and Geneva are both visited by these ghosts with messages about death. Years before the action of the book, Lutie was warned, "Death is the tribute we owe nature" (*High Hearts*, 39). Later she has another vision of Casimer Harkaway; this time he does not predict death but prepares her for her destiny—life: "Your existence is a prayer" (*High Hearts*, 230). On the eve of her wedding and of the war, Geneva learns from the ghost that "each person you kill is a soul you must bear like an unseen weight" (*High Hearts*, 10). The predictions come true in that Lutie does determine to live life as a gift, influencing all around her with her love and compassion. Geneva, on the other hand, retains a more cynical view of human nature, partly due to her battlefield experiences.

Interestingly, it is the women, black and white, who are most sensitive to these visions, to religion, and to the African beliefs. With the wisdom of age, Lutie is no longer afraid of the Harkaway Hunt; she wants to be able to read the signs that exist around her and are trying to tell her things about life: "What manner of magical events or creatures lurked between our version of reality and the creation of Almighty God, she wondered. Perhaps unicorns, centaurs, and griffins existed side by side with us just like the Harkaways and a tremendous jarring of our ordered existence would open our eyes and we would see them for an instant. Perhaps this war would shake the earth like a mighty earthquake. Who knew what creatures will emerge from the fissures?" (*High Hearts*, 40).

Another mythology that seeks to explain human history and justify the ways of man to man is history itself. Brown reread Herodotus and Thucydides in preparation for writing *High Hearts*. Characters continually refer to Greek and Roman mythology and history as they analyze events around them. As the new god of war for his generation, Mars Vickers wants to write the military history of the world to prepare America for future wars: "He believed progress outstripped the military's ability to assimilate it" (*High Hearts*, 129). He understands the changing technology of weaponry: "Those artillery boys never see who they're killing" because their guns have a much longer firing range than they did in Napoleon's day (*High Hearts*, 376). Instead of following a scholarly career, however, Mars is caught up in actual battle, modestly trying not to get promoted so that he can stay close to the heart of battle and close to his troops. He laments the fact that war has become a science since "Epaminondas developed the echelon, a column of men who would obey orders—turn right, turn left, go forward, fall back" (*High Hearts*, 354). Mars actually appreciates Geneva/Jimmy's enthusiastic and reckless style of battle. References by various characters to Napoleon, to "Nekra Gate, the death gate of Constantinople's hippodrome" (*High Hearts*, 179), to Hannibal's destruction of the Roman forces at Cannae (*High Hearts*, 378), and other scenes of battle violence provide an apocalyptic context in which to see the Civil War as the ending of another civilization through war. Southerners know their military history, but they have learned nothing from it to prevent war.

"The Slow, Steady Push of People Over Decades"

The only solution or hope that Brown offers in the face of the overwhelming stupidity of the human race throughout history is the possibility of change.[5] The optimist in her emerges as once again she promotes love for others and individual goodness as the only valid responses to social upheaval. Again, her idea of individual change does not mean becoming someone else but discovering/uncovering the true self beneath the artificial layers of class, gender, and racial conventions. As Lutie pronounces without quite knowing what it means, "Corruption is the beginning of change" (*High Hearts*, 346). Decay and destruction can provide for new growth. The violent upheaval of the war might shake loose our hold on tradition and allow new creatures to "emerge from the fissures" (*High Hearts*, 40). Lutie herself is one of those creatures. An unhappy woman before the war, grieving for the death of her infant son Jimmy and for the disintegration of her marriage after Henley's passionate affair with a beautiful slave, Lutie survives by communion with Emil, an imaginary pasha from Baghdad who visits her in her dreams, and by obedience to the conventional formalities of life. She loves her son Sumner but has distanced herself emotionally from her daughter and maintained a festering resentment against her slave Di-Peachy as the constant reminder of her husband's infidelity. She shares much of her life with Sin-Sin without giving the servant the respect she deserves as a human being. Work on the plantation and with the wounded soldiers gives her a new purpose in life and new insight into herself and others. She learns to value people for their inner qualities, not for their social status or appearances. Her suffering teaches her that others are not responsible for her happiness: "Only she could create happiness" (*High Hearts*, 394). As women throughout history, Lutie was taught to depend on men for her sense of worth and self; even her imaginary companion is a dominant male. She blames herself for her husband Henley's affair before she realizes that he is accountable for his own choices. Instead of letting her children discover themselves, she tries to force them into her own ideal. Fortunately, she is able to see the truth of her situation before her life is enveloped in misery and bitterness. She reconciles herself with her husband when she starts being honest and speaking from her heart. They are able to be friends for a while before his death, and she is surprised that she can miss him after hating him for so many years. Perhaps most indicative of her transformation, Lutie finds the courage and sympathy to help her gossipy neighbor Jennifer Fitzgerald overcome her grief at the gruesome death of her beloved son: "We must accept death and we must accept life" (*High Hearts*, 208).

Lutie's marital problems are echoed in the process of Geneva's self-discovery and emotional evolution. The married couples in the novel want to explain away their problems with the assumption that passion in a relationship is doomed to die, so they try to convince themselves that they are happy when they are not. Like her mother, Geneva is confined by the stereotypical roles of women, heightened by the pressures of being a Southern lady. Lutie knows that Geneva will discover what all women eventually learn, "there's one set of rules for us and another for them" (*High Hearts*, 5). Having always been "contented with the surface of things," Geneva does not think deeply about her future (*High Hearts*, 13). Feeling herself not to be as attractive as a woman should be, she is grateful for Nash's affections; as she later tells Mars, "I never was pretty, but when I trussed up in a dress he looked at me, you know, that way" (*High Hearts*, 377). Their healthy sexual appetite in the early days of their marriage, their physical attunement to each other, is not enough to sustain a lasting relationship. Hints of their future incompatibility surface early. When Nash appreciates a poetic remark that Geneva makes, she quickly decides not to tell him that her comment was something that Di-Peachy said years ago: "She wondered if not telling him was the same as lying. It was such a little thing" (*High Hearts*, 29). Yet this one difference is indicative of the many incompatibilities that inevitably emerge: "She irritated him by her ignorance. She cared nothing for the things he loved—books, good conversation, intellectual respect, and he cared nothing for the things she loved—horses, adventure, and war" (*High Hearts*, 220).

Like Brown, Geneva is a fine equestrian, a trait that distinguishes her from other women and initially attracts Nash to her: "Gawky and lacking in feminine graces off a horse, she was transformed into a graceful, mesmerizing person on one" (*High Hearts*, 29). But this athleticism becomes a barrier in their relationship when she decides to enter the masculine world of the cavalry. Her androgynous looks and riding skills allow her to infiltrate the military to be near her husband. She betrays her ambition, however, when she goes beyond the bonds of marital duty. Not only does she want to be with Nash, but she also wants "to see what's going on" (*High Hearts*, 29). This curiosity, this desire to be part of history, is not compatible with Nash's traditional view of femininity. In camp together, Nash is critical of her because she smells of leather and doesn't "know the meaning of the words insomnia or femininity" (*High Hearts*, 204). In a subconscious act of hostility toward her, Nash thinks of other women when they are making love, "women who looked and acted like women" (*High Hearts*, 204).

Her experiences as a soldier forever change both Nash's and Geneva's perspectives on life, love, and each other. Geneva blossoms when she is freed of all the "thousand and one false courtesies men shower upon women" (*High Hearts*, 76). Treated as an equal because of her skills instead of pampered for her sex, Geneva reads her brother's engineering books and enjoys physical competition. Jousting with Banjo or Mars or with the enemy on the battlefield, Geneva loses the privilege associated with name, class, and gender and is judged only by her individual merit and by her actions. She thinks "women are silly" because of the roles they have been assigned: "They sit around and sew and gossip and nurse the sick. You're better off as a man" (*High Hearts*, 105). Though Nash thinks that Geneva is becoming too much like a man for his tastes, Geneva is actually discovering her own womanly qualities without the artificial role requirements that burden the Southern belle. She is able to show compassion to Banjo and to Mars in a "feminine" way, by her touch, without making them uncomfortable. When she is with the troops, "for the first time in her life, Geneva had a goal outside her own self. She felt magnified, important, useful" (*High Hearts* 95). Meaningful work, whether it be the "feminine" occupation of nursing for Lutie, or the "masculine" job of fighting, gives a sense of self-worth and value.

When her father warns her about how threatening her invasion of male prerogative is to Nash, Geneva refuses to return to petticoats: "I found something, and I won't ever give it up! . . . . I found myself" (*High Hearts*, 307). Her newfound freedom allows her to follow her father's advice to "learn to see reality as it is, not as you wish it to be" (*High Hearts*, 306). She begins to stand up to Nash's unjust criticism of her and to be honest about their relationship: "I used to look up to you, but you're not the end all and be all. I'm out in the world now, and I've got a mind of my own" (*High Hearts*, 352). Even with her love of battle and glory, her patriotism for the cause, this honesty eventually forces her to question her attitudes toward the war. Formerly, she had exulted in being alive when she crossed battlefields littered with corpses. With the death of her brother and father and the wounding of Mars, however, Geneva begins to see the truth about the war, beneath the surface of adventure and excitement. When a young Yankee captain spares her life for her acts of bravery, she wonders why she is trying to kill such a noble man: "For the first time Geneva had an inkling of what she was doing, of what they were all doing. It was wrong. It was so profoundly wrong that she felt cold sweat trickling down her armpits" (*High Hearts*, 367).

By the time that she achieves this degree of wisdom, her relationship with Nash, whose conscience felt similar doubts about the validity of war, has deteriorated beyond repair. Their passion for each other dies (as the older couples had warned them to expect), but they still feel friendship and affection. Though his changing feelings frighten him, Nash begins to realize that he is more like a brother than a husband to Geneva. He cannot overcome his traditional view of what a woman should be, and his underlying sexism will not let him accept Geneva for the "simple love" that she offers (*High Hearts*, 220). Even without the war, their relationship would probably have been troubled, but the dramatic extremes of their situation sped up the process. When his archenemy Mars tries to apologize for the way he treated the couple (after he discovers that Geneva is Nash's wife), Nash cannot understand Mars's praise of Jimmy/Geneva: "Colonel, this is easy for you to talk about. You're married to the most beautiful woman in the world who is doing what she's supposed to be doing: nursing the sick and behaving like a lady" (*High Hearts*, 386). Nash is more captivated by external beauty and traditional feminine stereotypes than genuine love. Nash dies from an enemy bullet through his heart without every truly appreciating Geneva. But Nash is not to be blamed for his short-sightedness. So strong are the feminine stereotypes that Geneva herself maintains some of the same expectations about her femininity, even after her battle experiences. When Mars proposes to her after the war, her first reaction is, "I'm not beautiful" (*High Hearts*, 409).

The irony of Nash's exchange with Mars about Kate Vickers is that Mars realized the error of his own marriage as he tried to counsel Geneva and Nash. He had married for the possession of a beautiful, desirable woman, and "too late did he understand the meaning of the word partner" (*High Hearts*, 130). Kate did not share his sexual drive and his need for a family; Mars did not share her driving social ambition. Mars discovers that "love is harder than war," but is fortunate enough to find true love, the love of the soul, based not on appearances but shared experiences and values, with Geneva (*High Hearts*, 185). In fact, Mars is able to fall in love with Geneva before he learns that she is a woman, although Brown does not insist upon developing or exploiting for humorous potential this mistaken gender identity as she might have in *Southern Discomfort*. Geneva wants to be loved for being herself, for her athletic abilities, her courage, and not for any false feminine exterior, so it is appropriate that Mars accepts her as she is, as a soldier first. Like one of Shakespeare's comic heroines, she goes into the woods disguised as a boy seeking reunion with her lover, but she emerges a woman, in Brown's version, with a better, truer lover at the end of her arduous journey.

The other soldiers are surprisingly tolerant of Jimmy's attachment to Nash because of the respect that they have for Geneva's skills and the sympathy they have for his/her youth. Calling Jimmy and Nash "sister boys," sometimes tauntingly, sometimes playfully, the men are aware of but not appalled by the homosexual implications. Early in his observations of the odd couple, Mars is afraid that Nash is taking advantage of a boyish infatuation: "Sometimes a boy does swoon over a grown man before he become a man himself with grown man's responsibilities" (*High Hearts*, 117). Interestingly, homosexuality is seen as a phase that men go through, as verified by Greek tradition, according to Banjo: "In ancient Greece an older man would love and care for a younger man until the young one grew a beard" (*High Hearts*, 344). Brown toys with the potential of a homosexual longing in Mars's attraction to Jimmy, but backs away from following through with that implication; similarly, she does not explore Geneva's boyishness as an expression of lesbianism (though her closeness to Di-Peachy could hold some interesting possibilities). Instead she portrays those pseudo-gender variations in an acceptable family context. Geneva's love for her father is transferred to the older Mars, who sees in Jimmy the son he was unable to bear, while Di-Peachy's love for Geneva can be explained away as a sisterly bond. Opposing war, like Lutie, because she believes that people should leave other people alone and allow them individual freedom, Brown refuses to step in to judge these characters for their choices. Tolerant of human diversity, she does not analyze the psychological dimensions of their sexuality.

War not only allows change in personal self-definition and gender expectations but creates a climate for social change. Artificial distinctions of class and rank, based on birth or wealth, like the false constraints of sex roles, are swept away in battle. People are valued for their skills and their actions, not their inheritance. Entering the army as a private instead of an officer, Sumner prides himself on his abilities as an engineer, not as the son of a famous family. Banjo Cracker best reveals the social changes made possible by the war. This poor white befriends Geneva, who appreciates his shooting and riding talents. Because she herself is breaking gender barriers, she is an appropriate ally and bargains with Mars to get him a commission in the cavalry. From there, his talents are justly rewarded. Though the genteel women would probably have ignored him before the war, his humor and charm win their affections. Just as death is the great equalizer, war is an equal opportunity employer. Banjo and Geneva are clearly better soldiers than Nash and Henley. They not only survive but prosper.

Changes in racial attitudes are perhaps the most difficult to bring about. Portraying an array of black characters with different perspectives and backgrounds—the faithful servants, the dissatisfied mulatto, the silent lovestruck giant, the scheming rascals—Brown celebrates the diversity of the slave community and credits blacks for their many roles in the war and in Southern society. Unfortunately, as this list of types suggests, Brown has problems creating believable black characters, free from stereotypical traits. The black characters seem to exist to provide insight into the changes undergone by the white characters, not as full-fledged characters in their own right. As a group, the slaves are comparable to the women of the period because blacks and women are considered dependent, weak, and childlike, and both groups are used to justify male violence in the war. Sin-Sin is the faithful old-time servant, imbued with the black superstitions of magic and ritual, carefully in control of her power on the plantation, and cleverly manipulative of her superiors and subordinates. She functions as a contrast for Lutie, who has problems seeing Sin-Sin as an individual with feelings and thoughts of her own. Sin-Sin's nemesis Ernie June is repeatedly described as having eyes that "bug out."

It comes as no surprise to anyone (either the characters or the readers) that Di-Peachy is the illegitimate mulatto offspring of Henley and his beloved slave mistress. In the early chapters, Di-Peachy promises to be more interesting than she turns out to be when she drops out of the main plot line. She refuses to be the slave of a slave, to marry any black man, though all the men in the novel are attracted to her because of her extraordinary beauty. In some ways she is the Southern belle daughter that Geneva is not, which is another reason for Lutie's strong dislike of the girl. She eventually marries a white soldier whom she had nursed back to health. Though Banjo rises in social stature, and Geneva is accepted as a soldier, Di-Peachy cannot successfully break the color barrier as Geneva reveals in a mysterious afterthought when she ties up loose ends in the last chapter: "That's a sad story. They did get married, but the Fates and other people were not kind. I'll tell you that one after your honeymoon" (*High Hearts*, 411). We are left to imagine her fate as well as that of most of the other black characters. They do not experience the spiritual transformations that the white characters do, a disappointing omission on Brown's part. However, Brown plans to continue Di-Peachy's story in a future novel.

The reasons given in the novel for and against slavery provide part of Brown's commentary on war in general. She presents many of the traditionally espoused views. At first Lutie expresses the noblesse oblige perspective that the black race had been entrusted to the care of the white race: She "felt responsible for them to her peers and to God. Lutie never asked anyone if they wanted to be taken care of, but then she wouldn't have gotten a straight answer. No, Lutie was convinced no matter what, no matter when, the white race would have to care for the black" (*High Hearts*, 109). Eventually, she learns to see Sin-Sin as a real person and to divide her beloved land among her faithful freed slaves to work toward common goals of survival. Despite his privilege, Henley determines to free his slaves even if the government does not force him; his love for Di-Peachy's mother softens his position toward blacks. Along with other men of his generation, he feels responsible for the evolution of historical events toward war because he abnegated his public duty and allowed lesser men to take office when he should have been less selfish. Geneva expresses a more democratic view toward slaves than her mother, who criticizes her for befriending blacks. Because Geneva believes in individual merit, she accepts people, black or white, for what they are worth. Mars provides a more cynical look at the motives for war. As a worldly-wise military man, he often sees through the rhetoric of war to the underlying causes—human greed: "This war's been brewing since I was in the cradle. I'd a damn sight prefer it if the real reason—greed— was put forward for once and not this smarmy abolitionist hypocrisy" (*High Hearts*, 117). Like the other men in the novel, however, even the cynical Mars occasionally falls prey to the romantic notion of fighting the war for the honor and protection of Southern women.

Drastic conditions, like war, break the flow of the seemingly inevitable; the past does not have to be prologue. Religion provides the example of miracles, the improbable becoming reality for no apparent reason. The black tradition also proposes an element of magic to change the course of human events. Brown believes in the role of chance in human affairs and incorporates it into her fictional theory and world, in small doses: "Chance is not the negation of certainty but an active force in human affairs. It can be positive or negative. Chance is not irrational. The Romans called it Fortuna and it may well be fortunate. Every one of us has bumped into coincidence, a streak of good or bad luck, and sometimes we've even had premonitions which have helped us. Those are examples of chance. How can you write about life and not use this aspect of it? Just don't overuse it" (*Starting from Scratch*, 109). Of course, war provides many opportunities for such chance occurrences that change the path of individual and social history.

Historical Romance and the Civil War Novel

To make her revisionist version of history more acceptable, as has been noted, Brown utilizes a conventional historical fiction format. Like her idol Mark Twain, Brown blames some of the South's problems on the romanticism found in Sir Walter Scott's popular historical novels: "Romances glorifying personal combat infected males of all ages, to say nothing of the ladies who thought themselves damsels of purity inspiring their heroes" (*High Hearts*, 260). In her use of historical traditions, however, Brown attempts to combat some stereotypes of the genre. She has a difficult time trying to balance her long-standing anti-war sentiments with the genre's tendency to glorify battle. Just as the animal lover Brown gets caught in the position of defending her love of foxhunting, here she must reconcile Geneva's love of battle with her own anti-war stance. Changing the sex of the hero to female, she can escape some of the charges against her that she does indeed glorify the excitement of battle, because for the first time a woman gets to participate in the sacred ritual of battle usually reserved for the initiation of men. Since war provides Geneva an opportunity to discover her true nature, it must serve some useful function despite its horrors. Geneva's innocence (seeing only the surface of things) and her youth protect her somewhat from the corruption of war. Her will to live is an affirmation of life's eventual triumph over death. Since Brown portrays battle from the ground up, that is, from the soldier's point of view, she celebrates human cooperation and camaraderie and can express her usual criticism of the hierarchical forces that are responsible for human tragedy. She blames the politicians and profiteers instead of the lowly soldiers who are pawns in the hands of this power. She also balances the excitement and adventure of battle against gruesome details of slaughter and suffering. She carefully shows the consequences of actions, counterpointing battle charges with hospital amputations. In one of the most powerful scenes in the novel she describes Jennifer Fitzgerald's tragic confrontation with the puzzle pieces of her son's mutilated body. In a moment out of Greek drama, Brown demonstrates beautifully the inconsolable lamentations of the victims of war (see *High Hearts*, 166–67). No one can question Brown's ultimate horror at the results of war. The list of dead soldiers at the end of the text confirms the human cost of this episode in our history.

Besides Scott's romances, the other historical fiction with which this book must inevitably contend is Margaret Mitchell's *Gone with the Wind*. One reviewer referred to *High Hearts* as a "kind of feminist *Gone with the Wind*" perhaps without acknowledging that GWTW in many ways presents its own feminist issues.[6] Both Scarlett and Geneva are struggling against the confines of the Southern belle stereotype and find many opportunities for change in the upheaval associated with war. Scarlett manipulates her sexuality to achieve her goals in a way that is foreign to Geneva, but both temporarily assume roles in a male world (Scarlett through Frank Kennedy's business). Geneva finds fewer restrictions and social pressures inhibiting her evolution than Scarlett does, perhaps because she is originally less imbued with the Southern belle mystique or because Virginia produces fewer belles than Georgia (according to Mars Vickers in *High Hearts*, 199). Both Brown and Mitchell portray the social upheaval that equalizes classes, though Brown is more sympathetic to this leveling. Melanie was the primary character in GWTW who judged people on their individual merit instead of their social class. Because of her proper manner of handling situations and her genuine kindness, she was able to overcome many traditional prejudices to portray the book's ideal Southern lady, her strength grounded in tradition. Lutie reflects many of these same values and provides a direct parallel to Scarlett's beloved mother Ellen, the epitome of the Southern lady. Nash's lamentations over the death of a beautiful civilization and his weak stomach for soldiering connect him to Ashley Wilkes, while Mars's virility and cynicism echo Rhett Butler. In a direct allusion to Belle Watling, Brown even includes a prostitute with a heart of gold eager to help the Confederacy. Although it is impossible to write a Civil War novel that does not in some way draw comparison to GWTW, Brown's themes are her own. Her eighties vision of history and the possibility of human and social change to improve mankind even in the midst of destruction and chaos reverse the essentially nostalgic, backward-looking romance that Mitchell wrote for the Depression-era thirties.

Since historical fiction is a way to personalize the massive movements of history, Brown not only proposes a grass-roots view of battle from a local Virginian perspective and parallels the personal domestic with the national domestic policy, but she also explores the importance of story-telling as she tells the story of her small band of characters. Her reliance on original historical documents reveals how important it is for future generations that everyone tell her story. Comparisons of past and present are valuable. The stories of personal courage she researched from family documents are "breathtaking," she admits, wondering "if we have it today" (*High Hearts*, xvi). Without history some things fade from memory: "No one alive knows what it is like to be a slave. We may know what it is to be downtrodden, despised, deflected, and determined to win despite the odds, but not one of us knows what it is to be owned" (*High Hearts*, xii). Whites used their power to suppress black access to literacy as a means of social control. Finding a voice, learning to speak a new language of the heart, is to take control over one's destiny. Brown offers her book as a monument to the women and slaves whose sacrifice has yet to be officially commemorated.

In her choice of influences—historical fiction, the Bible, slave oral traditions, Greek and Roman history—Brown is aware of how these collections of stories provide clues to the characters about their lives and their place in history, but they cannot give any definitive answers. Lutie is frustrated by this reality: "First we saw the aurora borealis in the sky this winter and then that gigantic comet streaked across the sky and now I come to hear Casimer Harkaway spoke to my daughter. We've been given a talisman of insight and yet we can't decipher it" (*High Hearts*, 61). The stories may not be clear but they must be told. Because generals falsify documents for their own purposes, history books may not record or remember events accurately. The characters feel that their lives may be in vain: "One hundred years from now every person in church today will be dead. Will anyone remember us? Even my own blood kin? . . . . We'll be shadows, shadows dispensed with their sunlight, their problems, their triumphs. They won't believe that we loved, fought, sung, cried, and died nor will they care. Maybe we're already shadows and don't know it" (*High Hearts*, 339). Even if remembered in history, an individual's life gets reduced to a simple anecdote or a footnote in a textbook. Henley's chivalrous note apologizing to the Baron for dying before he could fight the appointed duel will be all that is remembered of Henley's life as it becomes emblematic of the Southern notion of a gentleman's honor.

Lutie eventually understands that "memory is the true function of age," for without a sense of history one is rootless and alienated from one's own life (*High Hearts*, 294). Part of the maturation process is discovered by Geneva and Di-Peachy when they learn of Di-Peachy's true parentage: "They cried for their new knowledge, for their lost childhoods, for their fear of loss and of death. They were women now, and they knew that not every story had a happy ending" (*High Hearts*, 311). Brown's novel is no exception to that rule. People survived the war, but they could not be untouched by the drastic events they had witnessed and acts they had perpetrated. Geneva fulfills the storytelling function of history by passing her Civil War memories on to the subsequent generations. As the aged Geneva recounts the novel's conclusion to her granddaughter, she advises her not to long for the excitement of those war days, especially as time distances us from the reality of the events and allows romanticism to color the truth: "When people tell about their war experiences, it sounds exciting. It was, but, honey, I saw things I'll never forget" (*High Hearts* 405). As she proceeds to recount the horrors, Geneva remembers vivid images: "It seemed as though the whole world died. Beautiful John Pelham was hit in the back of the skull with a shell fragment at Kelly's Ford on March 17, 1863. Never forget that" (*High Hearts*, 405).

Generational differences are perceived as Geneva talks to her granddaughter on the eve of World War I before America is plunged again into violence. As memory is the function of age, we should look to our elders, which youth never does, for wisdom. The granddaughter is excited by the war stories and not yet touched by their horrors. An earlier episode in the novel demonstrates the nature of youth even more clearly. When Geneva's company passes by a village where children are celebrating May Day, the men understandably become nostalgic for their own families. What the children want to see, however, are not the maypole fertility rites but cavalry maneuvers. While the men oblige the eager youngsters, Brown questions what effect the results of war (suicide, drug addiction, disabled veterans) might have on the next generation (*High Hearts*, xvi). On another level of this generational conflict, Geneva does not have the optimism and peace that Lutie was able to achieve in her lifetime. She laments to her mother, "I don't have much use for the human race. I love a few people, and that's all. I don't have your wide embrace, your high heart. There are other wars out there, Mother. They'll be worse. We haven't learned a thing" (*High Hearts*, 413).

It is not enough to learn the horrors of war as Geneva has experienced them first-hand. To achieve true wisdom and a "high heart," one must learn lessons of love. Brown returns to her transcendental vision of a world soul to express this philosophy through the character of Sin-Sin: "God give each of us little pieces of other people's souls even when we doan know them. When you sad like that, one of 'em dies. You see, honey, we all part of one another. Thass white folks' terrible curse. They cuts off everyone from them. They thinkin' they superior but they jes alone, and when they hear that coffin's hollow moan, it too late" (*High Hearts*, 350). Lutie achieves grace when she does not shut the door on life as Geneva does; she opens herself to experience by dividing her precious land with the faithful servants, marrying Banjo, working the soil, and adopting orphan children. She explains her philosophy to Geneva: "In death there is life, and in life, death. But in love, there is only life" (*High Hearts*, 333). The simple but profound answer to war's brutality and the shameful history of man's misdeeds is love, for, as Brown proposed in *Six of One*, "love multiplies."

Chapter Eight
Wish You Were Here: A Mrs. Murphy Mystery

In *Wish You Were Here* (1990), Rita Mae Brown continues her exploration of small-town Southern life, bringing the action into the present and exploiting the conventions of mystery/detective fiction in order to make her social commentary. Although her satire and humor remain intact in this new genre, Brown retreats from her usual lesbian concerns, creating instead one of her least flattering gay portraits in the closeted, sycophantic villain, Josiah Dewitt. Gender is not as much the issue in Crozet, Virginia, as divorce, which is viewed as a community rather than an individual issue, and murder, which provides an intriguing parallel to the death of romance. Parallels are also drawn between the human and the animal kingdoms as Brown "co-authors" the text with her pet cat Sneaky Pie Brown, who is transformed into Mrs. Murphy, one of the major animal character/detectives in the mystery and the inspiration for the "Mrs. Murphy Mystery" series that may develop from this first book. Perhaps because of the divine silliness involved in the creation of the cat characters, the inclusion of the delightful drawings by Wendy Wray, and the publication of the paw print signed "Author's Note" from Sneaky Pie, Brown seems more at ease in her plot and prose style, less contrived in her humor and situations, than she has been in many years and novels. Always a devoted animal lover, Brown is liberated here from many of her old diction and narrative habits when she is writing the sections by and about the animals. As the *New York Times* book reviewer sees it, Brown, like most cat lovers, is "obviously, if harmlessly, nuts" and her "tongue-in-jaws mystery tale" successfully makes the book's animal conceit "every bit as charming as Ms. Brown intends it to be."[1]

Social Satire and the Rural Landscape

A real railroad town between Brown's Charlottesville and Waynesboro to the west, Crozet is another incarnation of Brown's divided

community. Unlike *Bingo*'s Runnymede and *Southern Discomfort*'s Montgomery, Crozet does not have a significant boundary running through
town, but it is cut off from the rest of the world in its isolation. The
railroad and the post office are central symbols of the mountain town's
connection to the outside world. Hoping to avoid the "golden fungus" of
development that has spread into Charlottesville, the town's inhabitants
can maintain tenuous bonds to modern society without being invaded by
it.[2] Although the railroad discontinued passenger service in the seventies, the train still stops in Crozet by individual request. The characters,
especially the local Southerners, fear progress and its associated crime,
unemployment, and exploitation. What the train finally brings
them, however, is the return of the ostracized interracial couple in the
book's last scene; prejudice and local hypocrisy have been defeated as the
family is reunited. Some contact with modern-day tolerance of diversity
is desirable to counteract the stifling conventions of the past.

The history of Claudius Crozet's attempts to bring Virginia into the
future through the railroad is interspersed throughout the novel as the
characters consider the encroachment of the future and how it will affect
their lives. They do not want to be caught like North Carolina with "one
foot in the nineteenth century and one in the twenty-first and nothing in
between" (*Wish You*, 64). Balance between past and future is important
to living successfully in the present. Brown lambasts the politicians for
their wastefulness, their callousness toward the environment, and their
disregard of local interests as they plan highway bypasses to handle the
increasing population. The action of the novel proves that even in their
isolation the townspeople are not free from the problems of modern
society (greed, murder, deceit), but they must learn like the rest of the
Sunbelt South to negotiate their future, preserving the best of the past
and incorporating the best of the present.

Brown does not overly glorify small-town life in any of her books; she
is perfectly aware of the pettiness and hypocrisy that can thrive in
conservative isolation. It is clearly a fallacy that "human emotions were
less complex in a small town than in a big city," though some people
believe this rural stereotype and thereby become dupes of clever manip-
ulators like Josiah DeWitt in the novel (*Wish You*, 57). Early on, Brown
presents two conflicting visions of the small-town myth. Supposedly, in
a small town everyone knows everyone else's business; yet the townspeople are equally aware that if one keeps up the proper facade, no one will
bother to question the surface appearance. Manners are extremely important in her Southern social environment. The novel's heroine, nicknamed

Harry, is particularly affected by the complex social code as she is undergoing separation and divorce from her husband, Fair Haristeen. Although she has suspicions about her husband's former flirtatious relationship with the newly widowed Boom Boom Craycroft, Harry must visit the widow: "Not paying her condolences to Boom Boom would have been a breach of manners so flagrant it would be held against Harry forever. Not actively held against her, mind, just remembered, a black mark against her name in the book" (*Wish You*, 39). Fair's own visit to the widow is recorded with the simple comment, "It was correct of you to come" (even though Fair did not like the deceased man) (*Wish You*, 42). Manners control not only what people do, but what they cannot do. Because Harry is postmistress of Crozet and therefore aware of most of the town's social activities, she is assured of an invitation to all events: "No one dared not invite Harry, because it would be so rude" (*Wish You*, 11–12). All of the characters are aware of the sophisticated code of manners that affects everyone in a small town. If one obeys all of these rules, then, one's behavior is above suspicion. Reality is not as important as appearance. The novel's mystery ultimately hinges upon careful observation of these habits of behavior. Knowing people's routines allows the killer to plot the murders and escape detection temporarily, but this knowledge of people's habits also eventually helps the local detectives to solve the crimes.

Because people are expected to act in a certain socially acceptable way, characters surprise themselves and others when they tell the truth. Brown is interested in charting the progress of characters as they break through artificial boundaries that inhibit behavior. The shocking murders free people from the normal codes of action. The widow begins to realize the truth about her hollow marriage, while the pious Mrs. Hogendobber gets actively involved in deceit and espionage. Most important is the development of Little Marilyn Sanburne, who must break the powerful control of her domineering mother Mim, described by Brown in her cast of characters as "queen of Crozet and an awful snob," an "honorary man" in her power (*Wish You*, 10). Once again Brown satirizes the social pretension of one whose sense of self-worth is determined by her place on the social register: "She was a woman who needed external proof of her social status" (*Wish You*, 10). Although her own marriage is strained by her relentless social climbing, Mim insists on giving unsolicited marital advice to Harry, on controlling her daughter's upcoming wedding, and on rejecting her own son's successful marriage to a young black woman. To show her disapproval of such hypocrisy,

Brown humiliates Mim in one of her scenes of comic mayhem. Trying to impress her friends with her wealth and social status, Mim takes a group out on her specially decorated pontoon boat, only to have it sink ignominiously as Little Marilyn watches from the shore. The scene not only reveals Mim being put in her place but also shows the daughter finally rebelling against her mother's commands when she delays as long as possible before helping Mim.

By the end of the novel, Little Marilyn can invite her brother and his wife to her wedding over her mother's objections: "I'll speak to you any way I like. I've done everything you've ever ask of me. I attended the right schools. I played the appropriately feminine sports—you know, Mother, the ones where you don't sweat. Excuse me—glow. I made the right friends. I don't even like them! They're boring. But they're socially correct. I'm marrying the right man. We'll have two blond children and they'll go to the right schools, play the right sports *ad nauseam*. I am getting off the merry-go-round. *Now*. If you want to stay on, fine. You won't know you aren't going anywhere until you're dead" (*Wish You*, 229). Mim's comeuppance includes being duped by her crony Josiah as well as having to endure the socially embarrassing situation of her black daughter-in-law as matron of honor in Little Marilyn's wedding. But Mim does not remain unredeemed; she realizes that she will never dominate her daughter again and actually greets her estranged son at the train station. Stripped of her pretensions, Mim can at last be honest and break free of her own socially imposed restraints to be reunited with her family in a new relationship. If Mim can change, Brown suggests that there is hope for the whole community.

The detective formula allows Brown to explore beneath the surface of small-town manners and life in her search for the truth of the human heart. As one of the minor characters interjects about the murder mystery, "It's something right under our noses. Something we're used to seeing or passing every day, as well as someone we're used to seeing or passing. It's so much a part of our lives we no longer notice it. We've got to look at our community with new eyes" (*Wish You*, 218). To do this Brown has to break through certain Southern small-town stereotypes to expose the truth. As her main character she chooses a postmistress in what must be a direct allusion to Eudora Welty's nosy postmistress in her famous short story, "Why I Live at the P.O." Instead of a vindictive woman, we find a mature woman struggling with the painful realities of small-town gossip during her divorce as friends and loyalties are divided. The postcards that she inspects cleverly introduce the characters and provide clues for the mystery instead of revealing a simple snoopiness about Harry.

The murders provide a fascinating parallel to Harry's divorce. Harry learns more about the community as she investigates the murders, while at the same time she learns more about herself during the stressful process of divorce. With new honesty she can examine her relationship with Fair and realize why their marriage failed: "Sex brought them together and left them together for a while, but they weren't really connected emotionally and they certainly weren't connected intellectually. They were two reasonably good people who needed to free themselves to do what came next" (*Wish You*, 28). The reality of separation, however, involves disputes over money, lawyers, friends, and old jealousies. Not wanting to become one of those bitter divorced women, Harry must struggle to maintain her equilibrium and sense of individual identity. Harry muses that Mrs. Hogendobber's marriage was probably successful because her husband had "simply surrendered all hope of individuality" (*Wish You*, 24). That also seems to be the case with Mim's marriage to Jim Sanburne; he stops fighting her and lets her have her way even though he may disagree strongly. Harry's best friend Susan Tucker and her husband Ned, however, reveal how compromise and cooperation can lead to a happy union of two very different people. Harry must reestablish her sense of self before she can recover; even her nickname is taken from her husband's surname, not her own names. She distrusts herself for allowing her marriage with Fair to go on for so long after the passion has died: "What was I doing married to Pharamond Haristeen? Am I that far away from myself?" (*Wish You*, 72). Though marriage can indicate an abnegation of self that leads to feelings of alienation, Harry still defends the power of love. In her support of the interracial couple, Stafford and Brenda Sanburne, Harry extols romance: "Love whomever you could. It was such a rare commodity in the world, you'd better take it where you could find it" (*Wish You*, 126). This belief eventually leads her to sympathy for Fair's relationship with Boom Boom Craycroft. When he is arrested as the murder suspect, Harry discovers that Fair is innocent because he was having an affair with Boom Boom at the time in question. Yet she refuses to use this knowledge to her advantage in court during the divorce settlement. She too waits at the train station to welcome the arrival of the interracial couple, who symbolize the power of love to overcome differences and the triumph of emotion over social conventions.

In her alienation from self, Harry recalls Nickel in *Bingo* and, of course, reflects Brown's autobiography to a degree. Harry's references to the wisdom of her mother's axioms, her honest perceptions of other people's problems, her hatred of social pretense, her intellectual curiosity, her feminism (she lifts the mail bags rather than let a man do it for her)—all these traits come from Brown herself. Thus, when Harry criticizes her marriage to Fair for its sexual passion but lack of emotional and intellectual compatibility, one cannot help but make the parallel to Brown's relationship with Martina Navratilova. The separation of lovers, with its concomitant haggling over money and friends, clearly reflects Brown's experiences trying to survive after her breakup with Navratilova. She had to sell their house and suffer the emotional trauma of her ex-lover's new romance, but Brown eventually managed to remain friends without excessive bitterness. Her emotional support during this time came mainly from her heterosexual friends, like the Tuckers in this novel and the Frosts (Regina and Jackson) in *Bingo*.[3] In both books the protagonists learn that they must come to terms with themselves first before they are ready for involvement in any future romance.

All Creatures Great and Small

The animals in *Wish You Were Here* provide unique perspectives on this process of self-discovery as they reflect and reflect upon the human race. The animals, it seems, do not have to abide by the same social manners that hinder human beings. When Bob Berryman and Kelly Craycroft get into a scuffle at the post office, restrained by her sense of good manners, Harry cannot rush out to watch the fight as she would like to do. The animals have no such compunctions and can satisfy their curiosity without being stigmatized. In their discussion of human nature, the animals criticize humans for not listening to what animals are trying to tell them or even to each other. This lack of communication is a reflection of their alienation from their animal natures. They have lost their animal senses through ages of disuse, and they senselessly attack animals that they do not understand without seeing the bonds that all earth's creatures share: "Their fears and their inability to comprehend how animals are connected, including themselves, would bring everyone to a sorry state" (*Wish You*, 118). They are destroying species of animals and wrecking the environment without understanding that their own survival is also at risk: "They just won't realize they're another animal and the laws of nature apply to them too" (*Wish You*, 205).

Like Molly envying the toad's simplicity in *Rubyfruit Jungle*, Mrs.

Murphy perceives animal existence as pure unselfconscious being, a vivid contrast to human strivings: "What she couldn't accept was that these creatures worked and worked and they didn't enjoy what they worked for; they were too busy paying for things they couldn't afford. By the time they paid for the toy it was worn out and they wanted another one. Worse, they weren't satisfied with themselves. They were always on some self-improvement jag. This astonished Mrs. Murphy. Why couldn't people just be? But they couldn't just *be*—they had to be the best. Poor sick things. No wonder they died from diseases they brought on themselves" (*Wish You*, 118). Mrs. Murphy criticizes human competitiveness, humanity's relentless drive for material goods to fill the void of their own natures. As an honorary animal, so named by her pets, Harry also senses how superior animals are to humans in their "sheer delight in the moment" (*Wish You*, 23). Animals do not kill for pleasure or profit as do humans; people refuse to kill their weak, yet they rush off to war at the first provocation in a hypocritical moral system that the animals cannot fathom. Animal sexuality is not as complicated either: "Nothing is clear with humans, not even mating. A human being will mate with another human being for social approval. They rarely sleep with the person who's right for them" (*Wish You*, 205).

While praising the unique qualities of animal existence, Brown cannot resist anthropomorphizing her creatures as they gossip, vie with each other for human attention, and exhibit petty jealousies. Even marriages in the animal kingdom are somewhat difficult. Mrs. Murphy's dealings with her estranged first husband Paddy are a humorous reflection of Harry's own divorce. An astute observer of both animal and human behavior, Brown cleverly bases her creatures' actions on real animal habits. When they want to gain Harry's attention for their theory of the murder, for instance, they leave mutilated animal carcasses in imitation of the latest murder victim, surely an interesting interpretation of why cats love to bring their prey to show their owners.

Although Brown, as usual, tries to break down stereotypes to reveal the individuality of her characters, human and animal, she is forced by the mystery genre to make one of her characters a murderous villain. That she chooses a man who seems to be the only gay man in Crozet to be this villain apparently goes against her principles of political correctness. Although his sexuality is never firmly established by Brown in the text, Josiah's portrait is drawn from too many stereotypical homosexual characteristics for readers not to make the assumption that he is gay. Traditionally, hard-boiled detective novels and films have equated homosexuality with evil, perversion, decadence, and crime. Any sign of

effeminate behavior automatically brings suspicion upon such a character. Working more within the British school of crime stories (based on
logic and social observations of behavior), Brown nonetheless borrows
this American film noir theme of homophobia to work out her plot. In
this small town, the book suggests that only a frustrated homosexual
would have enough wit and sense of theater to perform these macabre
murders, displaying the bodies in gruesome poses, one ground up in a
cement mixer, another chopped into three puzzle pieces by a speeding
locomotive. The simple motive of greed is given for these horrendous
crimes; even in the Reagan eighties, lamented as times of "spiritual
famine," this seems rather a weak motivation unless the stereotype of the
villainous homosexual is being invoked to fill out the characterization
(*Wish You*, 22).

Usually favorable to her gay male characters, especially since she has
many close friendships with gay males in her own life, Brown turns upon
Josiah DeWitt for no apparent reason. She had created a rather stereotypical hairdresser queen portrait of Mr. Pierre in *Bingo*, but she at least
allowed him a dignified and noble role as father to Nickel's children. In
both of these portraits, however, Brown conveniently separates the men
from their sexuality; they are gay but essentially sexless. Mr. Pierre's
lover has died, but rather than seeking to fulfill his own sexuality, he
sacrifices himself to play the part of heterosexual father, toning down his
flamboyance for the sake of the children. Interested only in fine furniture
and wealth, Josiah spends his time accompanying Mim on her visits to
her socially significant friends and connections because her husband will
not go with her. Most of the other characters in the story assume that he
is gay based on the stereotypical clues about his perfumed handkerchief,
his witty repartee, and his snobbish behavior; his first postcard clue is of
Oscar Wilde's tomb in Paris. Part of Mim's comeuppance is to learn that
she has been a "fag hag" for years with Josiah, who has used her to gain
entrance into homes that he later returns to rob. He is too clever for his
own good; he cannot resist sending the postcards as clues or gossiping
with Harry as she stalks him in the secret tunnel. His desperate need for
attention and appreciation leads to his downfall. He remains the only
unredeemed character, devious until he is shot between the eyes by a
woman police officer. With so much astute character observation in the
details of the novel, it is disappointing that Brown chose to create such a
stereotypical villain.

Chapter Nine

Rita Mae Brown and Contemporary Literature: "I'm a Writer and I'm a Woman and I'm from the South"

In a *Publisher's Weekly* interview in 1978, Brown minimizes the significance of lesbianism in her works, insisting instead on her place as a Southern woman writer.[1] Although her early works particularly benefited from a strong gay readership, she did not want her work ghettoized into a narrow category that could be easily dismissed by mainstream audiences and critics. She elaborates on her complaint against the lesbian author label in her writer's manual: "If you're female and gay, watch out. You'll get one of two responses. You'll be told you write like a man. . . . The other response you get, and I confess that this is my favorite, is that you are a man-hater" (*Starting from Scratch*, 33). What both of these criticisms imply for her is that the works of men are considered more important than those by women and that the critical standards are different for male and female authors. Male writers, she explains (using Norman Mailer as an example), are rarely dismissed for creating weak or unbelievable female characters, while women writers are essentially judged by the type of male characters they create. All industries, including publishing and advertising, operate by means of "oppressed categories," the labels that keep "telling people they're different from one another" (Holt, 16). Brown insists that her fictional message is that "we're *not* different": "Sure there are some things different about being gay or poor, or black or old, but they're not so monumental as to be impediments to human communication" (Holt, 16).

Even though Brown consciously defies such labels, she cannot deny the significance of her sexuality in her artistic creations. In fact, she strongly believes that all authors must be, not androgynous as Virginia Woolf proposed, but bisexual: "In the beginning of everyone's work the dice are always loaded toward one's own sex or sex preference. Learning to unload those dice, to throw the bones honestly, is what maturity as an individual and as a writer is all about" (*Starting from Scratch*, 38). This sexual sensitivity is one aspect of the larger issue of knowledge of human behavior that is crucial to good writing: "The more you know about people, the better you'll be as a writer. Whites need to learn about blacks, Chicanos, Asian-Americans, and so on. Men need to learn about women, and straights need to learn about gays. Maybe those lives will never appear in your work but you will be informed, broadened, and deepened by learning from others" (*Starting from Scratch*, 34). Because women and homosexuals are socialized to exist in the dominant male straight culture, they are already knowledgeable about a range of behaviors and should, according to Brown's theories, excel as artists.

Despite her dislike of the label, Brown's role as a lesbian author is an influential one in contemporary literature. Her primary contribution to lesbian literature has been a sense of humor, a trait rarely found in earlier literature (before the 1970s), which deals primarily with the social stigma and personal traumas associated with the "perversion" of lesbianism. Critic Catharine Stimpson describes the two repeated patterns she finds in lesbian novels in English: "The dying fall, a narrative of damnation, of the lesbian's suffering as a lonely outcast attracted to a psychological lower caste; and the enabling escape, a narrative of the reversal of such descending trajectories, of the lesbian's rebellion against social stigma and self-contempt."[2] The "dying fall" pattern includes such noted lesbian texts as *The Well of Loneliness* by Radclyffe Hall, *Nightwood* by Djuna Barnes, and *The Group* by Mary McCarthy. Lesbian author/critic Janice Rule describes a similar transformation of the lesbian novel from these early bleak and depressing morality tales to a more realistic and positive understanding of lesbianism: "Self-sacrifice, moral guilt, a twisted psychology, and heterosexual salvation are still the preoccupations of many novels published today, but a new theme is emerging, the struggle of women to overcome prejudice and persecution, to overcome the attendant fear and guilt as well in order to be free to love."[3] The fiction of Rita Mae Brown is clearly in this new mode, that of the enabling escape, of literature in which the heroine is proud of her identity as a lesbian, is successfully rebellious against a crippling status quo. The closing prophetic cry in Hall's *Well of Loneliness*, "We are coming . . . and our name is legion—you dare not deny us," is echoed and fulfilled in Molly Bolt's assertion, "I'm here."[4] Although at times her novels can border on the polemical and the "too blatantly preachy," Brown's books are saved by their "arrogant humor, never-mind-the-consequences fury, and transcending tenderness" (Rule, 195).

The impact of her liberating works has been felt by lesbian readers and writers alike. Bertha Harris perhaps best expresses what Brown's books have meant to an emerging lesbian consciousness in literature: "The great service of literature is to show us who we are. . . . Lesbians, historically bereft of cultural, political and moral context, have especially relied on imaginative literature to dream themselves into situations of cultural, political and moral power. Twenty years ago, without Molly Bolt, we were Rhett Butler and Stephen Gordon and the Count of Monte Cristo. It is, of course, much more to the point to be Molly Bolt or Patience or Sarah or Mrs. Stevens. . . . the new lesbian hero is certainly safer for our mental health than Rhett or the Count or Stephen—we do not have to associate power and adventure with the penis any longer; we do not have to call on God to cure us of 'inversion' and wear male underwear any longer. . . ."[5] In contrast of the guilt-ridden consciousness of Stephen Gordon in *The Well of Loneliness* is the refreshing sexual honesty of Molly Bolt, a long-overdue change of the usual stereotypes associated with lesbian characters. According to another reader who was also deeply affected by Brown's innovative work, these new lesbian stories are "exciting because they present, anxiety and all, the girl next door. We follow the histories of women who neither behave as slaves nor imitate masters. As these stories unfold we discover that lesbians, too, have a sense of humor, which revelation elevates not only the literature but the popular image of lesbians out of the melancholic mire of adolescent experience."[6]

In a 1975 Modern Language Association panel, several lesbian scholars and authors attempted to define the emerging lesbian feminist literature. June Arnold's description of the books published by Daughters, Inc. catalogues traits that Brown was developing in her fiction during this era and afterward. According to Arnold, the contemporary lesbian feminist novel is departing from traditional plot-time structures to explore "experience weaving in upon itself, commenting on itself, *in*clusive, not ending in final victory/defeat but ending with the sense that the community continues."[7] This new plot structure also demands a different notion of the heroine: "There is an interinvolvement of women in a community" ("Lesbians and Literature," 29). As we have analyzed in earlier chapters, Brown's experiments with narrative structure through a manipulation of time, as found in *Six of One*, *Bingo*, *Southern Discomfort*, and *High Hearts*, are clearly related to her feminist views on the nature of history. Women must understand their past, as individuals and as women in a patriarchal society, in order to challenge the future. Since their history is often not written, much of it must be imaginatively conceived by artists. Her conscious use of anachronism and her perception of women's history through a modern sensibility, fictional characteristics that she is often criticized for employing, are Brown's methods of re-creating the past and finding her relation to it.

Arnold also notes that the political philosophy of feminism encourages authors to break down "the distance between the writer and the reader"; similarly, Brown frequently challenges her readers to become writers themselves ("Lesbians and Literature," 30). Her writers' manual expresses her ultimate belief in the joys and rewards of writing and its attainability through dedication and hard work: "Creativity comes from trust. Trust your instincts. And never hope more than you work" (*Starting from Scratch*, xi). Arnold defines the political purposes of lesbian feminist humor as dealing "with the absurdity of the patriarchy but also our own foibles, assumptions and presumptions which we discover during the learning of lesbian feminism" ("Lesbians and Literature," 30). Above all, the new lesbian author is completely honest: "The dyke author is committed only to the truth, having no stake in placating the culture—no life to lose either" ("Lesbians and Literature," 30). Although at times Brown laments being the only lesbian author in America (meaning that she is one of the few self-proclaimed lesbian authors and openly gay public figures), her honesty allows her the freedom to be outspoken in her views and outrageous in her humor without fear of reprisal.

Brown's special talent for blending her feminist political views with her traditional notions of family, place, and values earns her a unique niche in American literature. In her fictional world, the lesbian becomes the true inheritor of the ideals of the American Dream, for she must fight adversity in a harsh world, must work harder than a "normal" person to gain respect, must continually assert her identity and individuality to survive, must rebel against the status quo in order to gain success, and must pursue her future with unflagging optimism. With her Southern background as well as her lesbian sexuality, a Brown heroine is an outsider to mainstream culture who must earn acceptance by her strength, wit, and perseverance. Like most good American heroes, she distrusts the city, associating it with evil and corruption, and preferring instead the rural environment for its preservation of family values and its nurturance of the individual spirit. Brown's theme of adoption becomes an appropriate metaphor for the acceptance and tolerance of the outsider that she feels herself to be. Through her interest in communities of women, a theme common to women writers in general, Brown is able to explore the dynamics of society on a more personal, local level. As she goes in search of her mother's gardens, to borrow an image from fellow Southern feminist Alice Walker, Brown tries to find her place in history through an understanding of family, nuclear and extended.

Brown's fiction deserves examination also in light of the Southern literary tradition. As a self-proclaimed admirer of Mark Twain, Brown exhibits a similar political use of humor and satire to express her criticism of society. Like Twain, she detests hypocrisy in every form, often mercilessly satirizes the upper classes, celebrates the individual, expresses tolerance for racial/social diversity, and laments the evils of war. Like his, Brown's social satire is based on a strong sense of moral righteousness and indignation. But Twain is not her only Southern mentor. Brown reflects many of the truisms of Southern literature and culture in her fiction. Her fascination with place, with "roots," leads her to prove that one not only can go home again but also that one must go home. Although she is aware of the changing face of the Southern landscape, especially in *Wish You Were Here,* she looks to the past of the region for strength and sustenance, to the eternal verities of family, home, and love. She is proud of her Southern heritage, despite its negative traditions of racism and intolerance, because she believes in the fundamental goodness of people and their ability to rediscover their "root selves," freed from their social definitions and limitations. Although it probably would have been easier for her as a lesbian to live in the tolerant atmosphere of a large city, she chose a more isolated rural landscape to foster her writing career and remind her of basic human truths and values.

When discussing the male characters in *Six of One,* Brown also describes her notion of Southern values: "They are like the men I grew up with . . . good men who know the value of honest labor and who, like the women, are very Southern in their belief in a personal code of honor and in the land as a source of life. Perhaps that's my message, if any. I find that I am in a generation that doesn't understand cause and effect, doesn't recognize its dependence on that black soil laid down in the Mississippi Valley; nor does it care. That frightens me—the Southern philosophy is that the land is all there is, and that cuts across all barriers of rich and poor" (Holt, 17). Implied in this evaluation of the Southern spirit is a strong sense of the individual and the importance of the land as the great equalizer, two essential themes for expressing the democratic fervor of Brown. To her, the South is also a region rife with paradox and contradiction, which partly account for the proliferation of artists there. In her estimation, "Southerners are politically conservative but personally the most liberal people in the United States. It is an incredible paradox. In the South you can do anything you want as long as you have good manners. The personal freedom in the South is unequalled anywhere else in the United States" (Ranson, 3B). Thus the South not only is the appropriate place for her to live and work as a writer, but also accounts for the strange combinations of unique individuals one finds in her fiction.

Part of her genius as a social commentator is to reconcile the revolutionary aspects of her fiction (specifically, her sexually liberated and liberating characters) with the traditional American/Southern values of her mainstream audience. Stated simply, her philosophy of sex is: "Sex is a natural act. Nothing is unnatural, only untried" (*Starting from Scratch*, 37). Yet she is able to make sexual diversity acceptable through her use of humor and her association of sexuality with individuality. Being true to one's root self, one is free from a socially imposed notion of sin, of difference. Standing up for one's sexual identity becomes a powerful statement of individual freedom of expression in Brown's universe.

Because of her radical background and her fascination with human history, Brown believes in the power of language and literature to make a difference in the world. Writing is a political act as well as an individual expression of creativity. Although at times she seems willing to hide in the safety and security of the language ("When I sit down at the typewriter . . . I'm not thinking about belonging to anybody or any movement"), she ultimately believes that writing can help us to change our reality: "Life is a conversation between the dead, the living, and the unborn—between all that was and all that can be. Writing preserves this exchange and enables you and our generation to reach beyond the limits of our physical existence. . . . . Writing is a communal art. It brings us together over centuries and over national boundaries" (Carr-Crane, 4; *Starting from Scratch*, 203). Having been criticized by many of her lesbian feminist followers for "selling out" to the majority in her mainstream success, Brown still reveals in this comment her essential idealism and her continued commitment to art as an instrument for enlightenment and change. Keenly aware of the amount of hard work that goes into each work of literature ("I put a piece of paper in my typewriter and I wait until blood appears on my forehead"), Brown nevertheless remains dedicated to the craft of writing for the pleasure that it brings her: "I can say that writing not only makes me happy but brings me rapture. Happiness is in the animal brain and joy is in the cerebrum. Writing gives me both experiences of pleasure" (Maupin, 50; *Starting from Scratch*, x). When asked what the future holds for her, Brown proclaims with her characteristic enthusiasm, "More books, lots more books. Lots more screenplays and teleplays. I really love to write, and that's when I'm happiest" (Carr-Crane 4).

Notes and References

Chapter One

1. Carole Horn, "Rita Mae Brown: For Her, Being Different Really Isn't so Different Any More," *Washington Post*, 24 October 1977, C13; hereafter cited in text. The most comprehensive biographical article about Brown, other than individual interviews with her, is found in *1986 Current Biography Yearbook*, Charles Moritz, ed. (New York: H. W. Wilson Company, 1986), 71–74. I have relied on this entry for my overview of important dates and events of Brown's life and career.

2. Armistead Maupin, "Rita Mae Brown," *Interview*, February 1982, 50; hereafter cited in text. Rita Mae Brown, *Starting from Scratch: A Different Kind of Writers' Manual* (New York: Bantam Books, 1988), 8; hereafter cited in text as *Starting from Scratch*.

3. Lenore Fleischer, "Lenore Fleischer Talks with Rita Mae Brown," *Washington Post Book World*, 15 October 1978, E2; hereafter cited in text.

4. Charlene Ball, "Rita Mae Brown: Elusive and Charming as Ever," *Southern Voice*, 28 September 1989, 9; hereafter cited in text.

5. Rebecca Ranson, "Saving Power: Atlanta Playwright Rebecca Ranson Discusses Politics, Fame and Social Activism with Rita Mae Brown," *Creative Loafing*, 7 October 1989, 1; hereafter cited in text.

6. Karen Jackovich, "The Unthinkable Rita Mae Brown Spreads Around a Little 'Southern Discomfort,'" *People*, 7 October 1985, 81; hereafter cited in text.

7. Rita Mae Brown, *A Plain Brown Rapper* (Oakland, Calif.: Diana Press, Inc., 1976), 81; hereafter cited in text as *Rapper*.

8. Judy Klemesrud, "Underground Book Brings Fame to a Lesbian Author," *New York Times*, 26 September 1977, 38.

9. The Sagaris experiment is described in a volume edited by Charlotte Bunch and Sandra Pollack, eds., *Learning Our Way: Essays in Feminist Education* (Trumansburg, New York: The Crossing Press, 1983), 114–37.

10. Patricia Holt, "Rita Mae Brown," *Publishers Weekly*, 2 October 1978, 16; hereafter cited in text.

11. Jean Carr-Crane, "Unsinkable Rita Mae Brown," *Lambda Rising Book Report*, December 1988/January 1989, 4; hereafter cited in text. *Starting from Scratch*, 8.

12. Martina Navratilova (with George Vecsey), *Martina* (New York: Ballantine Books, 1985), 193; hereafter cited in text as *Martina*.

13. Stephanie Mansfield, "The Love Match Gone Sour: Rita Mae Brown,

Martina Navratilova and the End of the Affair," *Washington Post*, 13 August 1981, C1; hereafter cited in text.

14. Robert Julian, "An Interview with Rita Mae Brown," *Torso*, June 1989, 38; hereafter cited in text.

15. "Cheap Drills," *American Film*, December 1982, 12.

16. Ranson, 3B. Further clues to Brown's life after her separation from Navratilova might be gleaned from Diana Salvatore's apparent roman à clef *Love, Zena Beth* (Tallahassee: Naiad Press, 1992), a novel about a young Southern lesbian's passionate affair with a famous Southern lesbian author recently separated from a world renowned sports star.

17. Bennet Bolton, "Tennis Ace Retrieves Treasures from $ Million Lesbian Love Nest," *National Enquirer*, 2 June 1992: 3.

Chapter Two

1. "The Shape of Things to Come," *Rapper*, 115.

2. *Rapper*, 22. Rita Mae Brown, *The Hand That Cradles the Rock* (New York: NYU Press, 1971).

3. *Rapper*, 37. Brown's sensitivity to the difference between true leaders and media personalities is expressed most fully in her essay "Leadership vs. Stardom," *Rapper*, 139–50.

4. Martha Chew, "Rita Mae Brown: Feminist Theorist and Southern Novelist," in *Women's Writers of the Contemporary South*, ed. Peggy Whitman Prenshaw (Jackson, Miss.: University Press of Mississippi, 1984), 200; hereafter cited in text. Jan Clausen particularly criticizes Brown for her seeming abandonment of the radical feminist agenda: "It is a sobering experience . . . to read early 'underground' heroine Rita Mae Brown's musings on the joys of owning a Rolls Royce in a recent issue of *Savvy*." See *A Movement of Poets: Thoughts on Poetry and Feminism* (Brooklyn: Long Haul Press, 1982), 14.

5. Radicalesbians, "Woman Identified Woman," in *Lesbians Speak Out* (Oakland, Calif.: Women's Press Collective, 1974), 87; hereafter cited in text as "Woman Identified Woman."

6. This important essay may be found in Leslie B. Tanner, ed., *Voices from Women's Liberation* (New York: New American Library, Inc., 1970), 158–66.

7. In one essay Brown tones down her anti-male rhetoric to explain how she relates to men as friends because they are very supportive of her career and they provide her a different perspective on life from that of her female friends. See Rita Mae Brown, "Some of My Best Friends Are . . . Men," *Ms.*, September 1985, 66, 115–16. She has gone so far as to claim, "It's much easier for a man to love me than it is for a woman. It's been the curse of my life. I'm the last person in the world who should be a lesbian. I mean unless a woman's prepared to be right up there in the glare with me, I would be better off with a good fella" (Maupin, 50).

8. So important is this title that Robin Morgan used it to head her

chapter "Poetry as Protest" in her anthology *Sisterhood Is Powerful: An Anthology of Writing from the Women's Liberation Movement* (New York: Random House, 1970).

9. Rita Mae Brown, "Another Time in the Same Place," *Poems* (Freedom, Calif: Crossing Press, 1987), np; hereafter cited in text as "Another Time," *Poems*, when I refer to this introductory essay and *Poems* when I refer to her poems. Unless otherwise noted, I will refer to this edition of her poetry since it is more readily available than the original editions of her two volumes, which are out of print. Since this edition does not cite line or page numbers, I will refer to individual poems by title.

10. "On the Rooftop Where All the Pigeons Go to Die" is not printed first in *Poems* as it was in *The Hand That Cradles the Rock*; *Poems* begins with "Necrology," which also uses the imagery of death in its criticism of male culture.

11. Judith McDaniel, "The Transformation of Silence into Language and Action," *Sinister Wisdom*, 1978, 17.

12. For a discussion of the significance of poetry to feminism, see Jan Clausen, *A Movement of Poets: Thoughts on Poetry and Feminism* (Brooklyn, New York: Long Haul Press, 1982); hereafter cited in text.

13. Bertha Harris discusses the lesbian as "monster" in literature in her article, "What we mean to say: Notes Toward Defining the Nature of Lesbian Literature," *Heresies*, Fall 1977, 5–8. She explains, "Monsters, heroes, criminals and lesbians (and sometimes saints and gods) have the following traits in common: an ability to make a life outside the social norm that seems both enviable and frightening to those inside; an actual or imagined power to concentrate which may be either emotionally or intellectually expressed—but whose object is to solve a problem; marks of difference that are physically manifested and both horrify and thrill; a desire to avenge its own (and sometimes others') outcast misery: through destruction or through forcing a change in the world that will admit it and its kind; an ability to seduce and tempt others into its 'evil' ways; super-human power" (p. 7).

14. "The only alliance I would make with the Women's Liberation Movement is in bed," according to Abbie Hoffman; "The only position for women in SNCC is prone," according to Stokeley Carmichael. See Robin Morgan, *Sisterhood Is Powerful*, 35.

15. This alternate title was used when the poem was originally published in *Motive* in its March-April 1969 issue; see Joanne Cooke, Charlotte Bunch-Weeks, and Robin Morgan, eds., *The New Woman: A Motive Anthology on Women's Liberation* (New York: Bobbs-Merrill Company, Inc., 1970).

16. Rita Mae Brown, "To the Reader," *Songs to a Handsome Woman* (Oakland, Calif.: Diana Press, 1973), np. Although Brown does not mention Smith by name in her note, she admits love for this one "handsome woman" as her inspiration for the volume. She signs her note with "Kisses and Revolution."

17. Ephraim Katz, *The Film Encyclopedia* (New York: Putnam Publishing, 1979), 1067.

18. When asked about her relationship with Navratilova, Brown admitted that she generally preferred older women, possibly in a reference to Smith: "I'd always been attracted to the Grace Kelly-Dina Merrill kind of woman: older, sophisticated, repressed. Actually, I mean restrained, not repressed, because that restraint indicates there's something to hold back." See Maupin, 50.

19. Charlotte Bunch, *Passionate Politics: Feminist Theory in Action* (New York: St. Martin's Press, 1987), 218.

20. N.A., Review of *The Hand That Cradles the Rock*, *Choice*, September 1972, 810.

21. William Pritchard, Review of *The Hand That Cradles the Rock*, *Hudson Review*, Spring 1972, 120.

Chapter Three

1. Terry Curtis Fox, "Up from Cultdom—and Down Again," *Village Voice*, 12 September 1977, 41.

2. Bonnie Zimmerman, "Exiting from Patriarchy: The Lesbian Novel of Development," in *The Voyage In: Fictions of Female Development*, eds. Elizabeth Abel, Marianne Hirsch, and Elizabeth Langland (Hanover: University Press of New England, 1983); hereafter cited in text as Zimmerman 1983.

3. Marilyn Webb, "Daughters, Inc.: A Publishing House Is Born," *Ms.*, June 1974, 35–38.

4. Leslie Fishbein, "*Rubyfruit Jungle*: Lesbianism, Feminism, and Narcissism," *International Journal of Women's Studies*, March/April 1984, 155–59; hereafter cited in text.

5. James Mandrell, "Questions of Genre and Gender: Contemporary American Versions of the Feminine Picaresque," *Novel*, Winter 1987, 149–70.

6. Annis Pratt, *Archetypal Patterns in Women's Fiction* (Bloomington: Indiana University Press, 1981), 37; hereafter cited in text.

7. Rita Mae Brown, *Rubyfruit Jungle* (Plainfield, Vermont: Daughters, Inc., 1973; rpt. New York: Bantam Books, 1977), 3; hereafter cited in text as *Rubyfruit*.

8. Brown continues the sewer pipe metaphor as Molly later crawls through the drainpipe to Mrs. Bisland's home in search of Leota.

9. Throughout the novel Molly defines herself as a Southerner, recognizing that she is an outsider, and adamantly criticizes those who would make fun of her Southern accent or manners.

10. Brown claims to have been involved sexually with both boys and girls from age sixteen: "I maintained the impartiality of it until I was eighteen," she explains of her preference of women. See Dolores Alexander, "Rita Mae Brown: 'The Issue for the Future Is Power,'" *Ms.*, September 1974, 111.

11. Brown's own biography reveals strong emotional bonds to a man at this time of her life; she was even engaged shortly to Jerry Pfeiffer and later shared an apartment with him in New York City. She cites him along with Martina Navratilova as the two great loves of her life. See *Starting from Scratch*, 17.

12. Florence King, *Southern Ladies and Gentlemen* (New York: Bantam Books, 1975), 34–36; hereafter cited in text as King 1975.

13. Mark Twain, *The Adventures of Huckleberry Finn*, in *Anthology of American Literature*, Vol. II, ed. George McMichael, 3rd ed. (New York: Macmillan Publishing Company, 1985), 477.

14. The Horatio Alger books reveal this inherent contradiction; though preaching the virtues of hard work, Alger's plots eventually turn upon a quirk of fate to lead to the hero's success. See John Tebbel, *From Rags to Riches: Horatio Alger, Jr., and the American Dream* (New York: Macmillan Company, 1963), 14.

15. Mary McIntosh, "The Homosexual Role," *Social Problems*, Fall 1968.

16. Dennis Altman, *Homosexual: Oppression and Liberation* (New York: Avon Books, 1973), 237.

17. Janet Weihe, Review of *In Her Day*, *Library Journal*, 1 December 1976, 2510.

18. Deborah Core, "Rita Mae Brown's *In Her Day*," *Sinister Wisdom*, 1976, 88; hereafter cited in text.

19. Rita Mae Brown, *In Her Day* (Plainfield, Vermont: Daughters, Inc., 1976; rpt. New York: Bantam Books, 1988), 2; hereafter cited in text as *In Her Day*.

20. Brown's friend Mychelle Smiley is identified as the "real Adele to my and the world's delight" in Brown's dedication to *In Her Day*.

Chapter Four

1. Rita Mae Brown, "Special Mention," *Six of One* (New York: Harper and Row, 1978; rpt. New York: Bantam Books, 1979), np; hereafter cited in text as *Six of One*.

2. Alice Turner, "Books: Rita Mae Brown," *New York*, 18 September 1978, 60.

3. John Berger, *Ways of Seeing* (London: Penguin Books, 1972), 11.

4. Cynthia MacDonald, Review of *Six of One*, *Washington Post Book World*, 15 October 1978, E2.

5. Ironically, the book is prophetic, for shortly after its publication Brown meets lover Martina Navratilova and moves into a Southern mansion.

6. This story of Nickel's rescue is actually the story of Brown's own adoption. See Horn, C1, C13.

7. S.K., Review *Six of One*, *Times Literary Supplement*, 7 December 1979, 104.

8. Rita Mae Brown, *Bingo* (New York: Bantam Books, 1988), 291; hereafter cited in text as *Bingo*.

9. For example, see Ball, 9.

Chapter Five

1. Gary Davenport, "The Fugitive Hero in New Southern Fiction," *Sewanee Review*, Summer 1983, 442.

2. Rita Mae Brown, *Southern Discomfort* (New York: Harper and Row, 1982), 11; hereafter cited in text as *Discomfort*.

3. According to Navratilova, Brown thought of herself as a man trapped in a woman's body; see *Martina*, 193.

4. This aspect of love is similar to Alice Walker's outlook in *The Color Purple*, where Celie eventually tolerates Mister, the man who had brutalized her physically and emotionally, after she has experienced loving Shug Avery.

Chapter Six

1. Rita Mae Brown, "Genesis," *Sudden Death* (New York: Bantam Books, 1983), vii; hereafter cited in text as *Sudden*.

2. Amy Wilenz, Review of *Sudden Death, Village Voice*, 19 July 1983, 35; hereafter cited in text.

3. N.A., Review of *Sudden Death, Booklist*, 1 March 1983, 825.

4. Marcelle Thiebaux, Review of *Sudden Death, Best Sellers*, July 1983, 120.

5. Mary-Ellen Mort, Review of *Sudden Death, Library Journal*, April 1983, 756.

6. Carmen's marriage to a total stranger contrasts sharply with Grace's marriage to Payson in *Southern Discomfort*; although theirs could also be seen as a marriage of convenience, their genuine love, friendship and respect for each other prevent Brown from condemning their sexual dishonesty as she does Carmen's in *Sudden Death*.

Chapter Seven

1. Florence King, "Rita Mae Brown's Tomboy Scarlett O'Hara," *Washington Post Book World*, 4 May 1986, 3.

2. Rita Mae Brown, "Foreword," *High Hearts* (New York: Bantam Books, 1986), xi; hereafter cited in text as *High Hearts*.

3. High Hearts, xiv.

4. Although Brown does not cite Reston's book in her bibliography, a similar interpretation of Civil War history is presented in James Reston, *Sherman's March and Vietnam* (New York: Macmillan, 1984).

5. In her reevaluation of her political activism, Brown writes, "Change, it becomes apparent, is not as convulsion of history but the slow, steady push of people over decades." *Rapper*, 13.

6. Diane Cole, "Catch Up Time," *Ms.*, June 1986, 32.

Chapter Eight

1. Marilyn Stasio, "Crime," *New York Times Book Review*, 16 December 1990, 33.
2. Rita Mae Brown, *Wish You Were Here* (New York: Bantam Books, 1990), 1; hereafter cited in text as *Wish You.*
3. After her separation from Navratilova, Brown thanks her local friends for their support: "They were awfully good to me, I must say. They came up that driveway and sat in my house for a long time with me. Those are real friends. And all the people who came up that hill are straight." See Julian, 38.

Chapter Nine

1. Holt, 16.
2. Catharine Stimpson, "Zero Degree Deviancy: The Lesbian Novel in English," *Critical Inquiry*, Winter 1981, 364.
3. Jane Rule, *Lesbian Images* (Garden City, New York: Doubleday & Company, 1975), 188; hereafter cited in text.
4. Radclyffe Hall, *The Well of Loneliness* (1928; rpt. New York: Avon Book, 1981), 437.
5. Bertha Harris, "What We Mean to Say: Notes Toward Defining the Nature of Lesbian Literature," *Heresies*, Fall 1977, 6.
6. Cathy Cruikshank, "Lesbian Literature: Random Thoughts," *Margins*, August 1975, 40.
7. June Arnold, "Lesbians and Literature," *Sinister Wisdom*, 1976, 29; hereafter cited in text as "Lesbians and Literature." Other women on the MLA panel were Sandy Boucher, Susan Griffin, Melanie Kaye, and Judith McDaniel.

Selected Bibliography

PRIMARY WORKS

Novels

Bingo. New York: Bantam Books, 1988.
High Hearts. New York: Bantam Books, 1986.
In Her Day. Plainfield, Vermont: Daughters, Inc., 1976; reprint New York: Bantam Books, 1988.
Rest in Pieces. New York: Bantam Books, 1992
Rubyfruit Jungle. Plainfield, Vermont: Daughters, Inc., 1973; reprint New York: Bantam Books, 1977.
Six of One. New York: Harper and Row, 1978; reprint New York: Bantam Books, 1979.
Southern Discomfort. New York: Harper and Row, 1982; reprint New York: Bantam Books, 1983.
Sudden Death. New York: Bantam Books, 1983.
Wish You Were Here. New York: Bantam Books, 1990.

Poetry and Non-Fiction

The Hand That Cradles the Rock. New York: New York University Press, 1971.
A Plain Brown Rapper. Oakland, Calif.: Diana Press, 1976.
Poems. Freedom, Calif.: Crossing Press, 1987.
Songs to a Handsome Woman. Oakland, Calif.: Diana Press, 1973.
Starting From Scratch: A Different Kind of Writers' Manual. New York: Bantam Books, 1988.

Screenplays

I Love Liberty (co-author). Dir. Norman Lear. ABC, 1982.
The Long Hot Summer, Part One. Dir. Stuart Cooper. NBC, 1985.
The Long Hot Summer, Part Two (with Dennis Turner). Dir. Stuart Cooper. NBC, 1985.
My Two Loves (with Reginald Rose). Dir. Noel Black. ABC, 1986.
Slumber Party Massacre (original title, *Sleepless Nights*). Dir. Amy Jones. Prod. Roger Corman. 1982.
Rich Men, Single Women. Prod. Aaron Spelling. ABC, 1989.

SECONDARY WORKS

Books and Parts of Books

Abbott, Sidney, and Barbara Love. *Sappho Was a Right-On Woman: A Liberated View of Lesbianism.* New York: Stein and Day, 1972. Dedicated to RMB "for starting it all."

Abel, Elizabeth, Marianne Hirsch, and Elizabeth Langland, eds. *The Voyage In: Fictions of Female Development.* Hanover, New Hampshire: University Press of New England, 1983. Includes Mary Anne Ferguson's essay "The Female Novel of Development and the Myth of Psyche" and Bonnie Zimmerman's "Exiting from Patriarchy: The Lesbian Novel of Development."

Auerbach, Nina. *Communities of Women: An Idea in Fiction.* Cambridge, Massachusetts: Harvard University Press, 1978. Examines selected works of nineteenth-century British and American fiction to explore the nature of family, community, and history.

Bunch, Charlotte. *Passionate Politics: Feminist Theory in Action.* New York: St. Martin's Press, 1987. Collection of essays by Brown's fellow Furies Collective member, written from 1968 to 1986, including a section on lesbian feminism.

Bunch, Charlotte, and Sandra Pollack, eds. *Learning Our Way: Essays in Feminist Education.* Trumansburg, New York: The Crossing Press, 1983. Includes essays by Jackie St. Joan and Susan Sherman about the Sagaris experiment in feminist education, with which Brown was involved.

Clausen, Jan. *A Movement of Poets: Thoughts on Poetry and Feminism.* Brooklyn, New York: Long Haul Press, 1982. Author examines the significance of poetry to the feminist movement and the need for a feminist aesthetic.

Cockshut, A. O. J. *Man and Woman: A Study of Love and the Novel, 1740–1940.* New York: Oxford University Press, 1978. Includes chapter on "The Lesbian Theme" in the development of the novel.

Cooke, Joanne, Charlotte Bunch-Weeks, and Robin Morgan, eds. *The New Woman: A MOTIVE Anthology on Women's Liberation.* New York: Bobbs-Merrill Company, Inc., 1970.

Davidson, Cathy N. and E. M. Broner. *The Lost Tradition: Mothers and Daughters in Literature.* New York: Frederick Ungar Publishing Co., 1980.

Deckard, Barbara Sinclair. *The Women's Movement: Political, Socioeconomic, and Psychological Issues.* New York: Harper & Row, Publishers, 1983. This history details many of the political maneuvers within the women's organizations during the time Brown was active in the women's movement.

Freedman, Estelle B., Barbara C. Gelpi, Susan L. Johnson, Kathleen M. Weston. *The Lesbian Issue: Essays from SIGNS.* Chicago: University of

Chicago Press, 1985. This collection includes feminist essays that had been published in the feminist journal *Signs* from Autumn 1982 to 1984.

Fritz, Leah. *Dreamers & Dealers: An Intimate Appraisal of the Women's Movement.* Boston: Beacon Press, 1979. Considers some of the problems in the organization of the women's movement, including her evaluation of the "lesbian revolution."

Galana, Laurel and Gina Covina. *The New Lesbians: Interviews with Women Across the U.S. and Canada.* Berkeley: Moon Books, 1977. These interviews portray lesbianism as a positive experience, reflecting the new attitude toward homosexuality addressed by Brown in her fiction.

Greene, Gayle and Coppelia Kahn. *Making a Difference: Feminist Literary Criticism.* London: Methuen, 1985. Includes essay by Bonnie Zimmerman, "What Has Never Been: An Overview of Lesbian Feminist Criticism."

Hirsch, Marianne. *The Mother/Daughter Plot: Narrative, Psychoanalysis, Feminism.* Bloomington: Indiana University Press, 1989.

Hoagland, Sarah Lucia and Julia Penelope, eds. *For Lesbians Only: A Separatist Anthology.* London: Onlywomen Press, Ltd., 1988. Includes "Woman Identified Woman" and article on the Furies, among other separatist documents.

Humm, Maggie. *Feminist Criticism: Women as Contemporary Critics.* New York: St. Martin's Press, 1986. Includes consideration of lesbian and black critical aesthetic.

Katz, Ephraim. *The Film Encyclopedia.* New York: Putnam Publishing, 1979.

Kuda, Marie J., ed. *Women Loving Women: A Select and Annotated Bibliography of Women Loving Women in Literature.* Chicago: Lavender Press, 1974.

Lesbians Speak Out. Oakland, California: Women's Press Collective, 1974. Personal essays, poetry, prose, and graphics by and about lesbians, including works by Judy Grahn, Martha Shelley, and Rita Mae Brown.

Moi, Toril. *Sexual/Textual Politics: Feminist Literary Theory.* London: Methuen, 1985.

Morgan, Robin, ed. *Sisterhood Is Powerful: An Anthology of Writings from the Women's Liberation Movement.* New York: Random House, 1970.

Myron, Nancy and Charlotte Bunch, eds. *Lesbianism and the Women's Movement.* Baltimore, Maryland: Diana Press, 1975. Political essays primarily by members of the Furies Collective, including "The Shape of Things to Come" by Rita Mae Brown.

Navratilova, Martina, with George Vecsey. *Martina.* New York: Ballantine Books, 1985. Popular biography of Martina Navratilova that reveals details of her relationship with Brown.

Papachristou, Judith. *Women Together.* New York: Alfred A. Knopf, 1976. A *Ms.* book including reprints of important documents and manifestos concerning the women's movement.

Pratt, Annis. *Archetypal Patterns in Women's Fiction.* Bloomington: Indiana University Press, 1981.

Rule, Jane. *Lesbian Images.* Garden City, New York: Doubleday & Company, 1975. This lesbian author surveys the history of lesbian fiction by focusing on key authors from Radclyffe Hall to Maureen Duffy; her chapter on "Four Decades of Fiction" includes commentary on *Rubyfruit Jungle.*

Tanner, Leslie B., ed., *Voices from Women's Liberation.* New York: New American Library, 1970. Anthology of articles on feminist issues, including Anne Koedt's "Myth of the Vaginal Orgasm," as well as essays by Naomi Weisstein, Martha Shelley, and Roxanne Dunbar.

Wicks, Ulrich. *Picaresque Narrative, Picaresque Fictions: A Theory and Research Guide.* New York: Greenwood Press, 1989.

Articles and Reviews

Alexander, Delores. "Rita Mae Brown: 'The Issue for the Future Is Power.'" *Ms.*, September 1974, 110–13.

Arnold, June and Bertha Harris. "Lesbian Fiction: a dialogue." *Sinister Wisdom*, Fall 1976, 42–51. These two respected black lesbian writers discuss the themes and politics of lesbian publications.

Ball, Charlene. "Rita Mae Brown: Elusive and Charming as Ever." *Southern Voice*, 28 September 1989, 9. Interview with Brown at the time of the publication of *Bingo.*

Benestad, Janet P. Review of *Southern Discomfort. Best Sellers*, May 1982, 44.

Brinson, Claudia Smith. "Cat Tales: Sneaky Pie's Kitty Crime Series Much Too Cutesy." *The State*, 23 December 1990, 5F. Review of *Wish You Were Here.*

"Brown, Rita Mae." *Contemporary Authors: New Revision Series.* Vol 35. Detroit: Gale Press, 1992, 70–74.

"Brown, Rita Mae." *Contemporary Authors.* Ed. Clare D. Kinsman. Vol. 45–48. Detroit: Gale Press, 1974, 73.

"Brown, Rita Mae." *Contemporary Literary Criticism.* Ed. Daniel G. Marowski and Roger Matuz. Detroit: Gale Research Company, 1987, 80–86. Biographical sketch followed by critical excerpts of reviews for books through *High Hearts.*

"Brown, Rita Mae." *Contemporary Literary Criticism.* Ed. Daniel G. Marowski and Roger Matuz. Detroit: Gale Research Company, 1981, 72–75. Earlier version of above entry, but contains different critical excerpts.

"Brown, Rita Mae." *1986 Current Biography Yearbook.* Ed. Charles Moritz. New York: H. W. Wilson Company, 1986, 71–74. Most comprehensive biographical essay, with excellent factual details gleaned from numerous sources.

Boeth, Richard. "Sewing Circle." *Newsweek*, 2 October 1978, 94–95. Review of *Six of One.*

Buchanan, Ron. *"High Hearts* and High Hopes: The Importance of Place in Rita Mae Brown's Novels." Unpublished essay, 1989.

————."The Love-Hate Rhetoric of Rita Mae Brown's Political Non-Fiction." Unpublished essay, 1991.

————."Whores, Honeys, and Hunks: Unconventional Love in Rita Mae Brown's *Southern Discomfort*." Unpublished essay, 1987.

Califa, Pat. "We Know What We Want: Lesbian Literature Meets the Sexual Revolution." *Sinister Wisdom*, Fall 1976, 67–70. Review of several books about lesbian sexuality.

Carr-Crane, Jean. "Unsinkable Rita Mae Brown." *Lambda Rising Book Report*, December 1988/January 1989, 1, 4. Interview with Brown at the time of the publication of *Bingo*.

Chew, Martha. "Rita Mae Brown: Feminist Theorist and Southern Novelist." *Women Writers of the Contemporary South*. Ed. Peggy Whitman Prenshaw. Jackson, MS: University Press of Mississippi, 1984, 194–213. Focus on political essays and their relationship to Brown's fiction.

Childress, Mark. Review of *High Hearts*. *New York Times Book Review*. 20 April 1986, 22.

Clausen, Jan. "The Politics of Publishing and the Lesbian Community." *Sinister Wisdom*, Fall 1976, 94–115. Brown is one of the feminist authors who respond to Clausen's questionnaire about feminist versus mainstream presses.

"Cheap Drills." *American Film*, December 1982, 12. Review of *Slumber Party Massacre*.

Cole, Diane. "Catch Up Time." *Ms.*, June 1986, 32, 34. Includes review of *High Hearts*.

Core, Deborah. "Rita Mae Brown's *In Her Day*." *Sinister Wisdom*, 1976, 87–88.

Cruikshank, Cathy. "Lesbian Literature: Random Thoughts." *Margins*, August 1975, 40–41. Includes mention of *Rubyfruit Jungle*.

Damon, Gene. "When It Changed, or Growing Up Gay in America with the Help of Literature." *Margins*, August 1975, 16–18. Includes photograph of Rita Mae Brown.

Davenport, Gary. "The Fugitive Hero in New Southern Fiction." *Sewanee Review*, Summer 1983, 439–45. Includes commentary on *Southern Discomfort*.

Denham, Alice. "Southern Belles Lettres." *The Nation*, 19 June 1982, 759–60. Includes review of *Southern Discomfort*.

De Stefano, George. Review of *Before Stonewall*. *The Nation*, 6 July 1985, 25–26.

Fishbein, Leslie. "*Rubyfruit Jungle*: Lesbianism, Feminism, and Narcissism." *International Journal of Women's Studies*, March/April 1984, 155–59.

Fleischer, Leonore. "Leonore Fleischer Talks with Rita Mae Brown." *Washington Post Book World*, 15 October 1978, E2.

Fludas, John. Review of *Six of One*. *Saturday Review*, 30 September 1978, 52.

Fox, Terry Curtis. "Up from Cultdom—and Down Again." *Village Voice*, 12 September 1977, 41. Review of *Rubyfruit Jungle* and *In Her Day*.

Gardiner, Judith Kegan. "On Female Identity and Writing by Women." *Critical Inquiry*, Winter 1981, 347–61.

Garrett, George. "American Publishing Now." *Sewanee Review*, Summer 1988, 516–25. Review essay of books about publishing, including commentary on *Starting from Scratch*.

Gottlieb, Annie. "Passion and Punishment." *New York Times Book Review*, 21 March 1982, 10, 29. Review of *Southern Discomfort*.

Review of *The Hand That Cradles the Rock*. *Choice*, September 1972, 810.

Harris, Bertha. Review of *Rubyfruit Jungle*. *Village Voice Literary Supplement*, 4 April 1974, 34–35. Reviews of books from the new publishing house, Daughters Press.

————."What we mean to say: Notes Toward Defining the Nature of Lesbian Literature." *Heresies*, Fall 1977, 5–8. A consideration of the lesbian as "monster" in literature.

Henze, Shelley Temchin. "Rita Mae Brown, All-American." *New Boston Review*, April 1979, 17–18. Review of *Rubyfruit Jungle, In Her Day*, and *Six of One*.

Review of *High Hearts*. *West Coast Review of Books*, July 1986, 32.

Holt, Patricia. "Rita Mae Brown." *Publishers Weekly*, 2 October 1978, 16–17.

Horn, Carole. "Rita Mae Brown: For Her, Being Different Really Isn't So Different Any More." *Washington Post*, 24 October 1977, C1, C13.

Review of *In Her Day*. *Choice*, January 1977, 1433.

Jackovich, Karen G. "The Unthinkable Rita Mae Brown Spreads Around a Little 'Southern Discomfort.'" *People*, 26 April 1982, 74+.

Jarvis, Jeff. Review of *The Long Hot Summer*. *People*, 7 October 1985, 13.

Julian, Robert. "An Interview with Rita Mae Brown: She's Tough and Tender and Always Right on Target!" *Torso*, June 1989, 34+.

King, Florence. "Rita Mae Brown's Tomboy Scarlett O'Hara." *Washington Post Book World*, 4 May 1986, 3, 8. Review of *High Hearts*.

Klemesrud, Judy. "Underground Book Brings Fame to a Lesbian Author." *New York Times*, 26 September 1977, 38.

Kort, Michele. "The Name of *Bingo*'s Game Is Mediocrity." *Lambda Rising Book Report*, December 1988/January 1989, 4.

Krieger, Susan. "Lesbian Identity and Community: Recent Social Science Literature." *Signs*, Autumn 1982, 91–108. Review essay of literature concerning "how lesbian communities both affirm and challenge the individual lesbian's sense of self."

Langer, Ingeborg. Review of *Six of One*. *Best Sellers*, February 1979, 336–37.

Langsam, Allegra. Review of *Sudden Death*. *The Cabirion and Gay Books Bulletin*, Fall/Winter 1984, 22–23.

Larkin, Joan. Review of *In Her Day. Ms.*, April 1977, 44.

Review of *The Long Hot Summer. Variety*, 23 May 1985, 50.

"Love of Liberty." *The Nation*, 3 April 1982, 387–88. Review of *I Love Liberty.*

Mandrell, James. "Questions of Genre and Gender: Contemporary American Versions of the Feminine Picaresque." *Novel*, Winter 1987, 149–70. Includes consideration of *Rubyfruit Jungle.*

Mansfield, Stephanie. "The Love Match Gone Sour: Rita Mae Brown, Martina Navratilova and the End of the Affair." *Washington Post*, 13 August 1981, C1, C8.

McDaniel, Judith, June Arnold, Sandy Boucher, Susan Griffin, and Melanie Kaye. "Lesbians and Literature." *Sinister Wisdom*, Fall 1976, 20–33. Publication of a seminar panel conducted at the Modern Language Association in December of 1975.

MacDonald, Cynthia. Review of *Six of One. Washington Post Book World*, 15 October 1978, E1, E3.

Marchino, Lois. "Rita Mae Brown." *American Women Writers, Vol. 1*. Ed. Lina Mainiero. New York: Frederick Ungar Publishing Company, 1979, 257–59.

Marty, Martin E. "I Love Liberty." *Christian Century*, 17 March 1982, 294–96.

Maupin, Armistead. "Rita Mae Brown." *Interview*, February 1982, 50.

Mays, John Bentley. "Earth Mommas at the Garden Party." *Maclean's*, 13 November 1978, 67–68. Review of *Six of One.*

Miller, Mark Crispin. "Patriotism Without Tears." *New Republic*, 14 April 1982, 22–24. Review of *I Love Liberty.*

Mitchell, Judith. "Search and Find." *Voice of Youth Advocates*, February 1983, 17–18. Summary of Mitchell's dissertation "Changes in Adolescent Literature with Homosexual Motifs, Themes, and Characters," which includes commentary on *Rubyfruit Jungle.*

Nelson, Martha. "B Movies." *Ms.*, June 1983, 33. Review of *Slumber Party Massacre.*

Parks, Adrienne. "The Lesbian Feminist as Writer as Lesbian Feminist." *Margins*, August 1975, 67–69. In a special issue of *Margins* dedicated to "Lesbian Feminist Writing and Publishing."

Pritchard, William H. Review of *The Hand That Cradles the Rock. Hudson Review*, Spring 1972, 120.

Pritchard, William H. Review of *In Her Day. Hudson Review*, Spring 1977, 151–52.

Ranson, Rebecca. "Saving Power: Atlanta Playwright Rebecca Ranson Discusses Politics, Fame and Social Activism with Rita Mae Brown." *Creative Loafing*, 7 October 1989, 1B, 3B.

Rowan, Diana Newell. "Juts and Wheezie: Time to Settle Down." *Christian Science Monitor*, 22 November 1978, 22. Review of *Six of One.*

Sheff, David. "When Norman Lear Raises the Flag, Nearly Everyone in Town Salutes." *People*, 22 March 1982, 101–03. Commentary on *I Love Liberty*.

Review of *Six of One*. *West Coast Review of Books*, November 1978, 41.

South, John, Michael Glynn, Jeffrey Rodack, and Roger Capettini. "Explosive Gay Scandal Rocks Women's Tennis." *National Enquirer*, 31 July 1990, 20–21. As in *Sudden Death*, the threat of lesbianism among female tennis stars is considered scandalous; Martina Navratilova is criticized for her relationship with Judy Nelson and a public display of affection after a win at Wimbledon.

Stasio, Marilyn. "Crime." *New York Times Book Review*, 16 December 1990, 33. Review of *Wish You Were Here*.

Stimpson, Catharine R. "Zero Degree Deviancy: The Lesbian Novel in English." *Critical Inquiry*, Winter 1981, 363–79. Stimpson claims that *Rubyfruit Jungle* replaced *The Well of Loneliness* as the one book that all lesbians now read.

Thiebaux, Marcelle. Review of *Sudden Death*. *Best Sellers*, July 1983, 120.

Tone. Review of *My Two Loves*. *Variety*, 23 April 1986, 56.

Turner, Alice K. "Books: Rita Mae Brown." *New York*, 18 September 1978, 60. Review of *Six of One*.

Webb, Marilyn. "Daughters, Inc.: A Publishing House Is Born." *Ms.*, June 1974, 35–38. Includes review of *Rubyfruit Jungle*.

Wiehe, Janet. Review of *In Her Day*. *Library Journal*, 1 December 1976, 2510.

Wilenz, Amy. Review of *Sudden Death*. *Village Voice*, 19 July 1983, 35.

Zimmerman, Bonnie. "Beyond Coming Out: New Lesbian Novels." *Ms.*, June 1985, 65–67.

———."The Politics of Transliteration: Lesbian Personal Narratives." *Signs*, Summer 1984, 663–82. Review essay includes discussion of *Rubyfruit Jungle* as a personal lesbian narrative.

Index

The Author

Carol Ward received her B.A. and M.A. in English from the University of South Carolina and her Ph.D. in American Literature from the University of Tennessee. She is currently an Associate Professor of English at Clemson University where she teaches courses in film studies and film/video production. In 1989 she published *Mae West: A Bio-Bibliography* with Greenwood Press. Her award-winning video documentary *In the Eye of the Hurricane: Women's Stories of Reconstruction* (1991) examines the lives of eight women in the small coastal village of McClellanville, S.C., as they struggle to put their lives back together in the wake of Hurricane Hugo. A regular reviewer for *Independent Spirit* and *Southern Quarterly*, she has written about many regional film/video projects, exhibiting her long-term interest in films made in and about the South.

GAYLORD
F